Digital Mediation

Digital Mediation

Stephen Walker MA (Oxon), FCIArb
Solicitor and Accredited Mediator

Bloomsbury Professional
LONDON • DUBLIN • EDINBURGH • NEW YORK • NEW DELHI • SYDNEY

BLOOMSBURY PROFESSIONAL

Bloomsbury Publishing Plc

50 Bedford Square, London, WC1B 3DP, UK
1385 Broadway, New York, NY 10018, USA
29 Earlsfort Terrace, Dublin 2, Ireland
BLOOMSBURY and the Diana logo are trademarks of Bloomsbury Publishing Plc

Reprinted 2024

British Library Cataloguing-in-Publication Data

A catalogue record for this book is available from the British Library.

ISBN: PB: 978 1 52652 574 1
ePDF: 978 1 62652 576 5
ePub 978 1 52652 575 8

Typeset by Evolution Design and Digital (Kent)
Printed and bound by CPI Group (UK) Ltd, Croydon, CR0 4YY

To find out more about our authors and books visit www.bloomsburyprofessional.com. Here you will find extracts, author information, details of forthcoming events and the option to sign up for our newsletters

Preface

Dispute resolution is going digital. No longer DR (dispute resolution) it will soon be DDR (digital dispute resolution).

Will this be a good thing for mediators? Will mediation as we know it survive? Seeing the answer through all the hyperbole, anxiety, criticism and boosterism is not easy. As a jobbing mediator I wanted to find out what it all meant for mediation users – clients, advisers and mediators. Should we be full of enthusiasm for the next Axial Age of AI? Or should we be full of despair as humanity sleepwalks to extinction? The reactions are very mixed.

What is yours? Are you a utopian, a dystopian or justhopian? In other words, are you embracing the digital mediation world as a better place, avoiding it as a worse place or just waiting to see and hoping for the best?

Mediation is one player in the DR space. Our competitors include arbitrators, adjudicators, early neutral evaluators, conciliators, ombuds and judges. They are all going digital, aren't they? Well certainly judges are. Sir Geoffrey Vos, Master of the Rolls in England and Wales, has told them so and defined digital justice as 'an entirely smart system that operates online or even on-chain'. He reinforced the point by concluding that 'GPT-4 or other advanced machine learning is likely to transform the work that lawyers need to do and possibly even in the slightly longer term the business of judging'.

So, if we are to have a digital justice system what will the consequences be for mediation? What do mediation users have to do? That's what this book looks to find out.

This book is about Digital Mediation (DM) and its subset OLM – online mediation. Mediation does not exist in a vacuum. Over the last three years thanks to Covid and lockdown the way we mediate has changed. What will happen in the next three years? The digital debate has been going on for a few years now but was turbocharged by ChatGPT. 30 November 2022 was a momentous date for us all including mediators. But how do you understand what is going on? So much is happening so fast. It's very difficult with all the hype frenzy and excitement.

I'm not an AI expert. I'm a digital immigrant, ie born before 1980. I'm a civil and commercial mediator based in London. I've done over 900 mediations including more than 250 online. I've written six books on mediation all with the same purpose – to help users of mediation get the best out of the process. As with my other books the emphasis in this one is on the practical. Looking at things which mediation users can use now. How to cope with digital technology that is available now and not to just speculate on what may happen when the Vos revolution takes place or as yet uninvented technologies become available. You can read Richard Susskind for that (see Chapter 2).

The book is in four parts. You can dip into those that are most relevant to you.

Part A Digital mediation: threat or promise?

Chapter 1 gives a snapshot of the scene and discusses the five main drivers for change.

Chapter 2 looks in more detail at the Vos-Susskind Digital Justice System and what this means for mediators.

Chapter 3 examines what digital mediation is. It's an elastic term. Some of the semantic confusion is cleared away and DM is explained in simple non-technical terms.

Chapter 4 looks at whether we should worry about DM – from the point of view of clients, advisors and mediators. There is an update on mandatory mediation which is closely linked with online mediation and as at September 2023 is a hot topic in the UK.

These digital changes are underpinned by AI. This is another elastic term. Chapter 5 picks a way through the hype and frenzy. And looks in particular at what ChatGPT is, how it works and what it can do. You will find a bluffer's guide on how to use it and do prompt engineering.

Chapter 6 focuses on what AI can do for mediators and gives worked examples of how ChatGPT can be used by mediators and those preparing for mediations.

Part B OLM: first choice or second best?

OLM is the form of digital mediation which we are currently using. Again, the reaction to it has been mixed. Chapter 7 considers why some don't like it. Chapter 8 considers why others prefer it. There are pros and cons. Chapter 9 shows you how are to weigh them up and choose which format – online, in-person or hybrid – is best for your mediation.

Part C Getting OLM right – how to do it

Whether we like it or not online mediation is here to stay. The 2023 CEDR Mediation Audit reports that there were in the order of 17,000 civil and commercial mediations in the year to September 2022 and that 'within the 17,000 figure, the latest Audit **confirms the emergence of online mediation** with 64% of commercial cases being conducted online. This figure is well below the 89% that we saw during the pandemic period but seems to show that **the nature of the field has permanently changed.**' (emphasis added)

Chapter 10 looks at the online platforms focusing on Zoom which is the industry standard and market leader. You will find advice on what kit to buy and how to use it. Don't worry if you don't know how to sign a document on your smart phone – this chapter shows you how to do it!!

Chapter 11 walks you through how to run a zoom mediation, with experience-based tips, scripts and checklists. Chapter 12 explains what is different about communicating online and how to do it well. Learn how you should look and sound to get your message across on camera.

You still need documentation. Chapter 13 takes you through an online mediation agreement and explains the differences. And tips for drawing up settlement agreements online, including using ChatGPT.

Working online especially, if you are also working from home, brings its own physical and mental challenges. Chapter 14 looks at these and gives experience-based guidance on what to do to keep your energy levels up and your stress levels down.

Part D How to sell yourself online – getting mediations in

Going digital and doing things online doesn't just change the way you do mediations: it also changes how you attract mediations. You still have to get the work in.

Chapter 15 distils the essence of marketing online.

Chapter 16 explores how to sell yourself online. Schmoozing and boozing is not the same online. But you can still generate business.

Chapters 17, 18 and 19 go into detail about the three keys elements of online marketing – Websites, Videos and Social media. You can't market online without them. Don't worry if you're technophobic, allergic to Facebook or suffering from blogger's block. These chapters will walk you through it all. You will be supported by checklists, templates, scripts and real-life examples.

Chapters 20 and 21 grasp the two nettles that most of us really dislike about self-promotion: Pitching and Networking. Can you do them at all online. Yes, you can. And these chapters show you how.

Some of the topics are also covered in my other books. Duplication and repetition has been kept to a minimum. But I have included cross references to the other books. In addition, there are links to websites which I have found particularly useful for mediating online.

Stephen Walker

November 2023

Stop press

Churchill v Merthyr Tydfil Borough Council [2023] EWCA Civ 1416

In this case the Court of Appeal, in judgment handed down on 29 November 2023, unanimously concluded that:

> 'The court can lawfully stay proceedings for, or order, the parties to engage in a non-court-based dispute resolution process provided that the order made does not impair the very essence of the claimant's right to proceed to a judicial hearing, and is proportionate to achieving the legitimate aim of settling the dispute fairly, quickly and at reasonable cost.'

Mediators have welcomed this judgment. Given the judicial direction of travel as described in this book it was not unexpected.

Dedication

To Alison with all my love and thanks.

Perhaps not the most romantic 40 year anniversary present
but the most heartfelt.

XXX

Other books by Stephen Walker published by Bloomsbury Professional

Mediation Behaviour: Why We Act Like We Do (2021)

Setting Up in Business as a Mediator (2nd Edn, 2020)

Mediation Advocacy: Representing and Advising Clients in Mediation (2nd Edn, 2018)

FAQs for Mediators (2017)

Mediation: An A–Z Guide (2016)

Contents

Chapter 1

Why do I need to read this book?

To assess and build your digital resilience. Mediation is in an intense period of transition. All mediation users – mediators, clients and advisers – need to be able to navigate their way through it. We are facing a trifecta – three things are happening at the same time:

1 We are coming out of the Covid-19 pandemic.

On 5 May 2023 the Director-General of the World Health Organization, Dr Tedros Adhanom Ghebreyesus, declared the pandemic to be officially over, and: 'This trend has allowed most countries to return to life as we knew it before Covid-19.'

Perhaps we would like to go back to how mediation was in 2019 but can we? Lockdown changed the way we did things. We went online. How are those changes being integrated into how we mediate?

2 AI and ChatGPT are taking the world digital.

The process of digitalisation has been underway for years. ChatGPT has reignited it. It's going to be as big as the internet or threaten humanity with extinction. See **Chapter 5**.

3 The Digital Justice System is being introduced in the UK.

As part of the general digitalisation of our lives, the Master of the Rolls, Sir Geoffrey Vos, has vowed to 'radically rethink' civil justice. Aided and abetted by Professor Richard Susskind he is on a digital mission which includes getting rid of physical courts and making mediation mandatory.

How will mediation be affected? How will mediators, advisers and their clients cope?

In this book I try to make sense of what is going on, offer guidance on ways through and discuss how to improve digital resilience. This is a time of uncertainty for mediation. As mediators we know that our clients find uncertainty troubling. How do we view uncertainty ourselves?

What's your mindset? Ask yourself – are you a:

Utopian	Everything will be much better. There has never been a better time to be a mediator.

1.01 *Why do I need to read this book?*

Dystopian	Everything will be much worse. Mediation as we know and love it is finished.
Justhopian	Things will be different but not too bad or too different. Let's hope for the best.

One thing is for sure. All mediation users will have to do their best to understand and adapt to digital mediation in all its different forms and iterations. So, let's find out what it is.

What is digital mediation (DM)?

1.01 The short answer is carrying out mediation digitally. But what does digitally mean? The technical answer is doing something using digital devices or methods. Electronic technology generates, stores, and processes data in one of two states: positive and non-positive. Positive is represented by the number 1 and non-positive by the number 0.

So, if you use a computer, iPad or smartphone to mediate you are mediating digitally. But that is only the technical definition. It sounds simple and straight forward. In fact, the implications of digitalisation for mediation both as a process for resolving disputes and as a service industry are immense. For both mediation and mediation users, digital is disruptive. Read **Chapter 3** for a fuller answer.

Digital is a more than technology. It is a different mindset – a different way of looking at the world and doing things. Data, computing power, and speed are all available to us in ways that has never been experienced before. We can do things differently. Not just better but differently. Learn more **in Chapters 5** and **6.**

Non-digital mediation

1.02 Recall the classic definition: mediation is a voluntary confidential process where the parties to a dispute invite a neutral third-party to help them facilitate their own solution to their own problem.

Recall the classic process:

- Mediation was in person. Participants travelled to the mediation venue. We brought bundles of documents with us. Each team in its own room and spent the whole day together. Everyone stayed until the end.
- Mediations opened with a Joint Opening Session. Everyone – mediator, parties and representatives – sat in the same room. Mediators gave their opening address, and the parties were encouraged to state their positions. Usually, the representatives attacked each other's clients. After that they returned to their own rooms and the day continued in caucus sessions.
- Mediators shuttled from one room to another. Leaving homework for each room so that they did not become bored or disengaged. Downtime was a real problem.

- Through NLP (Neurolinguistic Programming)-based questioning mediators delved below the surface of positions to explore interests and needs. They engaged in reality testing by challenging what they were being told about the law, the facts and the prospects. Half the day was spent exchanging information and arguments before any offers were formulated, let alone made.
- An offer was made and rejected. A counter-offer was made and rejected. A further offer was made and rejected, and so on. Eventually the Deal Zone was identified. With the mediator's help the parties reached the strike point – a deal was struck!
- Then there was further haggling over the wording of the settlement agreement as the lawyers tried to improve the deal for their clients through the drafting.
- Eventually the settlement document was agreed and signed.
- And then you had to travel home.

This is the TradMed model.

Will the leopard change its spots?

1.03 'If we want things to stay as they are, things will have to change'? These were Giuseppi Lampedusa's much quoted words in *The Leopard*. Do they sum up the current dilemma for TradMed? How resilient will the TradMed model be? How much will it have to change?

The TradMed model has been under challenge in UK for some time, even pre-Covid:

- Mediation has not been voluntary in any real sense for a while. The courts enforce contractual clauses to mediate. They impose sanctions if you don't mediate. And recently, as we shall see, the Ministry of Justice (MoJ) is introducing mandatory mediation for some types of disputes (see **4.16**).
- Mediation has never been confidential in the absolute sense. Courts can compel mediators to give evidence about what happened at a mediation. Financial information about costs is not privileged.
- Clients don't always choose their mediator. In court-annexed or scheme mediations the mediators are appointed.
- Evaluative rather than facilitative mediation is becoming more popular. Especially in commercial mediation where mediation and arbitration can now be combined within the same dispute resolution process.

Back to the trifecta – what is going on?

Coming out of Covid and Lockdown

1.04 2020 was the year that online mediation (OLM) became established. AV meetings had been used for years. But somehow AV had never really taken off. Hence the profitable business travel industry. Why was this?

1.05 *Why do I need to read this book?*

Despite the obvious advantages of saving time and money and the greater convenience, AV meetings were seen as second-best. Many still feel that they are. You really need the personal touch – to shake people's hands, to look them in the eye, to offer them a drink. All desirable and helpful for sure but are they essential?

Covid changed all this. Lockdown transformed the ways that we resolve disputes. The legal system embraced AV. Telephone hearings had been routine in the UK long before 2020. Now trials as well as hearings, both civil and criminal, took place using AV.

Mediators are converted/baby Zoomers

1.05 Mediators embraced OLM enthusiastically. In truth they had no choice. Thought leaders who had eschewed OLM became overnight converts, even zealots. LinkedIn filled up with enthusiastic first time Zoomers. Here are some examples:

Andrew Wilkinson a well-known mediator in the Midlands posted: 'I did my first remote mediation today and despite some initial reservations, I'm a convert. It saved cost and time and I'm sure everyone appreciates being able to reflect and contemplate difficult decisions in their own space.'

Henrietta Jackson-Stops who now runs IPOS commented that these comments 'reflect many of those made by our clients in the recent weeks – all, despite their initial reservations, being impressed and surprised by the process and the technology. I agree that this will certainly change the way we do things in the future.'

Shaun Jardine said 'The genie is out of the bottle. Online mediation will continue to save a fortune. Not sure if I was asked to go back to London or any city to conduct a face-to-face mediation I would accept. In fact, I do know. I wouldn't.'

Eileen Carroll the doyenne of mediation in the UK and co-founder of CEDR said in December 2020: 'Having mediated now extensively online, I wonder why we didn't use this mediation medium more.' Quite!

From therapy room to pool party

1.06 OLM has changed the mediation process. Mediating digitally is a different mindset.

Mediation is no longer an intensive immersive experience where everyone took a whole day out of their work or life. Then travelled to a mediation venue and spent the day in their private room where they were encouraged to do nothing else but focus on the mediation.

Now, mediation is more like a pool party than an immersive therapy session. People dip in and out. This reflects two things.

- The flexibility of online systems such as Zoom.

- The more distracted and distributed way of working and doing things which we all now adopt.

TradMed has had to adapt its ways of doing things such as

- Joint Opening Sessions.
- Pre mediation contact with clients and advisers.
- Detailed discussions about needs and interests.
- Timing of offers.
- Split sessions where mediations are paused and resumed on another date.

How and why it has done this is explored in **Chapter 9.**

Are we all online now?

1.07 There is no universal consensus about the way forward. Paul Sills, a New Zealand barrister and London-based international commercial mediator sums it up well in a recent book *Mediation beyond Covid*:

> 'After a period of confusion, there's almost like two definitive groups; the online camp and the not-online camp. I think we've all settled down a bit now, after the panic of the pandemic, and that led to more in-person situations.'

He then goes on to identify his camp: 'For me, that has huge benefits as a mediator and that's the environment I want to work in; I want to sit around the table with people.'

That's the mediators' POV. What about clients? Here is the director of marketing for one of the leading litigation funders posted on LinkedIn In September 2023:

> 'Traditionally, mediation involved physical meetings in neutral environments. However, the landscape changed drastically with the onset of COVID-19. Online mediation became a necessity, and it is here to stay. It provides a secure videoconferencing platform, replicating the traditional mediation experience while saving time and energy.'

He then goes on to give hints for successful online mediations (see **Chapter 9**).

This personal view is reflected in the 2023 CEDR Mediation Audit. They reported that the number of mediations has now started to rise again after the Covid/lockdown dislocation and is running at about 17,000 civil and commercial mediations a year in the UK.

> 'Within that 17,000 figure, the latest Audit confirms the emergence of online mediation with 64% of commercial cases being conducted online. This figure is well below the 89% that we saw during the pandemic period but **seems to show that the nature of the field has permanently changed.**' (*emphasis added*)

OLM is here to stay. Wil you use it or refuse it?

AI and ChatGPT

1.08 You cannot miss the hype, hysteria, frenzy, fear, and hope. See **Chapter 5**. Just trying to get a feel for what was going on was hopeless. As Professor John Naughton said: 'Trying to keep track of the madness has been like attempting to get a drink from a fire hose'. He was referring to the sudden and immense impact of ChatGPT.

ChatGPT is a pre-trained generative chat bot. Bill Gates thinks that it will change our lives in the same way that the internet did. Very few disagree. More realistically and more relevantly Sir Geoffrey Vos summed up the situation in his McNair Lecture in on 19 April 2023.

> 'As I have been saying for some time now, digitisation, and now generative AI, is going to change both the kind of disputes that need to be resolved and the way in which commercial parties will want and require them to be resolved.'

And he added:

> 'GPT-4 and other advanced machine learning is likely to transform the work that lawyers need to do and possibly even, in the slightly longer term, the business of judging.'

ALERT

If lawyers and judges will have to cope with AI why won't mediators have to do the same?

The Digital Justice System

1.09 The court process is going digital. This is the really big news for UK mediators and all mediation and court users. It has huge implications for mediation.

Who says so? Sir Geoffrey Vos says so. He spelt this out in his 2022 Roebuck lecture at the Chartered Institute of Arbitrators in London. The title was *'Mandatory mediation – the digital solution'.*

He explained that:

> 'But what I mean by digital justice is an entirely smart system that operates online, or even on-chain, to identify and resolve the issues between the parties in a far more streamlined and efficient way than the current pleading-based processes. Judges, arbitrators or experts will still be responsible for the ultimate decision making but routine or interim processes maybe automated and resolved by algorithms, always provided that the parties know what AI is deciding and retain the right of appeal to a human judge. '

Sir Geoffrey's aim is to embed mediation in the digital justice system. You can find the lecture at: https://www.judiciary.uk/wp-content/uploads/2022/06/Speech-to-CIArb-Chartered-Institute-of-Arbitrators-Roebuck-Lecture-2022-Mandatory.

It is well worth reading but its message is deceptively and disarmingly disruptive.

Look at what Lord Bellamy KC said in the Ministry of Justice's July 2022 Consultation Paper *Increasing the Use of Mediation in the Civil Justice System.* 'I also want to begin laying the groundwork for embedding mediation as an integral step in the court process more widely across the civil justice system.

He followed this up in the forward to the Consultation outcome issued on 4 August 2023 when he said:

> 'I am pleased to confirm the Government's intention to fully integrate Mediation into the court process for civil claims valued up to £10,000.' He went on 'we also aim later to integrate mediation within the resolution of higher value claims in the County Court: within the fast-track (£10,000–£25,0000 and multi-track (over £25,000).'

It is an established mediation truth that mediation takes place in 'the shadow of the law'. Since the law is going digital that shadow will be digital.

What are the main drivers for this change?

Clients

1.10 Covid and lockdown changed the way we went about our lives and businesses. Clients could not afford to put everything on hold. Traditional legal processes and physical courts could not cope. We all moved online for food deliveries, medical advice and court hearings. Mediation followed suit.

Clients found they liked it. The attractions are obvious and are examined in **Chapter 8**. See the CEDR 2023 statistics at **1.07**.

Judges

1.11 We have seen what the Master of the Rolls and the MoJ have said. Anyone involved in a dispute who wants to use the UK courts will have to change their skill set and mind set. They will have to go digital. The Master of the Rolls is introducing the Digital Justice System. This is explained in **Chapter 2**.

Politicians

1.12 The government wants to increase access to justice and to decrease the cost of the legal system. Linked with the Vos Plan for digital justice is another disruptive idea: mandatory mediation.

1.13 *Why do I need to read this book?*

Until recently, in the UK, the idea of compelling people to go to mediation if they did not want to, was anathema. Some senior members of the judiciary thought that it would violate the Human Rights Act 1998, Sch 1, Article 6 which gives the right to a fair trial. That has changed. Sir Geoffrey commissioned a report from a committee headed by Lady Justice Asplin. Their conclusion was that mandatory mediation was lawful and was not in breach of Article 6.

As explained in 1.09 following the report, the Ministry of Justice (MoJ) undertook a consultation exercise. The Consultation outcome was issued on on 4 August https://www.gov.uk/government/consultations/increasing-the-use-of-mediation-in-the-civil-justice-system-response-to-consultatiion

To start with this will only be for small claims, ie money claims in the County Court under £10,000. This is explained in **Chapter 7**. The stated intention is to gradually extend mandatory mediation to higher value claims. Mandatory mediation will have to be done online – either by telephone or AV or a combination. Why? There simply is not the physical space to accommodate hundreds of in-person mandatory mediations.

Sam Altman

1.13 Who is he? Not many people had heard of him until 30 November 2022. That was when his San Francisco start-up company Openai launched ChatGPT. Its impact has been extraordinary.

An enhanced version – GPT 4 – has been available since 14 March 2023 and they are working on ChatGPT5. Its success has been beyond belief. Within five days it had 1 million users. Within the first two months it had 100 million users. Netflix took three years to get 1 million users. Estimates from UBS are that by the end of February 2023 ChatGPT had 1 billion visits.

What does this mean for mediation and mediators? We see a lot of disagreement and hype about AI, digital justice and online dispute resolution (ODR). Cutting through it is not easy. Learn how in **Chapters 5, 6** and **8**.

Society

1.14 Apart from these pressures within the legal system there are other reasons why the mediation climate is going digital.

1 Clients are now digital. For many their working patterns have changed. We now have WFH (Working From Home), hybrid, smart, and agile working. In other words, people do not all congregate in a physical place at the same time for a particular reason. They work from home and communicate online. So why should they do anything different in order to mediate?

2 The gig economy. More of us work for ourselves. We often work from home. Mediators have always worked in the gig economy. Even within the legal profession which is notoriously conservative we see the growing emergence of the virtual law firm. More lawyers and their clients are adopting flexible working methods and organisations.

3 The generational shift. Anybody under 35 has a different attitude towards the way in which services are bought and delivered. They are far happier doing things online. The Millennials (or Generation Y) – those born between 1981 and 1996 and Zedders/Zoomers (or Generation Z) – those born between 1997 and 2012 are more concerned with work /life balance.

4 Evolution. Mediation has evolved since its emergence in the 1990s. The way in which we thought about mediation and mediated had changed over 20 years even before Covid. One way of looking at DM is to see it as simply the next stage in the evolution of mediation. Adopting a growth mindset, as Professor Carol Dweck might describe it, will make it much easier for us all to adapt and cope with the changes.

5 Mediation's competitors are going digital. Courts and arbitrations are going online. Online hearings are routinely use not just for interlocutory applications but also for trials. Dispute resolution is a crowded space. If mediators don't offer their services online, others – ombuds, arbitrators, conciliators, and early neutral evaluators – will.

ALERT

If all this sounds too theoretical it's not. Society produces the circumstances in which people have disagreements leading to disputes to be resolved. How can mediation be immune from these societal pressures for change? If it cannot be immune, how can it adapt?

That is why you need to read this book – to learn what digital mediation (DM) means for you. Whether you are a client in a dispute going to mediation, a lawyer advising clients and representing them at mediation, or a mediator, DM will affect you. This book is a manual to help all users of mediation: clients, advisors, and mediators, to make the best out of DM.

In a nutshell

1.15 The reasons why you should read this book:

Clients: You need to be aware of the opportunities to be able to judge whether you want DM. It has advantages – see **Chapter 9** – and disadvantages – see **Chapter 8**. Is DM the right choice for your dispute? Learn how to decide – see **Chapter 10**.

Advisers: You need to be able to advise clients appropriately. Mediation is done differently online. You want to represent them effectively and get the best outcomes. Learn how. See **Chapters 11** and **12**.

Mediators: You need to prepare for the digital climate change. Will it be a digital summer or a digital winter? All disruptions produce winners and losers. Which are you going to be?

1.15 *Why do I need to read this book?*

- The world is going digital.
- You need to be digitally aware and digitally resilient.
- Digital means disruption.
- Mediation is in a period of intense change.
- There will be embracers and resisters. Decide which you want to to be and prepare accordingly.

Part A

Digital mediation: threat or promise?

Chapter 2

The digital justice system: dream or nightmare?

In this chapter you will learn

- What the digital Justice system is.
- Why it is being introduced.
- What it means for mediators.

The digital justice system is coming. Is it the individual mission of a reformist Master of the Rolls or an inevitable expression of societal and technological shifts? If the digital justice system is not Sir Geoffrey Vos's baby it is certainly his ward of court. Richard Susskind will probably claim paternity. Who are these revolutionaries?

Sir Geoffrey Vos

2.01 Sir Geoffrey is the Master of the Rolls. This means that he is the President of the Civil Division of the Court of Appeal of England and Wales and Head of Civil Justice and the second in seniority only to the Lord Chief Justice. He took over as Master of the Rolls in January 2021. At his swearing in ceremony, he was described by the then President of The Law Society as 'an outstanding lawyer, a legal disruptor and the premier ambassador of the jurisdiction'.

He has been an advocate of reform and digitisation for several years. He appears to be a man on a mission. How likely is it that he will disrupt the English legal system as he says he will and leave mediation intact?

In his 2022 Roebuck Lecture to the Chartered Institute of Arbitrators Sir Geoffrey delivered his mission statement.

Here was his message:

> '**Many lawyers think that the highest pinnacles of digital justice are achieved by using Teams, Webex, Google Meet or Zoom for a dispute resolution hearing**, perhaps even involving arbitrators located in different countries. They might also think that the use of e-filing and PDF

bundles or a digital document disclosure programme will turn the current systems into state-of-the-art automation of the dispute resolution process. **I respectfully disagree.** These things are, of course, all fine.'

Recall from **Chapter 1** what he said:

> 'But what I mean by digital justice is **an entirely smart system that operates online, or even on-chain**, to identify and resolve the issues between the parties in a far more streamlined and efficient way than the current pleading-based processes. Judges, arbitrators or experts will still be responsible for the ultimate decision making, but routine or interim processes may be automated and resolved by algorithms, always provided that the parties know what AI is deciding and retain the right of appeal to a human judge.'
>
> [*Emphases added*]

He reiterated his message in the McNair lecture given on 20 April 2023. Recall his words from Chapter 1:

> 'GPT-4 and other advanced machine learning is likely to transform the work that lawyers need to do and possibly even, in the slightly longer term, the business of judging.' And possibly slightly tongue in cheek, he said: 'That much is probably uncontroversial.'

He identified a key premise 'that needs to be understood that businesses will ultimately not want to pay for things that are available free. And that applies as much to legal services and dispute resolution as to anything else.'

And so, he said:

1. 'dispute resolution will need to make as much use of generative AI as is consistent with user confidence.'
2. 'I think the AI will be used within digital justice systems and may, at some stage, be used to take some (at first, very minor) decisions.'
3. Litigation procedures will fundamentally change. For him pleadings, expert reports and witness statements are 'analogue concepts rooted in an analogue age which may be in need of a digital makeover.'
4. 'Generative AI may be able to trawl through masses of documents and identify the real issues both legal and factual dispute that require resolution'.

He may well be right. Mediators would welcome this.

And the process is underway. On 12 June 2023 the MoJ launched a new Online Procedure Rules Committee (OPRC) to help judges, legal representatives and litigants in person through online court procedures. It will oversee the development of rules for online proceedings across the civil, family, and tribunal jurisdiction **as well as data and behavioural standards for online dispute resolution before proceedings are brought to a court or tribunal**.

Sir Geoffrey's reformist thinking reflects the work done by the UK Civil Justice Council's Advisory Group on Online Dispute Resolution chaired by his co- disruptor Richard Susskind. Who is Richard Susskind?

Richard Susskind

2.02 He is a world thought leader in legal and digital developments. He chairs the UK's Civil Justice Council's Advisory Group on Online Dispute Resolution whose report in February 2015 recommended the establishment of Her Majesty's Online Courts (HMOC). Sir Geoffrey Vos has been a keen adopter of his views.

He has a well-developed sense of self. In his book *Online Courts and the Future of Justice* he said: 'I often joke that I write the same book every four years. Yet there is truth in this jest, in that my message has been consistent for almost 40 years – that we can and should find ways of using technology to improve the practice of law and the administration of justice.'

Susskind has been terrifying lawyers for several decades. The third edition of his book *Tomorrow's Lawyers* came out in February 2023. In this book and in his recent book written with his son Daniel, *The Future of the Professions,* he concludes that the outlook for lawyers and the professions generally is bleak. Many of the jobs that they currently do will be done by digital devices.

Does this affect mediation?

2.03 Although it is questionable whether mediation is a profession, his criticisms and predictions about the professions apply to mediation. Since he is also the IT Advisor to the Lord Chief Justice of England and Wales mediators and their clients need to pay attention to what he says.

What is driving this digital-legal transformation?

2.04 The main ones that Susskind identifies:

1 Saving money.

Greater efficiency and moving away from paper-based systems to digital systems.

2 Reducing the cost of litigation.

It is too expensive and cumbersome for many people. No one disputes this. The dispute is over how to effect the reduction.

3 Improving access to justice.

More people will be able access it if they can do from their own homes. You can see the reasoning behind all these revolutionary ideas in his book *'Online Courts: The Future of Justice.'* For him there is both a moral and a business case for the digital justice system.

(i) Moral

As he says 'based on what I believed to be right and good. It is rooted in a deeper set of convictions: that all human beings – whatever their capabilities, status, wealth and wherever they live and work – deserve and should be accorded equal respect and dignity – crucially for present purposes, this right to respect and dignity I believe, should be enshrined in and enforceable by the law. For this to be so, we need effective court systems and services that are genuinely accessible to all. And we do not have these today. Anywhere.'

Fine words. Stirring language. Ideals that very few would contradict. So difficult to oppose but equally difficult to implement. Do these words describe a vision, an illusion, or a fantasy? Susskind has had lawyers in his sights for years. He still has.

(ii) No need for lawyers

He doesn't think lawyers will be needed in the future. A key benefit of the digital revolution will be demystifying the process by reducing the need for expensive experts. You don't need lawyers to solve your disputes. Lawyers do solve your disputes, but you can solve them without them. That is his general thesis.

He states that 'although it is not a defining purpose of online courts to exclude lawyers from the process of litigation, they are generally conceived as a service that can be used without formal legal representation.' (p 153)

4 AI is key.

Developing and implementing artificial intelligence will be key. Eventually we will face the prospect of decisions being taken without any human intervention. That is what Sir Geoffrey Vos was saying in the McNair lecture quoted at para **2.01**.

Susskind goes on: 'a second generation of the systems can in principle be envisaged… When the determination will be made by some form of artificial intelligence (AI). Today, this may seem outrageous. Within two decades or so, use of AI may well be commonplace for appropriate cases, not least where traditional court service is not available.' (p 117)

He could well be right. Is there any reason not to believe that eventually AI systems will make decisions that are at least no worse than those of a human judge? After all, every day disappointed clients and lawyers think that a judge has made a mistake. AI can already interpret medical scans for cancer better than human consultants. Although for the moment most systems have a human oversight and double checking. See **Chapter 5**.

5 Feasibility.

A lot of what Susskind says makes sense. Mediators will ignore it at their peril. He is an intelligent man who has been around politics, law, and IT for most of his working life. He knows the realities of situations. There are problems. Many large-scale government IT projects have failed. Why will these new initiatives be any more successful? Of course, we hope we have learned from our mistakes in the past but…? Are you a utopian, dystopian or justhopian?

6 Irrational rejectionism.

Susskind knows that there will be resistance from lawyers. He is scathing about what he refers to as 'irrational rejectionism.' And he warns that: 'We should view with scepticism any blanket rejection of remote courts on the grounds of justice.' Mediators know about cognitive biases. We need to be careful not to allow motivated reasoning or naïve realism to influence our responses.

7 Private v public sector.

Susskind argues that the provision of dispute resolution services should be a public service. For him there is not much justification for involving the private sector. This is bad news for mediators.

So, the question is how likely is all this to happen and when? Sir Geoffrey said that the speed of change is likely to be both 'very fast and very slow'. This may be true but is not the least bit helpful for mediators.

Susskind says rightly: 'Bold attempts to replace the most complex and challenging work in revolutionary sweeps invariably do not succeed.' (p 247). But, on page 253 he talks about emergent technologies: 'By 2030, and possibly, much sooner, all courts round the world will have been transformed by technologies that have not yet been invented.'

The short answer is nobody knows. Within the next three years the chances are that:

- We will have pilots for the digital justice system. A fully fledged system will take much longer.
- Mandatory mediation having been introduced and expected to be operational from April 2024 will be extended,
- Generative AI will be changing things – how, when, and where will be the questions.

In any business three years is about the maximum that you can confidently plan for. After that events happen that you didn't even dream of, and which can radically affect your business. If you are a mediator working in the gig economy three years is your maximum time horizon.

Whether the Vos-Susskind revolution is a threat challenge or opportunity remains to be seen. But equip yourself. As Darwin said, 'To survive you have to adapt.'

Mediators have not expressed wild enthusiasm for 'embedding' mediation in the legal system. For many this will subvert its whole voluntary, alternative, creative philosophy and turn mediation into just another procedural step on the way to trial. They have also expressed doubts about the proposals for mandatory mediation, see **4.16**.

Words of comfort

2.05 Although Susskind's predictions and conclusions are dire for lawyers, they are not necessarily so bad for mediators. As he says: 'if we are to introduce an affordable public online dispute resolution system, it makes sense to relieve the parties of the expense of lawyers.' (p 153). Mediators have been selling themselves for decades on the same premise. After all, ADR was conceived as an alternative to litigation. The use of lawyers in mediation was not encouraged.

And let us not forget that, certainly in the UK, most mediators are not lawyers. Changing the way litigation is conducted and courts behave will influence mediation. Will mediation be delivered in the same smart way that the Vos/Susskind alliance envisages for litigation? See **Chapters 5** and **6**.

In a nutshell

2.06 What to do?

- Keep abreast of events.
- Check blogs and posts on LinkedIn to stay in touch.
- Learn the lingo so you can understand the debate.
- Devise your coping strategies.
- Keep your head out of the sand.

Chapter 3

What is digital mediation?

> In this chapter you will learn
>
> - The jargon – what it means and what it doesn't.
> - What the DM mindset is.
> - The ways digital mediation is delivered – phone, email, video, hybrid.
> - How AI can be used more.

Jargon busting

3.01 The Alternative Dispute Resolution (ADR) Ecosphere is awash with acronyms. If you want to have any credibility in the DM world, learn these.

Glossary and abbreviations

3.02

ADR	alternative dispute resolution
AI	artificial intelligence – an umbrella term not a technology
Algorithm	a process or set of rules to be followed in calculations or other problem- solving operations, especially by a computer
AN	automated negotiation
AR	augmented reality
AV	audio visual
B2C	business to consumer
C2C	consumer to consumer
ChatGPT	generative pre-trained chatbot issued November 2022 by OpenAI

Deep learning	another type of AI. It is a subset of machine learning that uses artificial neural networks to mimic the learning process of the human brain
DM	digital mediation
eADR	electronic ADR
EAI	emotional artificial intelligence
eDR	electronic dispute resolution
F2F	face-to-face
GPT	generative pre-trained transformer – artificial neural network based on the transformer architecture pre-trained in unsupervised manner of large data set able to generate novel human like text
ICT	Information and Communication Technologies
iDR	Internet dispute resolution
IRL	in real life
LLM	large language model-natural language processing programs that use deep learning to generate text and source code
ML	Machine learning – computers discover their own algorithms without being specifically trained by humans
M2M	machine to machine – the internet of things (IOT)
ML	machine learning is a subset of AI that uses algorithms to analyse huge amounts of data, learn from insights and make informed decisions
MMM	multi-media mediation
MODRIA	modular online dispute resolution implementation assistant
oADR	online ADR
ODR	online dispute resolution – a subset of DM.
OLM	online mediation.
Singularity	the point at which computers become more intelligent than human beings – ETA is 2040
TAME	technology assisted mediation
Telepresence	technology that allows a person to feel that they are present at a place other than their actual location in
TFN	technology facilitated negotiation
TPN	third party neutral
Video Conferencing (VC)	a way of holdings meetings in real time and face to face out without being physically in the same location
Zoom	video conferencing system that has been industry standard for mediation

What's the difference?

3.03 Mediators, mediation commentators and academics love arguing about definitions and acronyms. For years we have not been able to agree what ADR stands for. Was it Alternative Dispute Resolution or Amicable Dispute Resolution or Appropriate Dispute Resolution? Even now we cannot agree what ODR means.

ODR

Rachele Beretta of the University of Antwerp has recently surveyed the problem. She concludes that:

> 'online dispute resolution ('ODR') is a complex and multi-faceted phenomenon, whose rapid evolution appears to challenge harmonisation efforts and elaboration of universally accepted definition.'

She continues that it has become a buzzword to indicate any type of procedure that relies on ICT components and reiterates that 'there is no well-established definition of ODR nor is there uniformity of views in ODR literature regarding the distinctive features of ODR.'

Thirteen years earlier in 2020 Professor Jean Sternlight had asserted that 'the term 'ODR' obscures rather than aids analysis'. She advocated ceasing to use the phrase at all. Her 'critique is not that the wrong *term* is being used, but, rather, that it is not useful to group so many disparate processes under *any* single term.'

ODM

It is the same with online mediation. Different words are used to describe the same thing:

- remote mediation
- virtual mediation
- offline mediation
- online mediation
- video mediation

All this is confusing, unnecessary, and tiresome. While commentators, trainers and academics might debate these distinctions, active users of mediation don't need to dwell on them. To make things simpler in this book I am just talking about mediation. I use the following definitions:

- in-person mediation means mediation that takes place with people physically present together at the same time in the same place.
- online mediation (OLM) means when participants mediate without being physically present and use some form of digital communication – video conferencing, smart phone, e-mail, or a combination.

DM

DM is not a synonym for online or remote mediation.

In practice DM has several meanings:

- Using a digital device to communicate, eg a laptop or a phone.
- Using VC or telepresence as the system of communication.
- Using computer programs **to help you** do your job – technology assisted mediation (TAME).
- Using computer programs **to do your** job aka mediator replacement.
- Adopting a data driven mindset as a reality check.

DM Includes OLM and ODR but is wider.

- Smart systems – algorithm based, a subset of ODR. An example is Smartsettle. Look at the way that eBay settles millions of consumer disputes using smart systems every year.
- Technology Assisted Mediation – making use of AI. In a nutshell ODR can be described as a smart system using TAME (technology assisted mediation). This term has not really caught on. Technology can in theory assist in various ways. For example:
  - predicting outcomes at trial based on similar cases such as Smartsettle or Robert Hogarth's SettleIndex.
  - faster research – recent awards and court decisions using Search engineers like Google with or without ChatGPT.
  - faster calculations – the cost of money, DCFs (Discounted cash flows), interest rate effects.
  - faster and better document searching and review.
  - more accurate calculations of risk/probability – using programs.
  - greater use of real-time information for example valuations using Search engines with or without ChatGPT (see **Chapter 6**).

VC

Video conferencing (VC). In contemporary mediation practice this means using Zoom.

All this doesn't necessarily mean that ADR will come to stand for Automated Dispute Resolution. But it does mean that it will come to stand for Augmented Dispute Resolution.

In this section we are talking about using audiovisual (AV) systems to mediate, eg platforms such as Zoom, Teams. Mediating online by using blind bidding systems such as Smartsettle or SettleIndex in are discussed in **3.24–3.31**. Let's look at what OLM systems we already have and how they are evolving, even without the planned disruption described in **Chapter 1**.

Telephone mediations

Please read this section with **12.05–12.10**.

3.04 This the oldest version of DM/ODR/OLM, now well established in the UK both in the public and private sectors of dispute resolution

Public sector

3.05 In the UK public sector, His Majesty's Courts and Tribunal Service (HMCTS) runs schemes using court officials. They are employed civil servants who provide a one-hour free mediation conducted by telephone. They are limited to small claims, ie with a value of less than £10,000 (see gov.uk/guidance/small-claims-mediation service).

This is the type of mediation that the Ministry of Justice introduces in its mandatory mediation scheme (see **Chapter 1**). They intend to roll it out for larger value disputes and are planning to increase the number of civil servants to provide the service by seven-fold.

Private sector

3.06 Private sector mediators also offer telephone mediations. They are usually longer than one hour but rarely are more than three hours. The technology is straightforward. Conference calls are used. This sort of mediation is predicted to grow.

Consumer mediations

3.07 Consumer complaints schemes were set up after the European Consumer Rights regulations were introduced in 2014. These are often referred to as scheme mediations. They usually have a telephone mediation option with one-hour sessions. They are free to the consumer – the trader pays for the mediation. The settlement rate is high although this largely depends upon the attitude of the trader. Some traders make one offer and never negotiate up. Others are more flexible.

The disputes tend to be simple, usually with only a single issue and the values are low. Sometimes less than £1,000. Often, under £5,000. Mediators' charges are low – typically £100 an hour. Sometimes £35 an hour. Apart from low rates of pay mediators have to face other challenges.

ALERT

In the UK the Digital Markets, Competition and Consumers Bill has recently been published, see **Chapter 4**. The Bill:

- provides a comprehensive framework for ADR for consumer complaint disputes.
- raises the prospect of regulation for mediation providers in this sector.

Challenges

Unrepresented parties

3.08 Many of the parties are unrepresented. They are not used to legal disputes. They may not understand the implications of not settling and being engaged in litigation.

Educating parties

3.09 Mediators have to provide a lot of explanation and education. There is always a danger that mediators can slip from giving explanations into giving guidance or even advice.

To give yourself the best chance of helping the parties to reach a settlement within 60 minutes have pre-mediation conversations with both sides. These can vary from 5 to 25 minutes. Be disciplined: don't let people ramble on.

TOP TIP

- Don't be tempted to take a shortcut and omit the pre-mediation conversation even if it is only a couple of minutes to introduce yourself. (See the Checklist at **3.14**.)
- Accept that an hour's mediation is not 60 minutes. Almost never is it less. Nearly always, it is more.

Preparation

3.10 The biggest obstacle to settlement is lack of preparation. People don't put the effort into assembling the information they need to take informed decisions during the mediation. Often high-speed information gathering takes place during the mediation. That uses up time and energy!

Use your pre-meditation phone call to give guidance and encouragement about preparation.

Procedure

3.11 Usually, the shorter scheme mediations – for example disputes with insurers over warranty claims or with utility companies over water or electricity bills – are by telephone. Sometimes Teams or Zoom is used.

The parties rarely talk to each other. They talk through the mediator. Why? There is time pressure to get to the real issues. Joint sessions easily degenerate into rows with each side justifying their past conduct. They need to concentrate on what they want to do in the future.

Some mediation commentators think that these sorts of scheme mediations deprive the parties of their day in court. Experience shows that parties can express their outrage quite quickly and cogently. Rarely do they complain about not being heard. Most seem satisfied with the format.

Time pressure

3.12 The timetable is tight. Most mediations are scheduled for an hour. Time management is important. You need to move people along without them feeling railroaded.

Settlement agreements

3.13 Mediation agreements usually provide that there is no legally binding agreement until a document recording the settlement has been signed by both sides. This must be drawn up within the 60 minutes as well. Who does that? The mediator.

The conventional wisdom is that mediators should never draw up mediation agreements. That is not practicable or even desirable in these types of scheme mediations.

If you are not sure how to draft a mediation agreement, then learn. Mediators are told to acquire soft skills. That is quite true. It is equally true that mediators need to be adept and comfortable with hard skills as well. These include drawing up settlement agreements (see **Chapters 6** and **13**).

CHECKLIST FOR PRE-MEDIATION PHONE CALL

3.14 Introduce yourself. Give your name and very brief details of who you are.

Say that you want to have a short word about the process.

Explain that:

- It is confidential – including this phone call. You won't tell the other side what they tell you until they tell you that you can. And they must not discuss this with anyone else. Ask if that gives them a problem.
- It is voluntary – they can stop whenever they want.
- That its purpose is to try reach a settlement.
- Explain that you'll ring the parties. Speak to them. And then go and speak to the other party.
- You will send out an email giving your mobile numbers.

Ask them if:

- they have been to mediation before.

- they have been to court before. Explain that it's not like going to court.
- they have taken legal advice.
- they have any legal expenses insurance because sometimes they have helplines that they could use.

Explain that:

- everyone only has 60 minutes and will be pressed for time. Assure them that you do not want them to feel railroaded. If they think everything is going too fast, to just tell you.
- there is no legally binding settlement until all parties have signed a settlement agreement. This must be done within the 60 minutes as well. So, if we are not in the Deal Zone after about 45/50 minutes then we are likely to run out of time.
- you will draw the settlement agreement – it is short and simple, but it still needs to be done within 60 minutes.
- you will ring the complainant first. Speak to them for 5–10 minutes. And then speak to the other party.
- you will send an email giving your mobile numbers.

TEMPLATE OF A SHORT FORM SETTLEMENT AGREEMENT FOR A DISPUTE WITH A UTILITY COMPANY

Online mediation AB Logistics Ltd v Mega Water PLC

Settlement agreement

3.15 This agreement is made on **XXX 2023** between

(1) AB Logistics Ltd of XXXX (ABL)

And

(2) MEGA Water Ltd of XXXX (MWL)

Following an online mediation, the parties have agreed to settle their dispute on the following terms.

1 In full and final settlement of all claims that ABL may have arising out of the complaints and claims that it has made to MWL at the date of the mediation and in full settlement of all outstanding money on their account with MWL as notified by MWL to ABL at the date of the mediation ABL will pay to MWL the sum of £...... . For the avoidance of doubt this includes but is not limited to any charges for late payment or meter verification.

2 The money to be paid by 12 noon on XXX into MWL's account Bank:

Branch:

Sort code:

Account number:

Account name: REF.

3 The terms of this agreement are confidential between the parties and is intended to be legally binding on the parties.

Signed	Signed
For and on behalf of AB Logistics Ltd	for and on behalf of MEGA Water PLC

ALERT

1 Your voice is you in telephone mediations. Please read **Chapter 12** about voice. It is vital.

2 Brush up on your telephone techniques: see **Chapter 12**.

3 Learn the hard lesson. 60 minutes is not enough. You will spend more time than this and you will not be paid extra. So why do such mediations? Experience, getting your hours in, building up confidence. And keeping your telephone technique in good order. You need good telephone technique in all sorts of mediations.

Good news

3.16 The satisfaction rates appear to be high. Why?

- There is minimal disruption for the parties.
- They are in their own homes or offices.
- They have achieved an outcome.
- They are usually free to the consumer.

Email mediations

3.17 Email is used as is video for pre-mediation communication. Its use in mediations is relatively rare. Ten years ago it was very different. As Professor Noam Ebner said the 'One clear trend emerging from a review of e-mediation service providers is that the age of video has not yet arrived. The state of the art of e-mediation is very solidly text based.' Some mediators are still very keen on it. Graham Ross is particularly expert and experienced at it. He is the Founder and President of the Mediation Room (see themediationroom.com).

The advantages of email mediation are:

- You can deal with different time zones. It is asynchronous not synchronous.

- People who feel at a disadvantage speaking for example those with neurodiversity or whose language of choice is a different one can take the time to reflect and crystallise their thoughts in the written word.
- Communicating in writing can reduce misunderstandings – people are less likely to misremember or mishear what is said.

But the advantages of the written word can be matched by the disadvantages.

- Things are always received differently if they are written down as opposed to being spoken.
- There is less scope for informal discussion in writing than in oral communication.
- Messages may be less nuanced.

How to email

3.18 Conveying your message by email whether through information or persuasion is a skill. Keep in mind the following:

CHECKLIST FOR EMAILS

3.19

- Long documents in email don't work. Keep your emails short.
- Use short words, short sentences and short paragraphs. People cannot absorb long blocks of text. Especially on screen.
- Keep your point shorts. Number them.
- Avoid the use of emojis.
- Don't capitalise WHOLE WORDS – it is perceived as verbal bullying.
- Don't use emphatic punctuation!!
- Jokes backfire. Avoid them.
- Resist both overstatement and understatement. Nuances get lost in emails. Stick to simple plain language.

Video conferencing mediations

3.20 This has been the main format for online mediation for the last ten years and is likely to remain so for the next five years at least. Variations and development such as Virtual Reality (VR) and Telepresence are used to some extent. The metaverse and the use of holograms and avatars in mediation are causing a lot of excitement. No doubt this will be used in mediations in some way, at some time. But, for most mediators doing vanilla mediations in 2023 they not just science-fiction they are science fantasy.

Zoom and Teams are the most widely used platforms. See **Chapter 11** to learn how to make the best use of them.

Mixed media mediations

3.21 These are where video, telephone and email are used. In practice all three are used in most online mediations. What happens is:

The mediation is on Zoom. During the session participants also communicate through WhatsApp or SMS messaging. Information is usually conveyed by email either as a text or an attachment. For example,

- Where up-to-date accounts or redemption statements are required, these are emailed.
- Suggested wording for a particular clause is usually drafted by one side and emailed to the other.
- Offers are increasingly emailed to the mediator who discusses them with the offeror and passes them on to the offeree. Putting them in an email reduces the danger of confusion. The offeror thinks more closely about what they are writing down. The mediator doesn't mishear. The offerees don't mishear. And no none misremembers.

The mediator and participants can have private and confidential chats. This are usually by telephone but can be by WhatsApp or in a separate breakout room. All quite simple. See **Chapter 8**.

Hybrid mediations

3.22 This is where some participants are in person and others online. Hybrid can have different meanings:

- The mediation is in person but the pre-mediation arrangements take place online.
- The mediation is in person but some people do not attend in person. They may be in a different country or their attendance is only required for a short time for a particular issue. Take expert witnesses – instead of being in the room all day long racking up fees for their clients they can dial in on Zoom for an hour or so (see **Chapter 8**).
- Communication between the parties is by VC. The mediator is in one location. The parties are in separate locations. Some participants may be physically together in their solicitor's office. But they communicate with the other team and with the mediator by Zoom.

Semi-hybrids

3.23 A new variation is sometimes suggested: semi-hybrid. This is where one team are physically in one location with the mediator, but the other team are on

Zoom. Apart from where people are in different countries the rationale for this is unclear. Who does one team want to be able to talk to in person. Not the other side. The mediator? Why? Do they think that they can win them over?

ALERT

- Resist the suggestion if you can.
- The team on Zoom begins to feel that perhaps the other team who are physically with the mediator are being favoured in some way. This usually happens in the middle of the afternoon when frustration at not having concluded a deal starts to show.
- In fairness, the mediator might have established a better relationship with the team who are in the same venue. They may have unknowingly been showing this.

TOP TIP

- Give the simple reason for resisting semi-hybrids.
- If there is a perceived advantage to being physically with the mediator then all participants should be able to have it.

As we shall see in **Chapter 8**, OLM is a great leveller. As mediators, we want to minimise any imbalances of power not reinforce them.

AI based systems

3.24 These are the long-anticipated game changers. Their software captures the information, analyses it and takes a decision. There is limited if any human intervention.

eBay have used this for years. British Columbia uses a system like this for simple condominium disputes. There are now systems using AI to settle disputes. For example, the smartsettle system.

Graham Ross a UK mediator and ODR expert has explained how he used this system. A three-month dispute over £2,000 in unpaid fees claimed by a trainer was settled in less than an hour. No human mediator was involved. Previously a telephone mediation involving a human mediator had been tried and failed.

They operate at 4 levels.

Level 1: Problem diagnosis and onboarding

3.25 At the simplest level they are used as an information management system. The parties log in online and enter details about themselves, the nature of the dispute and their opponent.

By doing this they register their wish to participate in dispute resolution using this process. From that stage there can be human intervention in the sense that a mediator/arbitrator is appointed. Communications can be online or through emails. There is nothing new about email. Most communication both before and after the traditional in person mediation is by e-mail.

The software can go further and act as a triage system. Through a series of questions and answers the software can:

- assign the dispute into a particular category of dispute.
- identify options for dealing with it.
- describe the dispute and the different resolution processes.
- give information about the steps involved and how long the process takes.
- describe how other disputes of this sort have been resolved.

Mediation providers do this when they receive telephone calls and emails from disputants looking for a mediator. Most still use humans. But no doubt they are considering chatbots. This triaging is what the Digital Justice System envisages as a start (see **Chapter 2**).

Level 2: Electronic dispute resolution (EDR)

3.26 The next level is more sophisticated. The technology is the medium for negotiation. There is no human intervention. We are now in the sphere of automated negotiation. It is already being used.

Blind bidding

3.27 This is usually used where liability is not in dispute. The parties want to arrive at a settlement figure.

Double- blind bidding

3.28 There are two parties in a dispute. They agree to negotiate. Each side makes secret offers or bids. They are only disclosed if both offers match certain standards. Conventionally each participant submits up to three offers. If the bids of each party come within a predetermined range for example 5–30% or for a given amount of money, for example £5,000 a deal, is done at the midpoint.

3.29 *What is digital mediation?*

What this system does is to encourage the parties to reveal their bottom line offers and demands. By splitting the difference when the amounts are not far apart a deal is achieved.

Conventionally each participant submits up to three offers. They are only disclosed if both of them match a certain standard or if the bids of each party come within a predetermined range – for example 5–30%.

Visual blind bidding

3.29 The difference between this and Double Blind Bidding is that in Visual Blind Bidding what is kept secret is what the parties are willing to accept. There can be several parties. They agreed to negotiate using the system.

> They exchange visible proposals. The initial ones are usually over-optimistic. But they define a bargaining range. The software generates suggestions that fall within the range. The parties can continue to exchange proposals if they want, or they can suggest altering the mix. The suggestions are anonymous. The perceived problem of people losing face by accepting a suggestion made by another disputant is avoided.

At the end of the negotiations if the parties accept one or more packages (or one or more proposed decision values) there is a resolution. This agreement is determined by the software using an algorithm that rewards the party that moves earliest into the Settlement Zone. This is seen to be less threatening then just splitting the difference.

Insurance companies settling several thousands of small claims when there is no real dispute about liability are enthusiastic supporters of the system. But not all claimants are enthusiasts.

The Vos Digital Justice System envisages using EDR (see **Chapter 2**).

Level three: Technology facilitated negotiation (TFN)

3.30 The third level of sophistication is Technology facilitated negotiation (TFN). This is really where the technology becomes the fourth party at the mediation. It is not limited to providing a certain process: it also provides the parties and the mediator with specific advice.

The most obvious example is sophisticated risk or decision tree analysis. This helps the parties and their advisors to work through the possible permutations. There are decision-making platforms on the market for example see superdecisions.com or lucidchart.com. In the UK Robert Hogarth has recently introduced SettletIndex which describes itself as

'SettleIndex is a risk and decision analysis platform that enables lawyers and clients to assess, track and analyse litigation disputes. The software features financial modelling, reporting and key performance indicators, and structured data collection and analysis.'

Resource

Settleindex.com

3.31 At this stage there is usually some human intervention. The parties have been through the first two stages which are conducted entirely online. The second stage of automated negotiation has not led to a settlement. The parties can then if they wish move to the third stage where the TFN is appointed and participates in their discussions about settlement.

These discussions are carried on through the online mediation either by email or so that they can be real time interaction by Zoom or telephone. As an alternative the parties can choose to step out of the online process and attend an in-person mediation.

This is also envisaged in the Vos Digital Justice System (see **Chapter 2**).

Level 4: Robojudge

3.32 The fourth level of sophistication is where the parties submit the dispute to adjudication by the software. There is no human intervention. The computer tells the parties what the outcome is. There is no negotiation. There is automated decision-making.

The software predicts the outcome of the dispute based upon a dataset of civil disputes that has been pre-determined or settled through negotiation online and comes up with an expected outcome.

The parties can agree to be bound by this. Or they can simply accept it as a non-binding recommendation. Evaluative mediators often do this anyway in both in person or online mediations. The difference is computers use software and data sets: humans use personal experience and hunch. Which will clients prefer in the future?

This is where AI and ChatGPT in particular can be used (see **Chapter 6**).

Using AI

Mindset

3.33 As mentioned in **Chapter 1**, DM is not just a technology as described above. It is also a way of looking at situations. At the mediator.com conference on AI and The Future of Mediation in April 2023 Itai Brun, former head of Israeli Defence Intelligence, explained the research that they have been doing using ChatGPT as an intelligence analyst. The big point was generative systems like ChatGPT didn't just do things better than humans, they did things differently.

The most significant differences are that:

- they don't share humans' stubborn attachment to old beliefs.

- they don't share humans' equally stubborn resistance to new ideas that upset their old beliefs.
- they don't feel the need to justify themselves.
- they readily admit their mistakes.

Data based analysis

3.34 AI tools will enable more detailed analysis and quantification. Much of what takes place at mediation is in fact second-guessing what a judge will do. Generally, this is based upon hunch and experience. It can be very accurate. But AI-based systems for predicting judicial outcomes can be even more accurate. Richard Susskind reminds us of this constantly – referencing the well-known experiment involving Lex Machina which predicted the outcome of patent cases more accurately than patent attorneys. More importantly these AI systems may be seen as more objective by clients (see **Chapter 6**).

Jointly instructed expert systems

3.35 Will an AI predictive system come to be seen as the jointly appointed third-party expert? We are all familiar at mediations with finding two valuers looking at the same information coming up with widely different valuations. They nearly always favour the party that has commissioned their report and paid their fee.

Will we get to a stage where jointly appointed experts are replaced by jointly appointed expert systems? (See **Chapter 6**.) We have seen how ChatGPT can provide information depending on the questions that are put to it. Will we be able to formulate the shared assumptions that are necessary to bring about a shared assessment of a situation? Even if we don't get to that point soon, we may get to the point where a list of key questions or key information is supplied to an expert system for it to provide an Early Neutral Evaluation (see **Chapter 6**).

Risk Analysis

3.36 Quantification will be used more. Not just for forecasting the outcomes of cases at trial but also for pricing up the risk of doing better at trial after litigation than you could do today through negotiation. One way of doing this would be using an Expected Value (EV) calculation. See **Chapter 6** for a worked example using ChatGPT. Or for gaming different settlement and negotiation scenarios and strategies. Working out the probability of a particular response from the other party and their likely counter-offers.

Behaviour analysis

3.37 For fans of in-person mediations a crucial part of the process is that participants see each other. They believe that body language can be revealing and helpful (see **Chapter 8**). They can read each other's real thoughts. They can go beyond the surface to see what is really driving the others' decisions.

What if you could rely upon your digital device to analyse the behaviour of the other participants. One that could tell you who was lying, who was feeling nervous and whether or not when they angrily rejected your latest offer they were in truth thrilled to have received it so early in the process. Far-fetched, a little creepy? Perhaps but Emotional AI (EAI) – is on the way (see **Chapter 5**).

In a nutshell

3.38

- DM is a different way of looking at situations and making decisions about them.
- DM is data driven and digital.
- OLM is already used, and it will be used more.
- Decide if you are a utopian, dystopian or justhopian.

Chapter 4

Do I have to worry about DM (digital mediation)?

In this chapter to you will learn

- The challenges of DM.
- Why lawyers don't like OLM.
- Should mediators fear DM.

The answer is: Who is asking? Are you a mediator, a lawyer/adviser, or a client?

First, let's be sure what we mean by the word '**worry**'.

1 Being **aware.** You need to be aware whether you are involved in mediation or not. Why? DM is the future. DM is new and challenging and something you will need to know about even if to work out how best to resist it.

2 Being **concerned.** If you are already familiar with mediation you need to be concerned about change. Digital mediation is different from in-person mediation. Don't doubt that. See **Chapter 8**. Will you be digitally resilient or digitally resistant?

3 Being **anxious.** If you are a mediator, do you have to worry about whether things will be worse or better for you? Yes. This is the big question. Will mediators still have work? Will lawyers have work to send to mediators? Will clients still have problems to send to lawyers or will they have found another way of dealing with them? Will mediators follow lawyers on their reported journey to extinction? That after all seems to be the end game of the Susskind mission (see **Chapter 2**).

Let's look at the question from the points of view of clients, advisers and mediators.

Clients

4.01 There are two separate scenarios. Mediation through the court system, ie the public sector, and mediation through the private sector.

4.02 *Do I have to worry about DM (digital mediation)?*

Public sector

4.02 The court system will become digital and mediation is becoming mandatory (see **Chapter 7**). At the point of entry, which is Tier 1, a case officer will assess whether your case can be settled without going to a judge. This will be done online.

To start with mandatory mediation will only be for cases with a monetary value of less than £10K. But the intention is to extend it to all cases (see **Chapter 1**). Mediation will be free and be carried out by court officials on the phone. So, to get the best outcome, brush up your telephone technique (see **Chapter 12**).

But will I get my day in court? Will it be fair? Will I get justice? All good questions. The big point for the time being is that you will not be forced to settle. You choose whether to accept an offer from your opponent. That is in the short term. But longer term will systems like SmartSettle take over?

You will not have your day in court in the sense of turning up in a court building before a judge and putting your case either yourself or through a lawyer. You will be on your own on the phone. You will have an hour of the case officer's time who is trying to mediate between you and your opponent.

Clients need to be concerned about

Is an hour long enough?

4.03 There is no agreement amongst mediators about this. Some say it is. They point to scheme mediations which already exist, and they work. Others say you need least at least two or three hours. Or as minimum you need the opportunity to extend the time if you are making progress during the one-hour mediation but cannot reach a final settlement. In theory extra sessions are easier to arrange online than in person.

Experienced mediators confirm that disputes can be settled surprisingly quickly or surprisingly slowly. Long running disputes can be settled in a very short time. Small scale even trivial disputes can take hours or sometimes days. Parkinson's Law tells us that work expands to fill the time available. So do mediations. If people in a dispute really want to settle the dispute, they will. If they really don't, they won't.

As discussed in **Chapter 3** time is used by mediators as a tool for process management anyway.

Will I be heard?

4.04 You will have an opportunity to say what you want to say. Even though the session is only an hour, and you may not end up with a concluded settlement you should feel that at least you have had the chance to be heard. Research from the existing online telephone mediation schemes show a high level of user satisfaction.

Will it be fair?

4.05 You don't have to settle. As the Ministry of Justice's consultation document makes clear it needs to win and retain the public's confidence and to ensure that mediators are properly trained and accountable.

As it says on p 19:

> 'A key aim of our work on accreditation and regulation is to improve public confidence in the civil mediation services that they receive.'

The MoJ proposed the creation of a National Standard for mediation. This would be a publicly available document, setting out a set of requirements that mediators could choose voluntarily to adhere to, in order to demonstrate that their services were of a high quality. The BSI, the UK's national standards body, would lead the development of this with the participation of the mediation sector.

However, this was not carried through to the Final Consultation document. Instead, the MOJ said at paragraph 15:

> 'Given the strength of this existing self-regulation, we have concluded that statutory regulation of the entire Civil Mediation Council would be disproportionate.'

And went on in paragraph 18 to say:

> 'We will continue working with stakeholders in the sector to enhance standards and improve public confidence in the provision of civil mediation services as we prepare to introduce integrated mediation to higher value claims.'

ALERT

There is more to effective telephone mediations then just rocking up for a chat. You need to be properly prepared. To learn how to do this see **Chapter 12**.

Private sector

4.06 Mediators will mediate by telephone and AV – probably by Zoom. You need to be familiar with Zoom. Don't panic. Go to **Chapter 11** where all is explained.

You don't have to worry. Clients at mediation can rely upon the mediator as host to sort out the technical arrangements and on their adviser, if they have one, to act as the intermediary with the mediator (see **Chapter 9**).

4.07 *Do I have to worry about DM (digital mediation)?*

Advisers/Lawyers

4.07 Lawyers need to worry in all senses of the word about DM. Why? DM is a disruptor. There will be changes. How many, how big and how soon are the open questions.

As the senior partner of a well-known law firm in London said: 'Mandatory mediation is not going to make much difference. We'll just carry on as before.' In other words, he is not a fan of mediation and pays lip service to it. There are still lots of lawyers who do that. But will your clients continue to tolerate this as mediation becomes more available and easier and cheaper to do? Recall what Sir Geoffrey Vos said about clients being reluctant to pay more than they have to do for legal services (see **Chapter 2**).

Why don't lawyers like OLM?

4.08 As well as the disadvantages of OLM discussed in **Chapter 8**, lawyers have specific considerations.

Less billable time

4.09 An uncharitable view is that lawyers fear the negative impact of OLM on their time sheets. If you go to an in person mediation, you block out a whole day. There is the travel time as well. That's 10–12 hours of chargeable time. Marvellous!

You cannot do this if you are online, working from home. For a start there is no travel. You will be able to do other work. So will your client. They may expect you to be doing other work and not to be spending every minute of every hour of the day on their matter. You cannot clock up the same amount of recordable time.

At a mediation in 2020 that was held in person, although many participants wanted online, a QC said that he preferred online mediation because it meant that he didn't have to charge his clients for all the time he spent at mediation. When he attended in person, he had to charge for every minute. He was reluctant to do that, but he had to. Frankly, he did not sound wholly convincing, but the commercial point was not lost on his clients, whose next mediation took place online.

Fewer jobs

4.10 As Susskind predicts (see **Chapter 2**), there will be fewer jobs as smart systems reduce the need for lawyers and mediators. There may be some limited involvement in preparing for mediations and explaining the process to clients, but the actual time spent will be much reduced.

Lower fee income

4.11 This is the lawyers' traditional objection to any sort of mediation at all. Lawyers often see mediation as reducing their fees. ADR, they said, stood for

Alarming Drop in Revenue. From the dawn of civilisation, lawyers have been accused of running cases for fees. Some still do. Most don't.

Although the more candid do acknowledge the potential loss of income. At a recent commercial professional negligence mediation, a barrister told his clients: 'As I always say to clients at mediations – every time I help you settle a case, I am doing myself out of a juicy brief fee.'

To be fair they were saying this to emphasis the impartiality of their advice to settle and the objectivity of their risk-reward assessment of going forward to trial. They were encouraging their clients to think hard about rejecting the defendants' final offer.

Fee income will go down. There will be fewer trials. There will be less involvement in mediation. There will be earlier settlement. Less chargeable hours per case will be accumulated.

In the UK the extension from 1 October 2023 of the Fixed Recoverable regime for claims below £100K in value took effect.

But against this gloomy outlook for fee income think about how lawyers build their practices. They develop a base of happy clients. Lawyers need happy clients. They pay their bills. They come back. They tell others about you. And clients like online mediation.

Also,

- The volume and complexity of disputes is not going to go away. The population is increasing. Regulation is increasing. So are expectations.
- There is unmet need. Thanks to greater accessibility and flexibility of online mediation more cases will come into the system which previously been dropped or not even started.
- Mandatory mediation means that more cases will go to mediation earlier. There will be less trial work. Potentially, cases will not run for as long so that there will be less chargeable time per case. But even if the income per case is less your profitability should go up. There will be lower operating costs. Lawyers will need fewer staff. So, lower turnover but higher profits.

ALERT

- Lawyers will have to adapt and relearn. And this is always uncomfortable.
- As the Master of the Rolls said on 29 November 2023:

  'Dispute resolution cannot be about paying lawyers. Dispute resolution has to be about helping people sort out their problems'.

  Churchill v Merthyr Tydfil Borough Council [2023] EWCA Civ 1416.
- And don't forget, lawyers are inherently conservative. That is both a strength and weakness.

4.12 *Do I have to worry about DM (digital mediation)?*

Change will be driven by client demand

4.12 Clients want outcomes: lawyers want incomes.

As Sir Geoffrey Vos said, clients will not want to pay for what they can get for free (see **Chapter 2**).

Loss of control

4.13 OLM separates lawyers from their clients. They cannot control them. They cannot support them. Being online fragments the team. Lawyers and their clients say that they find it harder to discuss things and come to conclusions about difficult topics unless they are all physically together (see **Chapter 8**).

These fears may be felt more by lawyers than clients. At a recent online insolvency mediation everyone was in separate locations. The liquidator's solicitors asked the liquidator if they would be going to the solicitors' offices. The liquidator expressed surprise. 'Why?' They asked. 'You are in the south east and I'm in the north west.' (See **Chapter 7**.)

Less fun

4.14 Taking a day out of the office can be a welcome break from your daily routine. A change is as good as a rest. Although in-person mediations are intense and tiring, the break from routine is stimulating and refreshing.

Mediating online is less fun. The theatre is missing. Barristers are particularly worried about this. The whole process is more sterile and muted. They find that being online takes the emotion out of things. Although this reduces the drama, they generally see this as a positive. Distressed or angry clients find thinking about risk-reward ratios more difficult. Contrast that with therapist mediators who are particularly concerned about the expression of emotions. For them the suppression of emotion hinders settlement. As Brown and Marriott say in *ADR Principles and Practice* (4th edn, 2019) 'Supressed anger can sabotage attempts to reach an agreed resolution'.

On the other hand at a contested probate mediation a client said that there was less drama online. And added: 'Sometimes you can have too much drama.' Indeed you can!

Mediators

4.15 The light bulb moment.

Question: how many lawyers does it take to change a light bulb?

Answer: How many can you afford?

Question: how many psychotherapists does it take to change a light bulb?

Answer: Only one, but it really must want to change.

Question. How many mediators does it take to change a light bulb?

Answer. None – mediators facilitate you finding your answer to your problem and changing the light bulb yourself.

Do mediators fear change in the way that lawyers seem to? Are they as conservative? The 2023 CEDR Audit tell us 67% of mediators who were reasonably experienced were lawyers and the average age is 54 (women) and 63 (men). As we know, lawyers are inherently conservative. And the older you get, the harder it becomes to adapt to change.

By temperament, mediators are not disruptors or entrepreneurs. But they are curious. When mediating, they urge people to be open minded, they want to explore with the participants the possibilities of change. They investigate different points of view and attitudes and alternatives. But they do that for other people, not necessarily for themselves. Is this mental flexibility and curiosity a transferrable skill?

Many mediators openly say that prefer in-person mediation.

Ethelwald Mendes a highly experienced advocate and mediator and member of the Board of International Academy of Dispute Resolution replied to my LinkedIn post about online mediation.

> 'I'm not a fan of the online mediation, but there are situations when online meetings can help. My reasons for avoiding wholly online mediations are:
>
> 1. Discussion during meditation is trust based and without trust there can never be good negotiation. The mediator has very little opportunity to establish trust and rapport and being f2f helps.
> 2. When parties are in remote locations their focus is not absolute, there is a tendency to multitasking which affects the quality of the negotiations.
> 3. When f2f the mediator is able to get parties to repair ruptured relationships which in remote settings is difficult.
> 4. Remote location of parties tends to make the parties lack effective listening and for parties to take hard stands as the remote settings don't help in delivering sympathy/ empathy or care or concern.
> 5. In remote settings body language which is a good indicator of behaviour is difficult to discern.
>
> So I would request parties to accept f2f at some point of time before giving up on mediation whilst using ODR as a starting point. And if successful then it's great.
>
> I know in today's world parties agree to contracts by digital signatures but still two people at two different places create issues of jurisdiction.'

For further discussion of these points see **Chapter 7** Why don't we like OLM?

These mediators describe themselves as people persons. They want human contact. They want to interact with people. Recall what Paul Sills said in **Chapter 1**.

4.15 *Do I have to worry about DM (digital mediation)?*

Mediating online reduces this element of personal interaction and contact. Should they fear that smart systems will make them redundant completely?

The well-known US mediator Phyllis Pollock does a weekly blog. Recently she has been posting about AI. She is concerned about the effect on mediation. She asked questions of ChatGPT. Here is its response:

> 'In summary, while AI can be a useful tool in mediation, it is unlikely to fully replace human mediators in the foreseeable future. The unique human skills and abilities that mediators bring to the process are difficult to replicate with current AI technology.'

And here is her conclusion:

> 'Wow! For now, my job is saved!
>
> But seriously, AI is very much a thing of the present and will be used more and more in various aspects of our lives. As ChatGPT noted, while it cannot entirely replace a human mediator because the personal touch and judgment will always be needed, it is capable of taking over some of the tasks performed by the mediator. I am not sure I am comfortable with that thought!
>
> ... Just something to think about.'

Another mediator Bruce Greig from the UK posts a newsletter that provides 'Interesting articles about mediation which will surprise you' did the same thing.

> 'The robots are coming. What happened when I asked the GPT-3 artificial intelligence system to provide mediation/litigation advice?
>
> Spoiler: it is truly mind-blowing, but still some way to go before the robots take over.'

Another mediation thought leader and champion of online training Aled Davies posted on LinkedIn.

> 'Software is eating the world' wrote Marc Andreessen in his 2011 essay.
>
> But it doesn't seem to be dining out on mediation, yet...
>
> Forget about robot mediators for now.'

Is this wishful thinking? After all mediators want to hear reassuring words from ChatGPT about the continuing need for human mediators. ChatGPT has not applied its mind to the question. It has no mind to apply. It regurgitates what others have said when they have applied their minds. Most of them will have been mediation theorists, commentators or mediators who want mediation to retain a role for human mediators (see **Chapter 5**).

We can see how AI is likely to disintermediate swathes of professionals. Lawyers and accountants have been identified as being particularly vulnerable. Is it going to disintermediate mediators?

My guess is that sooner rather than later clients and their lawyers will be inputting prompts to Generative AI and asking for likely outcomes or suggestions for settlements. If the outputs confirm the prompter's views, they will be seen as authoritative. If they don't, they will be seen as unreliable. If they don't do either, they will be seen at best as indicative and at worst as a waste of time.

Mandatory mediation: oxymoron or oxygen?

4.16 If mediators want to stay mediating, they must contemplate adapting to new markets, new clients and new processes. Take the example of mandatory mediation (see **Chapter 2**).

Mediators are displaying an inherent conservatism. At a workshop organised by CEDR in 2022 on mandatory mediation most of the comments were about how it could not work and in fact it was not really mediation. The problem is the difficulty in accepting that the traditional eight-hour mediation model will not work for new types of mediation. You cannot shoehorn that model into a one-hour phone mediation or Zoom mediation.

Suggestions that participants will need to do a lot of pre-mediation preparation involving filling in forms and supplying information are fanciful. People who use one-hour mediations, particularly if they are litigants in person, don't want to do all this text-based preparation. The MOJ recognised this in its Final Consultation document; para 7: 'We acknowledge that, in a system where participation in mediation is required, the burden of attending this mediation should be light.'

The MOJ's announcement in August 2023 provoked strong reactions on LinkedIn.

For example:

Janeen Achtar FCIArb. Arbitrator, Mediator and Trainer. Former Law and ADR Prof./ Lecturer posted:

> 'Free one hour long mediation session! This is not mediation and no mediator should agree to this.'

Chris Breedon, Accredited Mediator and Trainer at Prospero Professional Solutions posted:

> 'I wish there was a dislike button on the options. Mandatory mediation just isn't mediation. There's no empathy and it's only driven by an inefficient judiciary and so called "professionals" after a quick buck. The fact there are sanctions for those wanting to exercise their right to access to justice is disgusting.'

Alan Sharland of CAOS Conflict Management, based in London, who has 24 years' experience as a Mediator, Conflict Coach, Facilitator, Trainer and Consultant in Mediation and Conflict Management processes, posted:

4.16 *Do I have to worry about DM (digital mediation)?*

> 'For some strange reason the coercive, system-led, bureaucratic approach used in divorce mediation is now being applied to other areas of mediation within the legal profession. Are there any comparative studies to indicate that coercive/compulsory mediation is more effective as a model? No, but it returns the whole process to being taken over by legal practitioners, to being ridiculously bureaucratic and to being the very opposite of the purpose for its original introduction within that context for using it.
>
> Compulsory/coercive mediation is NOT mediation.'

Ed Johnson a commercial mediator in the north west of England posted:

> 'Good news – more mediation; bad news – making it free to devalue the profession (IMHO)'

And there was comment from the mediation academics.

Professor Bryan Clark of The University of Newcastle in the UK posted:

> 'My own view is that mandatory mediation is not per se objectionable and can have its uses in encouraging use and potentially providing positive, sustainable outcomes. On the current plans I would note that **assisted telephone, shuttle negotiations seem a poor substitute for real mediation** and that in a time when online mediation is becoming recognised as an efficient proxy for in person settings, it seems a shame that option is not being explored. One hour telephone mediation does smack of the cheapest possible option. ' (emphasis added)

But guess which option clients prefer? Yes: the cheapest.

Aled Davis of the Mediator Academy said in the August edition of the *Cube* Newsletter:

> 'While the expression mandatory or compulsory mediation is not actually used, what this means is that parties will be automatically referred to an hour's free telephone mediation before any court action proceeds.
>
> Yep, that's right telephones.
>
> The government has set some ambitious KPIs for this project, estimating that it will positively impact 92,000 claims and 180,000 parties per year and free up close to 5,000 sitting days per year.
>
> The mediation community is largely supportive of the move, despite some expressing concerns as to whether an hour on the phone can really be described as mediation. Other jurisdictions will be watching this development closely (and having a giggle about telephones), to see what impact integrating mediation at this level has before, as indicated in the government report, extending it to higher value claims.
>
> But really telephones – c'mon lads that's so British!'

On the other hand, CEDR organised a masterclass on September on Mandatory Mediation of Small Claims – Lessons from New Zealand, in which James South and Haamid Ben Fayed explained the work of the Residential Tenancy Tribunal mediation service which operates a one-hour telephone model. It achieves an 86% settlement rate and is well regarded by landlords and tenants.

In any case, doesn't saying that a one-hour telephone mediation is not mediation sound arrogant? Who says it is not? What is their authority for saying this? Perhaps it does not fit into the traditional definition and model of mediation. But that doesn't mean that it is not a new iteration of mediation. It shares the classic characteristics.

- It is a confidential process.
- It may not be voluntary any more in the sense that you have to attend a mediation. It is still voluntary in the sense that you do not have to settle if you don't want to. It is up to the parties whether they settle or not.
- It is where the parties try and find their own solution to their own problem.
- It is not adjudicative.
- It involves the participation of a neutral third party.

Mediators may well have to abandon purist rigidity and doctrinal orthodoxy. Mediating online whether by phone or VC, whether because you are required to or you have chosen to is another way of mediating.

Are mediators' fears justified?

4.17 Yes, to a large degree. So, the question then becomes, what can mediators do to protect themselves from the adverse consequences of these changes?

It has been said many times that the only way to predict the future is to create it. How can mediators do this? Who speaks for them?

One of the great difficulties that UK mediators face is their lack of collective voice. There is no one body for mediators. Traditionally, mediators have resisted being corralled into a single regulatory body. They are individualists. Mediation is not really a profession, it is a cottage industry. Lots of individuals working in the gig economy.

Will the Civil Mediation Council (CMC) step up to the challenge? There are encouraging signs. As from 2023 they have a new chair. The first time they are not led by a retired male High Court judge. Moving to mandatory mediation will prompt louder calls for regulation. Recall what the MOJ Consultation paper said at **04.05**. Interestingly, the previous resistance from the mediation community seems to be decreasing. The 2023 CEDR Audit reported that:

- 88% of mediators agreed that the field should be regulated.
- 76% supported the proposition that there should be a single regulatory body for setting and monitoring professional standards of practice by commercial mediators and dealing with public complaints against mediators.
- 82% thought that the CMC should be the regulator. Although we can expect turf wars with other professional or quasi professional bodies which want to take on the role, such as the CIArb.

4.18 *Do I have to worry about DM (digital mediation)?*

Lawyers also supported regulation:

- 76% in favour of regulation.
- 75% in favour of the CMC being the regulator.

The roadmap seems to be drawn. Will anybody read it and follow it?

Will OLM be a threat or an opportunity?

4.18 As pointed out in **Chapter 1**, CEDR reported in 2023 that:

- the number of mediations has now started to rise again after the Covid/lockdown dislocation and is running at about 17,000 civil and commercial mediations a year in the UK.
- 64% of them are being carried out online.

So, you can legitimately conclude that online mediation will produce more work for mediators. But what sort of work will it be?

Lower value mediations.

- Scheme mediation providers are expecting to eventually employ mediators themselves to provide the service in-house rather than use panels of self-employed mediators.
- The mandatory mediation for small claims will use employed court officials rather than private practice mediators. Whether they will continue to do this as mandatory mediation is applied to larger value disputes is another matter.

Again the 2023 CEDR Audit provides insight:

- The oversupply of mediators continues. Although increasing numbers of mediators described themselves as Advanced – ie, reasonably, or very, experienced – 49% undertook fewer than ten mediations a year.
- There is plenty of capacity and appetite for mandatory mediation which as explained in **Chapter 1** will be done nearly entirely online.

Will OLM make money for mediators?

Lower fee income

4.19 Fee rates have been declining for some time. The 2023 CEDR Audit which reported that (see **Chapter 16** on Pricing):

- Average fees of the less experienced mediator group for a one-day mediation have increased by 20% over the last two years to £1,781. Most of them do fewer than four mediations a year.
- Average fees for more experienced mediators have decreased by 8% to £3,893.

- Overall conclusion is that: there is considerable surplus capacity within the Mediation marketplace and that, if they achieve a sustainable income level, the majority of mediators are currently more concerned with gaining experience through taking on more cases than they are with increasing fee rates.

This is a pragmatic and realistic approach for mediators to take. After all, the more mediations you do, the more mediations you do. Subject of course to the proviso that you do them well. If you don't then you will not get referrals and repeat business. But then do you deserve to?

The market is trying to find the price point that makes sense for both customers and mediators. There are some anomalies. Nearly all mediation providers have introduced fixed-fee time-limited schemes for lower-value mediations – under £10,000. This is partly to meet demand created by the increase in court fees but also to provide work for novice mediators.

What will mediators be paid?

4.20 For non-scheme online mediations, the going rate for disputes with a value of under £3,000 is £100 plus VAT an hour.

For disputes between £3,000 and £10,000 the customer pays £600 plus VAT and the mediator receives £500.That includes preparation. There is no overtime. It is up to the mediator whether they allow the mediation to continue after three hours but they will not be paid if it does.

This can produce anomalies. For some schemes mediators are paid £500 for a three-hour online mediation for a dispute between £3,000 and £10,000. For an in-person mediation of the same value they will be paid £665 out of the £1000 charged to the customer. So, it is more profitable for a mediator to do the three-hour £500 online mediations as they have no travel costs or time. It will not be long before the prices are re-aligned.

See the extract below from the 10th CEDR Audit.

Income expectations

4.21 'In order to provide a baseline for any upcoming discussions about mandatory mediation and an expected increase in the number of cases if the remit was to extend into case values above £10,000, we asked mediators about their billing practices on typical lower value cases. These figures provide some insights on working and billing practices on individual cases.

However, because many mediators will work a portfolio of case values, this data may not, when taken in isolation, present an accurate view of individuals' broader aspirations.'

4.22 *Do I have to worry about DM (digital mediation)?*

Case value	Median hourly rate £	Average case length – hours	Total fee £
Under £10K	150	5	750
£10K–£25K	175	7	1,225
Over £25K	250	11	2,250

A mediator who completed a training course on Zoom mediations did one online mediation in eight months. He was paid £500 for three hours' work. He does not complain about the rate of pay. If he did two a day every day, that would be the equivalent of £20,000 a month. He would be happy with that. But the work was not coming in.

Two years ago, he was worried that having done the training several months ago he was becoming deskilled in the technology. Now in 2023 he is wondering whether he should insist that all his mediations should be online and is offering free demos and trials for those who are still sceptical or just unfamiliar with it.

Mediators must treat DM as an opportunity. If we treat it as a threat, we will go into defensive mode. That will not help us preserve our market share. Don't forget Dispute Resolution is a marketplace and there are lots of competitors – arbitrators, adjudicators, ombudsmen as well as judges who don't want to be made redundant.

Richard Susskind has been telling us for decades that lawyers will have to change the way they work. He is right. Mediators will have to as well.

Mediation trainers

4.22 Mediation training has not changed much over the last ten years apart from some of it now being done online. That was to preserve the income of the trainers during lockdown. The safe model of mediation, which is taught on most courses, will need to change to accommodate the changes that are coming.

If you want to offer OLM, go on a course. You need to feel confident in the technology. Fumbling the tech during a mediation will dilute confidence in both the process and in you.

Specialised courses in OLM are available. Most are online so the tutors and your fellow students could be anywhere in the world. The going rate in the UK seems to be about £600 plus VAT for a 12-hour course. This is spread over several sessions and is conducted online. There is some live tuition, but it is given online in much the same way as a webinar. About half the time is spent on learning how to use the technology. The rest is spent on training mediators how to use new techniques to deal with people online rather than face-to-face in person.

Course providers report that most of the people they train are non-lawyers. They come from an increasingly diverse background of occupations and ages. More young people are applying for the courses. They are hoping to make a career in mediation. They are also digital natives. Will they be at a competitive advantage compared with the average commercial mediator? After all, only 8% of civil and commercial mediators are below the age of 40 according the Tenth CEDR Audit.

What is in it for mediators?

4.23 In practice, if you offer online mediation you will have a commercial edge if you can say that you have received specialised training. See Chapter 9.02. As can be seen from both recent MOJ announcements and the CEDR audit the competence of mediators is a hot topic. For more tips on marketing go to **Chapter 15.**

How does the future look?

4.24

- Online mediation is here to stay. It will grow.
- Mandatory mediation is inevitable. It will increase the use of online mediation.
- Mediators will not make a lot of money out of mandatory mediation until the tipping point of using the public sector and being applied to bigger ticket disputes is reached.
- But they will mediate more and learn more.
- Trying to hold onto the traditional mode is not likely to bring mediators work or income.
- Yes, regulation is more likely.
- Fixed recoverable costs in litigation are coming. Will this have a knock effect for mediation? On present plans who can say? The chances are they will increase the demand for mediation in the lower value disputes as it makes sense to avoid the rather meagre recoverable costs of attending trial.

What do mediators have to do?

4.25

- Build up their digital resilience. How?
- Learn about OLM.
- Train in it.
- Offer it.
- Learn and practise prompt engineering (see **Chapter 5**).
- Sign up to ChatGPT and open it on your device at mediations (see **Chapter 6**).

Business management

4.26 How you start and develop your business online is different. See **Chapter 10** on Marketing.

4.27 *Do I have to worry about DM (digital mediation)?*

In a nutshell

4.27

- Learn how to conduct OLM.
- Recognise that OLM is both a threat and an opportunity.
- The MOJ mandatory mediation scheme will not make mediators lots of money. It will provide more low paid jobs for in-house and freelance mediators.
- If you don't offer OLM someone else will.

Chapter 5

AI: End or beginning?

In this chapter you will learn

- What ChatGPT is
- What ChatGPT can do
- How to prompt engineer
- How AI will influence mediation

Stop press

5.01 The answer to the question is both.

AI is the beginning of the end and the end of the beginning. We should not worry. After all It's quite conceivable that humanity is a passing phase in the evolution of intelligence. Who says so? The godfather of AI, Geoffrey Hinton. His work on neural networks underpins generative AI so he is worth listening to.

Another British intellectual titan gave a gloomier prediction. 'The rise of powerful AI will be either the best or worst thing to happen to humanity.' This was the bleak conclusion of Professor Stephen Hawking in 2016. He was a compelling presence. Confined to a wheelchair by motor neurone disease, with his voice synthesiser and a brain as big as the planet, exploring and explaining the mysteries of the universe.

Seven years later in 2023 we are facing the same question. This time with a lot more urgency. The reason? The explosion of interest and comments and anxiety by the arrival of ChatGPT in November 2022. As we saw in **Chapter 1** its success and impact has been phenomenal.

The media – social and traditional – are full of comments and news. There is an incendiary mixture of hope, hype and hysteria. New apps and rivals are introduced every week. We are approaching saturation level. How do you keep up? How do you understand what's going on. You can't. Recall from **Chapter 1** how Professor John Naughton described it 'trying to keep track of the madness has been like attempting to get a drink from a fire hose'.

Comment, analysis, and predictions pour out. Tech bros, academics and politicians are all making announcements and pronouncements. Mediators reading or listening to them will recognise behaviours seen at mediation – rationalisation, confirmation bias, motivated reasoning. Does anyone have any idea of what is going on and what is likely to happen?

Let's take a look.

Can we understand what AI is and what it could do, not for humanity in general perhaps, but just for mediation? To start, let's clear up some confusion. Check the definitions in **Chapter 3**.

Definitions

5.02

- AI/Artificial Intelligence – not one technology but an umbrella term for various technologies.
- GPT – generative pre-trained transformer – artificial neural network based on the transformer architecture pre-trained on large data sets of unlabelled text, and able to generate novel human-like content.
- ML – machine learning – is a subset of AI that uses algorithms to analyse huge amounts of data, learn from insights and make informed decisions.
- LLM – large language model – natural language processing programs that use deep learning to generate text and source code.
- Deep learning is another type of AI. It is a subset of machine learning that uses artificial neural networks to mimic the learning process of the human brain.

What are the tech bros, academics and politicians saying?

Utopians

5.03 'AI is going to be as big as the internet and mobile phones' predicts Philip Jensen BT's chief executive.

Leaving aside ChatGPT for the moment AI is already making lots of people happier, more productive, and efficient. You have to balance the upsides and downsides.

Professor Yorick Wills who won the Loebner prize for AI in 1997 with his creation of Converse which produced Catherine, an investigative journalist, said:

> 'people see the benefits, they can't imagine living without intelligent phones. People are aware that there are dangers and there are positives, and this is always true of science. Atomic energy has brought enormous benefits; it's also brought enormous dangers. There is nothing new here. Lots of science is both frightening and enormously beneficial.'

And 'AI is just like that.'

Emad Mostaque, Founder of Stability AI, thinks AI is one of the most important inventions in history – 'somewhere between fire and the internal combustion engine.' Although he signed the general letter in March 2023 calling for a pause of six months on training AI systems he confirms that: 'I'm more on the utopian side than the dystopian'.

But as he points out: 'I have a different approach to everyone else in this space, because I'm building narrow models to augment humans whereas almost everyone else is trying to build an AGI to pretty much replace humans and look over them.'

Medics

5.04 AI already helps doctors identify organs for transplants and scan images of lesions to detect if they are cancerous more accurately than humans can. On 12 May 2023 it was reported in *The Times* that AI was able to diagnose heart attacks more quicky than human doctors.

For example, as reported in the Times on 6 March 2023 the NHS is using an AI program, known as MIA (mammography intelligent assessment) to check breast cancer scans. To start with the scans will be assessed by the software and two human readers. If all three agree the patient is given the all-clear. If there's any disagreement a second clinician looks at the scan. In time it is hoped to replace one of the two human readers.

In England GPs use eConsult which is a digital triage system.

Elephants

5.05 Wildlife conservationists are using AI powered wildlife cameras to identify poachers without the need for Wi-Fi long-range radio or cellular coverage.

Customers

5.06 AI can improve productivity in the service industry. Just think of how we buy tickets, book hotels, carry out banking transactions, which have been transformed by AI. In the UK services count for 79% of output and 82% of jobs. The potential impact is enormous. Mediation is a service industry. What will be the impact?

Dystopians

5.07 Geoffrey Hinton quit his job at Google to be able to speak out more freely. He said 'this technology which ought to be wonderful… It's being designed in a society that is not designed to use it for everybody's good.' He is worried that it will reinforce inequalities, biases and fault lines in society rather than ameliorate them.

His concerns are shared by two other AI luminaries.

5.08 *AI: End or beginning?*

Professor Stuart Russell in an interview on 13 May 2023 said that he thought that politicians had been well trained by the technology industry to avoid heavy-handed legislation. He is in favour of more legislation and regulation. And he said 'we have sort of got the message and are scrambling around trying to figure out what to do.... It's a sort of what you would imagine might happen if we really did detect an alien civilisation'.

Mustafa Suleyman co-founder of DeepMind says that: 'I think that there are some fundamental boundaries which we should not cross. There is no reason to add autonomy to the systems. There is no reason to add recursive self-improvement – these would be design choices that we don't need to add yet until they can be proven to be controllable and safe.'

Noam Shazeer a former Google engineer who is behind Character.AI, which lets people create famous characters to interact with, says:

> 'We get all kinds of emails. Things like 'I'm ??have no friends, I was depressed. This makes me feel good. Thank you, this saved my life.' It's not what we set out to do, but it just stands to reason. There are a lot of lonely people in the world.'

Yuval Noah Harari the historian worries about the ability of AI to create 'fake intimacy' and therefore influence us. As he puts it 'Democracy is a conversation, and conversations rely on language. When AI hacks language, it could destroy our ability to have meaningful conversations thereby destroying democracy.'

Harari writes fascinating and popular Big History – full of big themes and ideas.

Even Sam Altman told the US Congress that government regulation could be critical in minimising the substantial risks that AI carries.

And in England education leaders are worried about the threat to education. As Sir Anthony Seldon said AI could bring the biggest benefit since the printing press but that the risks were 'more severe than any threat that has ever faced schools'.

In August 2023 AI was added to the UK's list of security threats along with pandemics, terrorism and nuclear war.

Justhopians

5.08 The situation could go either way say Oxford Professors Sir Nigel Shadbolt and John Tasioulas of the Institute of Ethics in AI. They summarised the current situation in an article on 7 May 2023:

> 'The reason we fear this technology is because it has the potential to penetrate so many areas of our lives and do damage there – from the potential destruction of jobs to the development of autonomous weapons systems which could violate the laws of war. There is also a more general fear that AI will begin to replace everyday interactions and that we will soon be living in a more dehumanised world.'

This is spot on.

They came up with six ways to contain the threat of AI.

1. Don't fall prey to the doom mongers.

   All human experts exaggerate the significance of their own expertise and academics always disagree.

2. Just because we can, it doesn't mean we should.

   AI is not an unstoppable process. Human beings can stop the machines and give them direction. Do we have the will to do this?

3. Learn from the past: don't over-regulate.

   We don't need to panic that a new area of technology necessarily means a new area of law. We already have the means to regulate it.

4. Stop following the ethical experts.

   Look at what is happening in Taiwan, which has been using digital technology to enhance citizen participation via the discussion platform called Polis. They gather opinions and turn them into insights that have informed policy making.

5. Search for a truce in the AI arms race.

   China and the US are competing for dominance. No one wants to give their opponents an edge by easing up on their own development. But see the increasing calls at government level for a nuclear weapons style system of regulation of AI.

6. Help it become a force for good.

   AI can be a force for good. Look at the significant progress in biology and medicine. Already others are seeing the benefits, such as musicians, speech writers.

Being university professors, Shadbolt and Tasioulas advocate for more education and information. Join the conversation. It's our responsibility. If we don't like the world that AI creates for us, we will only have ourselves to blame.

Challenging, encouraging sentiments. Will they turn out to be pious academic exhortations to behave correctly or the nuggets for calls to action that policy makers can take?

The Oxford professors are right – we are worried about the loss of jobs and the loss of humanity. Should we be?

ChatGPT – the hype and the hysteria

The enthusiasts

5.09 According to Richard Susskind who one might guess from **Chapter 2** is an enthusiast: 'ChatGPT is the most impressive system I have seen in 40 years of working on artificial intelligence.' Bill Gates supports him: 'AI is a revolution to change life like the web did.' says Gates (*The Times* 23 March 2023). But then Microsoft is a big investor in OpenAI.

5.10 *AI: End or beginning?*

What do others say? You can quickly get the flavour by scanning the headlines in The Times. Here they are for the month of April 2023

The Times 2023

1.	AI will obliterate humans if not shut down, warns expert	1 April
2.	Italy bans ChatGPT over data fears	1 April
3.	AI in the sky to spot drivers using phones	3 April
4.	AI journalists proved to be lazier than the real thing	4 April
5.	World must wake up to speed and scale of AI	4 April
6.	Certified deep fake video in court for AI signatures	5 April
7.	Common sense to use artificial intelligence	6 April
8.	ChatGPT makes false sex claims	7April
9.	AI could hasten the four-day week	7 April
10.	Virtual reality app removes patients from their anxiety	8 April
11.	Using a fork is latest way AI sticks it to humanity	11 April
12.	We'd be mad to slow the progress of AI now	11 April
13.	Fake news has frightening effect on trust says BBC boss	12 April
14.	AI humans plot and gossip like us	15 April
15.	Chatbot keep google boss up at night	18 April
16.	Artist snaps photography award with AI image.	18 April
17.	Spy chief briefs ministers on the dangers of AI	19 April
18.	Spotify pulls hit that used AI to clone star's vocals	19 April
19.	Schumacher interview was with chatbot	19 April
20.	Humans crave each other, not AI perfection	20 April
21.	AI rest my case: robotic judges poised to revolutionise courts	20 April
22.	Oasis album made with AI shows how bands could live forever	21 April
23.	ChatGPT used for degree by half of Cambridge students	22 April
24.	Pause or panic: battle to tame the AI monster	22 April
25.	Needs improvement – are used for end of year reports	24 April
26.	Local paper hires report to write stories using AI	24 April
27.	Protecting jobs will not be easy in the age of ChatGPT	24 April
28.	2023 PwC to invest $1 billion on AI bean counters	27 April
29.	Remote work poses threat to the Bar	27 April

The doubters

5.10

1 The software lacks creativity, originality and empathy.

As Professor Hannah Fry said: 'ChatGPT is producing nothing original. It may have the prose of a scholar, it has the conceptual understanding of a potted plant.' And she is an enthusiast.

2 It lacks wisdom.

Professor Mike Woolrich from the University of Oxford's Department of Computer Science said AI was useful for producing some of the tasks to do with processing language but warned:

> 'we shouldn't treat them as sages. You shouldn't go to them and ask for advice about your life or who you should vote for ... or whether climate change is real.

As he concluded AI often 'gets things wrong in a very convincing and plausible way.' But then so do lawyers. Is there a way to cope?

What about the workers?

5.11 A research report dated 26 March 2023 by Goldman Sachs concluded: 'the potentially large effects of artificial intelligence on economic growth by Briggs and Kodnani estimated the AI is capable of content generation and could do 25% of all the work currently done by humans. As they say extrapolating these estimates globally suggests that generative AI could expose the equivalent of 300 million full-time jobs to automation.'

As a 2021 UK government report concluded, the more AI takes over our jobs the more human the jobs that remain will become. We will do jobs, precisely because humans want humans to do jobs.

Technology replacing human workers is not new. Alarm clocks for example replaced knocker uppers – those people employed to knock on bedroom windows with long sticks to get factory workers out of bed. Refrigerators meant the milk could be stored and did not have to be delivered fresh by the milkman.

What is new is that the technology is not attacking physical jobs but jobs where people sit at computer screens. And that is an increasing number of us.

Which jobs are at risk? Which are safe? According to Martin Ford author of *Rule of the Robots: How Artificial Intelligence Will Transform Everything* you can look the ones that are going to be relatively insulated in three categories. Jobs that require:

1 Creativity. You're not just doing formulaic work – you come up with new ideas. But not all creative work will be immune. For example, graphic design, music composition can be done by AI.

2 Nuanced human relationship skills. For example, nurses, business consultants, investigative journalists, spies.

3 Being mobile and dextrous while problem-solving in unpredictable environments. For example, electricians, plumbers, and care workers.

Is there some wishful thinking here? Look at the Writers Guild of America strike that began on 2 May 2023 and as at 9 September 2023 is still going on. They are complaining both about residuals from streaming and about limiting the use of ChatGPT to research and facilitating script ideas – not being used to write them.

Greg Jackson Chief Executive of Octopus Energy explained that office jobs will be transformed. He described how in just 16 weeks Octopus's AI had gone from answering zero customer messages to doing the work of 250 people and doing it very well. He says that at the moment Octopus AI writes messages but within a few weeks it will make decisions and carry out actions too. It won't just tell you your balance but also suggest changing payments and do it for you.

Martin Sorrell, advertising supremo, thinks that call centres will be replaced by chatbots in answering consumer enquiries.

In August 2023 Thomson Reuters published a report, *Future of Professionals.*

They conclude:

> 'it is undeniable that the future of work is set to be revolutionised, driven by the power of AI.
>
> 'The exact transformation brought about by professionals is still unfolding, awaiting its full resident realisation. This topic certainly divides opinion... In the area of transformative value exchange, professionals must reassess and redefine what it means to be an advisor.'

Will mediators have to adjust to see themselves as advisors or even to redefine their role?

John Maynard Keynes, one of the world's greatest economists, wrote *Economic Possibilities for Our Grandchildren* in 1928. He predicted that Nirvana would arrive within 100 years (ie by 2028) when technology would solve mankind's economic problems and we would live in an age of leisure and of abundance. Everybody might want some work to do – 15 hours a week should be enough but for the rest it would be leisure, pleasure, and plenty. We are in 2023 – 95 years later and only 5 years away from Nirvana – and the average work week in the private sector is 34.4 hours. We are not there yet. Will AI get us there more quickly?

Comforting word

5.12 Two thoughts to bear in mind:

- As economists remind us, technological innovations have tended to create more jobs than they destroy. But will you be in a newly created job or a recently destroyed one?
- ChatGPT will not put you out of a job. Someone using ChatGPT will. But is this a distinction without a difference?

So,

- Will our current predictions be any more accurate?

- Where are mediators going to fit into this?
- And any way what is ChatGPT?

How does ChatGPT work?

5.13 ChatGPT is a completely different type of chatbot.

Neil Saunders, mathematician at Greenwich University, sums it up: 'The LLM designers successfully turned the problem of semantics – the arrangement of words to create meaning – into statistics, matching words based on their frequency of prior use.'

In essence it is a statistical probability model. The big difference between it and previous versions of chatbots is that it has context. The earlier ones had a keyword base. This has contextual understanding. It uses NLP, not Neurolinguistic Programming, but Natural Language Processing. You ask it to do something. This is known as a prompt. You ask it in natural human language. Your words are converted into numbers. It does this by splitting your text into chunks of characters known as tokens which commonly occur together. A token could be a word like 'is' or 'conflict' or 'ing' or 'tion' or punctuation marks such as '?' or '!'

The tokens are allocated to a 'meaning space' where there are words of similar meaning. The system's 'attention network' makes connections between different parts of your prompt. It starts a response to your prompt. The attention network has calculated a probability for each of the tokens in its vocabulary that it is the most appropriate one to use next in the sentence that it is generating. The secret sauce is that using auto-regression, where a word is generated, the result is fed back which generates a second word, and the second word is fed back which generates a third word and process is repeated.

All done at incredible speed. Three things make this possible:

- gigantic unimaginable quantities of data;
- algorithms capable of learning from them; and
- the computational power to do it.

Most of the data that ChatGPT was trained on came through snapshots of the entire Internet from 2016–2019 taken from a database called Common Crawl. It has been fed billions of words. The text includes news articles, social media posts, chat rooms, Wikipedia, books, transcript of real conversations etc. In simple terms it looks for patterns and how they fit together. It elicits patterns based on that data and uses patterns as a framework for answering questions.

All this data was fine tuned in the language model by both supervised learning and RLHF (Reinforcement Learning from Human Feedback). Openai claims that this use of human AI trainers is what makes ChatGPT stand out.

Originally as critics pointed out it was not connected to the internet, unlike say Bing Chat. Now it is.

As all lawyers and mediators know, the answer you receive depends on the question you ask. So, you need to be careful what you ask ChatGPT. This is known as prompting. A whole new range of jobs called prompt engineers has been created (see **5.20**). And it seems that the better your questions are, the better the answer is. But it's not infallible, as we will see below.

ALERT

ChatGPT is just a machine loaded with software and data. Although residents in some Japanese care homes have found that they can relate to a robot as a carer and talk to and build a relationship, a robot is not a sentient being.

But it is so easy to think that there is and to behave accordingly (see **Chapter 6**).

The Elza effect is the tendency to attribute human characteristics to nonhuman things like robots or computers. We even see faces in piece of toast or in clouds. Evolutionary psychology has predisposed humans to do this because we look for intention and meaning in order to understand what is going on.

With ChatGPT we need to accept that we are dealing with probabilistic calculation machines. They have no intention, no emotions, they just carry out pattern recognition. There are plenty of instances of people forming relationships with their chatbot. Studies have found that we are happy to have therapy with a chatbot and that chatbots can be more empathetic than doctors.

Decades ago, Alan Turing realised that computers, to be competent and able to do something well, don't have to be able to comprehend. They don't have to understand what they're doing. This makes them very useful servants.

He devised the Turing test – originally called the imitation game – which is whether you can tell if one of the parties to a conversation is a computer or a human. Chatbots are becoming more difficult to distinguish from human conversationalists. So the flea market test has been suggested as alternative – can a robot imitate the behaviour of a flea market trader. See the video on diplomacy.edu/blog.

This is what Professors Shadbolt and Tasioulas identified as one of the biggest worries about generative AI (see **5.06**).

Do you want to see how it works?

Getting started

5.14 Login or signup. Go to chat.openai.com.

- Log onto the website chat.openai.com.
- Sign up create an account using your email address or if you have one connect with your Google or Microsoft account.

- On the left hand side, you will see the New Chat button and your Chat History.
- Click New Chat.

At the moment it is a freemium service. The basic version is free but you have to pay for more advanced features. How long it will stay free is another question. If you want to use the Chat-4, the latest and better version, you pay for it.

You **will** be amazed at how fast and responsive it is. You **may** be impressed by the quality of its responses, or you may not. See **Chapter 6**.

If you know something about the subject that you are asking it about, expect the responses to seem banal. After all what it is doing is regurgitating text that it has been fed. At best it could be called combinatorial thinking. Putting different bits of data together in a way that is not self- contradictory. But is it original thought? A big question for some. The commentators are commentating at length. But does this matter for mediators?

Since in the UK most civil and commercial mediators get their work from lawyers, let's look at what lawyers are doing.

Lawyers

5.15 Lawyers, who are usually seen as a conservative profession, are using AI. On 15 February 2023 Allen & Overy announced the introduction of an AI program called Harvey across their global network of offices.

Wim Dejonghe, Senior Partner at A&O, said: 'This announcement marks a new era for A&O and the legal industry. Harvey AI is not just another platform, but a game-changer that will enable us to deliver unprecedented value, efficiency and innovation to our clients.'

This seems to echo the prophetic words of Richard Susskind (see **Chapter 4**).

What AI can do for lawyers

5.16 Thomson Reuters concluded that lawyers and accountants see AI as a way of improving client communication:

- Automating drafting and editing: most of us find it easier to revise than draft from scratch.
- Keeping clients in the know: identifies trends and impacts of regulations faster than humans.
- Improved readability: expresses complex information and ideas in simple terms.
- Research: much quicker and better at distilling findings.

5.17 The consensus is that AI could be truly revolutionary for improving our lives. But, of course, there are downsides. See the section below.

There is also the issue of client confidentiality. Everyone wants to know who owns the data, where it is, who can access it. Providing this reassurance is work in progress.

Accuracy

5.18 Is the product of the research accurate? As we have already seen ChatGPT is prone to make mistakes, make things up, simply tell lies. They call it hallucinations. So human checking is still thought to be necessary.

As a legal professional responded in the Thomson Reuters research: 'There is a tendency to use AI large language models as the **shortcu**t to the answer rather than as a tool to enhance the answer. If people are not strictly guided toward using AI towards the latter purpose, training in general will suffer as early career professionals will no longer work to understand the outputs but rather use the output as their legal advice.'

> **ALERT**
>
> See the sad case of the New York lawyer.

ChatGPT is not perfect No one at the moment pretends that it is. Examples of its imperfections can be seen in the headlines in **5.10**.

Then there is the cautionary tale of Stephen Schwartz, a New York attorney, who has been fined by the court in the following unprecedented circumstances.

Mr Schwartz's firm was acting for a client suing an airline over alleged personal injury. They prepared a brief for court in the usual way and cited previous cases as precedent.

The airline's lawyer said that they could not find these cases. The judge investigated and found: 'six of the submitted cases appear to be bogus judicial decisions with bogus quotes and bogus internal citations.' ChatGPT had made them up. This is a most graphic illustration of its tendency to hallucinate, ie invent things, tell lies, mislead. What is worse is that the lawyer checked with ChatGPT and it is reported that this exchange followed:

Lawyer: 'Is *Varghese* a real case?' Referencing *Varghese v China Southern Airlines Limited,* one of the cases that could not be found.

ChatGPT: 'Yes'.

Lawyer 'What is your source?'

ChatGPT responds that the case is real and can be found on legal reference databases such as LexisNexis and Westlaw.

Schwartz explained to the judge that he had never used ChatGPT before for legal research and was 'unaware that its content could be false'. Does this tell us more about ChatGPT or about American lawyers? After all, ChatGPT 3 came in the bottom 25% of the American Bar Exam. ChatGPT4 came in the top 25%.[1]

And something similar happened in a case in the UK where at the county court in Manchester a litigant in person asked ChatGPT for authorities that supported their case. ChatGPT obliged. Sadly, some of the references were fictitious. It had made them up.

Now we all know. You have been warned. Embrace AI. Don't surrender to it.

The AI systems will improve. And let us not forgot that the product of human research can be inaccurate. You always need to check. For the moment we humans and machines still need each other.

Will we need lawyers?

5.19 As Allen & Overy said: 'One of the brilliant things about Harvey is that you don't need to train people to use it; you just need to provide them with a short, simple list of parameters and tips (which we've done), it's quick, pain-free, and inexpensive to roll-out' and 'for some tasks, such as quick drafting, summarising and comparing documents, ChatGPT is already better than junior lawyers.'

And it's not just international Magic Circle firms that are making use of this technology for international business. At the other end of the scale members of the public are using it to challenge parking ticket fines. Sean Bosley, a sales consultant, used GPGPT. He said: 'I typed "write an appeal to a penalty charge notice for driving through Gatwick Airport". I have received a final notice but never received a first notice of the penalty. Straightaway it came back with a great response.' His appeal was successful.

The technology Is already being used in courts. In Columbia one of the most technologically connected countries in the world, Judge Juan Manuel Padilla said when using ChatGPT in a children's medical rights case: 'this artificial intelligence helps us to produce very understandable sentences, good wording and so on.... Anticipate the decision of the court may take, as it is supported by the principle of equality in the use of precedents.'

But he emphasised it does not make judges lazy as 'The decision remains autonomous and his or her own.' Yes, but for how much longer?

As mentioned in **Chapter 2** the Master of the Rolls, Sir Geoffrey Vos said in his McNair lecture: 'GPT-4 or another advance machine learning is likely to transform

1 *The latest version of the artificial intelligence program ChatGPT has passed the Uniform Bar Examination by 'a significant margin,' earning a combined score of 297 that surpasses even the high threshold of 273 set by Arizona.

GPT-4 took all sections of the July 2022 bar exam and earned a score so high that it approaches the 90th percentile of test-takers, according to researchers Daniel Martin Katz, a professor at the Illinois Institute of Technology's Chicago-Kent College of Law, and Michael James Bommarito, a professor at the Michigan State University College of Law.

ABA Journal Latest version of ChatGPT aces bar exam with score nearing 90th percentile

the work that lawyers need to do and possibly even, in the slightly longer term, the business of judging.'

In the UK we now have Court of Appeal authority. Lord Justice Birss told a Conference at the Law Society in September 2023 how he used ChatGPT when preparing a judgment:

> 'I think what is of most interest is that you can ask these large language models to summarise information.
>
> 'It is useful and it will be used and I can tell you, I have used it.
>
> ' ... I thought I would try it. I asked ChatGPT can you give me a summary of this area of law, and it gave me a paragraph. I know what the answer is because I was about to write a paragraph that said that, but it did it for me and I put it in my judgment. It's there and it's jolly useful.
>
> 'I'm taking full personal responsibility for what I put in my judgment, I am not trying to give the responsibility to somebody else. All it did was a task which I was about to do and which I knew the answer and could recognise an answer as being acceptable.'

And what do clients think? As one former senior London market insurance executive and now entrepreneur said: 'It's nice having a lawyer you can ring up for advice but when I get it for free from AI…' .They are firmly of the view that AI will disintermediate whole swathes of professionals.

If lawyers go out of business, where will mediators get their work from? For civil and commercial mediators, lawyers are the main source of work in the UK. How will this impact mediators' marketing? See **Chapter 15**.

Lawyers will have to learn to prompt engineer. Some people think it will become the main element of their work. Perhaps it will be. But not for some time. If lawyers are going to learn prompt engineering will mediators have to do the same? Let's find out what it is.

Prompt engineering

5.20 What is a prompt engineer? It doesn't mean someone with a spanner turning up on time. Look at the job specification for a prompt engineer when Mishcon de Reya advertised for one on LinkedIn in March 2023.

Here is part of the job specification:

> **'Duties and Responsibilities**
>
> As a GPT Legal Prompt Engineer you will be responsible for the following tasks:
>
> - Work with our lawyers and our Practice Transformation team to understand the legal practice use cases to which ChatGPT, GPT3 and other large language models could be applied.

- Work with our business and legal operations professionals to understand the wider business use cases to which ChatGPT, GPT3 and other large language models could be applied.
- Design and develop high-quality prompts for a range of legal and non-legal use cases, working closely alongside our data science team.
- Evaluate and improve existing prompts to ensure they are effective.
- Stay up to date with the latest developments in natural language processing and GPT technology, incorporate these advancements into our work and take leadership in keeping our Strategy, Practice Transformation and Data Science teams up to date.
- Collaborate with the team to ensure that our use of language models is in line with ethical and regulatory requirements.

Skills/Experience

- A deep understanding of legal practice – probably (but not necessarily) including a degree in law or experience working as a lawyer.
- A deep understanding of law firm operations – probably (but not necessarily) gained from working at a law firm.
- Strong technical skills, including experience with GPT3 and other large language models.
- Excellent problem-solving skills and the ability to work creatively and independently.
- Strong communication and interpersonal skills, with the ability to work effectively with lawyers and other stakeholders.
- A passion for innovation and a desire to make a real impact on the legal industry.'

If you want to learn how to prompt engineer properly, you will have to undertake some training. Either work through one of the instruction books available such as Nathan Hunter's[2] or take a training course. There are plenty of them online.

Some you pay for and if you pass you are certified. Others are free.

https://www.udemy.com/course/prompt-engineering-for-ai/?utm

https://www.blockchain-council.org/certifications/certified-chatgpt-expert/?utm_

https://www.coursera.org/learn/prompt-engineering

For free courses

https://www.coursera.org/learn/prompt-engineering

https://www.classcentral.com/course/youtube-prompt-engineering-with-openai-s-gpt-3-and-other-llms-126224

2 *The Art of Prompt Engineering with ChatGPT: A Hands-On Guide* (2023).

Bluffer's guide to prompt engineering

Prompting

5.21 Instructions are known as prompts. The more you give and the more specific you can be in your requirements the better the outcome.

Three keys things to know:

1. Speak in ordinary conversational English. You do not have to rely upon keywords. Just give it instructions as though you were giving instructions to a new colleague.
2. Use proper grammar and punctuation.
3. It works on feedback. If you don't like what you receive first time tell it. Telling it what you like, what you didn't like and what you would like to see instead improves the responses.

For example,

> 'I liked your prose style and the concise paragraphs. But I didn't like the way that you kept repeating the same sentence structure'.

If you don't like the title of your blog, ask it to create three more choices.

Clarification

5.22 Ask for clarification: 'Please explain why the example is relevant to my question.'

Changing things:

Be clear what you want to keep and what you want to change.

For example, 'Could you improve the conversational tone of the language? Make sure you don't change the structure of the content of the paragraphs.'

How long:

OpenAI has not set a precise character limit. Responses tend to cut off at about 500 words or 4000 characters. It can start mid-sentence. This limit is being increased.

You can ask just to continue or go on. If you upgrade to ChatGPT plus you will have a 25,000-word limit.

You might ask ChatGPT to write a short message and get a long essay instead. Or the other way round, you want a detailed description and you get a one liner.

Just ask it to make it shorter or longer.

Longer pieces:

ChatGPT may seem to have infinite capacity but it can be overloaded. If it suddenly stops in mid-sentence just reply with 'continue.' But if you are writing a 20-page presentation or a business plan you might have to take a different approach.

Try chunking: that is dividing the work into smaller individual units.

Role-play

5.23 Asking ChatGPT to play a role generates better results. For example, 'Act as my editor for my article in my newsletter.'

Or if you want to write a blog in a particular style say George Orwell or JK Rowling ask it to pretend to be or act as George Orwell or JK Rowling and write a blog for you about mediation and AI.

Specify

5.24 If you use a prompt 'how does the solar system work?' you will get a response. It will be quite general. If you use a prompt 'explain how the solar system works' you will get a more detailed one.

Guardrails

5.25 You can't ask whatever you want to. Safeguards, notice guard rails, have been built in. Questions that are deemed hateful, sexist, racist or discriminatory in any way are off-limits.

Other uses

5.26 You can use ChatGPT:

- to access an Excel spreadsheet;
- to write you code to develop your new website (see **Chapter 17**);
- to update your profile on LinkedIn. You need to give examples of profile that you like and then ask ChatGPT to use those as a template. Here's an example of an approach.

Example

5.27 'OK. I'm going to teach you the LinkedIn profile style. I will give you a profile and you will remember it, analyse its style, and re-formulate in your mind what the LinkedIn style is. I will reply with 'got it' each time. '

5.28 *AI: End or beginning?*

Testing ideas.

One of the things that ChatGPT has proved to be good at is as a sounding board. Do you have an idea say for an article or a blog? Try it out on ChatGPT.

Ask it for a summary or outline of the topic.

Look at individual headings and ask for more detail on at that point.

You are not trying to get ChatGPT to write your text for you but to help you organise your thoughts. Is this better than a piece of paper and a Mind Map? Or digitally speaking a whiteboard. Try www/miro.com.

Prompt Engineering or PE as no doubt it will soon be called is like skiing. Easy to learn, hard to master. For help see the sample cheat sheets in the Appendix 1.

Perhaps if Stephen Schwartz had used better prompts he would have prevented his problems. For example, as the Master of the Rolls suggested, he could have asked:

> 'Can you confirm that the case of Varghese is reported at such and such a reference, and that it decided such and such a point. Had he done so, he might have received a more accurate answer.'

So get practising prompting.

Rivals

5.28 ChatGPT may be seen as the first. It may enjoy first mover advantage. But already there are rivals, and more are being developed. The biggest one is Microsoft Bing chat which uses open eyes GPT-four model as the basis for its answers but you have to download the Edge browser to use it. Bad luck for Chrome and Safari users.

The biggest non-GPT competitor to ChatGPT is Google Bard. This is based on its own language model LaMDA.

Some people prefer ChatGPT to Google Search (see **Chapter 6**). But the consensus seems to be that there will be integration.

As of 31August 2023 the Chinese version was released – Ernie – by Baidu, operator of China's largest search engine. Will this rival Silicon Valley's dominance?

ALERT

- There are potential copyright issues. At the moment, this is particularly contentious with images and art. A class action has been brought in the US against Microsoft, GitHub and OpenAI.
- Openai say that you have the right to reprint, sell, merchandise anything that was created with ChatGPT or ChatGPT plus. At least this means you will not get sued by OpenAI.
- The bigger and more difficult topic of copyright law and generative AI is a matter for debate.

Where are we in September 2023?

Remember the Gartner cycle. The five phases in the Hype Cycle are:

1 Technology Trigger,

2 Peak of Inflated Expectations,

3 Trough of Disillusionment,

4 Slope of Enlightenment,

5 Plateau of Productivity.

At the moment we have definitely passed Phase 1 and are now on the upward path of Phase 2. How far we have to climb before we reach the peak is the interesting question.

As at June 2023 probably the best we can do is adopt the approach of Professor Wendy Hall of Southampton University and who said that 'I think everyone's got to get a grip, get out of the hype, and understand that this is a learning curve.'

To give yourself an idea of some of the issues that will be relevant for mediators, try these questions. Abstract, general, even philosophical without doubt. But expect the response to them to be part of the context in which we will be mediating in the short to medium term.

- How will it affect human behaviour. Will we as human beings in the long-term act differently towards each other? If yes – then how will this affect mediators and the way that we do our work?
- Can we just give our disputes to an AI system and accept the answer?
- What about judgement, discretion, empathy, fairness?

These questions will keep thinkers, thought leaders and conference organisers busy for years to come. Mediators may have to deal with them, not just talk about them, and have to do so rather more quickly.

We have seen what AI could do for other jobs, in particular lawyers. Read **Chapter 6** to learn what AI can do for mediation.

In a nutshell

5.29

- Generative AI is an existential challenge.
- Things will be different.
- Some of the hyped hysteria has subsided.
- Mediation will be affected.
- Things are changing all the time.
- Keeping up is hard but you have to try.

Appendix 1

Cheat sheets for prompting

These draw on ideas from Steve Nouri.

1. Content/copy

   Word count

   Subject

   Goal

   Call to action

2. Brainstorm any idea

   Generate a list of

   1] Specify subject

   2] Specific things

   3] How many ideas do you want

   4] Goal

   5] What do you want it to do?

3. Break down concepts for easier learning

   Prompt: 'Break down [any topic or skill] into smaller, manageable chunks or units, and provide a structured plan for mastering each one.'

4. Create a winning marketing strategy

   "I want you to act like a marketing specialist and develop a marketing campaign for a [product or service]. Use a variety of tactics and channels to reach the target audience and achieve specific objectives. Consider the competition, budget, and target audience when planning the campaign. be sure to track and analyze the results of the campaign and adjust as needed."

5. Learn to ask better questions

   Prompt: 'Guide me on how to formulate effective questions related to [topic or skill] that will promote deeper thinking and stimulate curiosity.'

6. Summarise books and articles

   You can extract new ideas and information in seconds.

   Prompts: Summarise the main points from 'Influence' by Robert Cialdini. And extract some killer quotes from it.

7. Talk with any experts

   Ask ChatGPT to become an expert in any field (entrepreneurs, teachers, guide, etc) Note – The prompt 'Let's play a game' is really important to enter the conversation.

8. Assist with decision-making

   Prompt: "Help me weigh the pros and cons of [decision or choice], and provide a suggestion based on the analysis."

9. Unravel complicated subjects:

   Prompt:

   'Break down [insert topic] into simple, beginner-friendly terms that anyone can grasp.'

10. Have ChatGPT mimic your writing style.

    Prompt

    'Examine the writing style in the text below and compose a 100-word piece on [insert topic]'

11. Teach ChatGPT to generate prompts for itself.

    Prompt

    'You're an AI assistant [insert profession]. Generate the top 5 prompts for yourself about [insert topic].'

12. Request ChatGPT's guidance on using ChatGPT.

    Prompt:

    'Design a beginner-friendly guide to ChatGPT, covering prompts, priming, and personas. Provide examples where needed and keep the guide under 300 words.'

13 Seek ChatGPT's advice for problem-solving.

   Prompt

   'As an expert career coach, I [describe issue]. Offer me a list of 5 potential solutions to address this problem.'

14 Generate new ideas.

   Prompt

   'I aim to [insert task or goal]. Generate [insert desired outcome] for [insert task or goal].'

   Test multiple prompt formulations:

15 Experiment with different phrasings to optimise the model's performance.

   Prompt 1: 'What are some tips for staying motivated while working from home?'

   Prompt 2: 'How can remote workers maintain motivation and productivity?'

16 Guide with examples:

Provide examples of desired outputs to help the model understand the context and format.

Prompt: 'Write an introductory paragraph for an article about the benefits of meditation, using a similar style to this example: 'The sun rises, and a new day begins. As the world awakens, there's a sense of calm that washes over the early morning hours. Just as the sun's gentle rays nourish the Earth, so too does the practice of meditation nourish the soul.'

17 Ensure input clarity:

Use clear and unambiguous language in your prompts to avoid confusion.

Chapter 6

What can AI do for mediators?

In this chapter you will learn

- What ChatGPT produces for mediators.
- What tasks AI can do.
- What blockchain and smart contracts mean for mediators.

We have seen how AI is helping healthcare, can it do the same thing for dispute resolution? Can AI help conflict resolution professionals do their job better, use their time and energy more efficiently and provide a better experience for their clients?

Let's ask AI?

Here are the responses from ChatGPT when I asked.

Question: What can AI do for mediators?

Response

Version A

6.01

'Artificial intelligence (AI) can assist mediators in various ways, including:

1. Data analysis: AI algorithms can analyze vast amounts of data, including legal precedents and case law, to help mediators understand the strengths and weaknesses of different parties' arguments. This information can be used to identify potential solutions and facilitate negotiations.
2. Communication: AI-powered chatbots can assist mediators in communicating with parties involved in a dispute. These chatbots can provide automated responses to frequently asked questions and assist in scheduling and organizing meetings.
3. Prediction and risk assessment: AI algorithms can analyze the past behavior of parties involved in a dispute to identify patterns and predict potential outcomes. This information can help mediators better understand the parties' interests and risks and facilitate discussions that lead to more satisfactory outcomes.

6.02 *What can AI do for mediators?*

4. Document analysis: AI-powered tools can help mediators analyze and summarize legal documents, such as contracts or agreements, to identify key terms and issues. This can save time and improve the accuracy of the mediation process.
5. Virtual mediation: AI-powered tools can facilitate virtual mediation, which can be more convenient and cost-effective than traditional in-person mediation. These tools can provide secure communication platforms and assist with the scheduling of virtual meetings.'

Comment

6.02 A bit bland and generic. Could we find out more? I used the well-known mediator's trick of asking the same question twice to see whether the response is the same.

Here is what I received. Please note that the two requests were made within 20 minutes of each other on the same day using the same device.

Response

Version B

6.03

'Artificial Intelligence (AI) has the potential to revolutionize the field of mediation by improving the efficiency and effectiveness of mediation processes. Here are some ways AI can help mediators:

1. Document Analysis: AI can analyze large volumes of documents related to a case and extract relevant information, allowing mediators to quickly and accurately identify key issues.
2. Data Analytics: AI can use data analytics to identify patterns and trends in the behavior of parties to a dispute, enabling mediators to develop more effective mediation strategies.
3. Natural Language Processing: AI can use natural language processing to interpret the language used in communications between parties, identifying key issues and areas of potential agreement.
4. Prediction: AI can use machine learning algorithms to analyze data and make predictions about the outcome of a dispute, helping mediators to identify areas of common ground and develop effective solutions.
5. Online Dispute Resolution: AI can facilitate online dispute resolution by providing an automated platform for parties to communicate, negotiate and resolve disputes.
6. Virtual Mediation: AI can support virtual mediation by providing real-time translation services, transcription and other services that help to bridge communication gaps.

Overall, AI has the potential to enhance the efficiency, accuracy and effectiveness of mediation processes, helping mediators to resolve disputes in a more timely and cost-effective manner.'

Comment

6.04 What do we learn? There is considerable overlap but there are significant differences.

The most intriguing is in the first sentence. Version A says the AI can 'assist mediators'. Version B says that AI 'has the potential to revolutionise the field of mediation.'

Version A talks about assisting mediators – helping humans. Version B talks about revolutionising the concept and process of mediation – replacing humans. Are they really saying the same thing? Is assisting mediators only a subset of revolutionising the field of mediation? I think that they are different and that they are both correct.

Let us look at how the chatbot responses apply in practical terms. The cross references are to the ChatGPT responses A and B. it appears that AI can influence mediators and Mediation in **7 ways**.

1 **Information gathering**

2 **Searches**

3 **Analysis**

4 **Reality testing**

5 **Document preparation**

6 **Presentation**

7 **Prediction**

What can it do in practice?

Information gathering

Responses A and B, para 1

6.05 Even now mediators still receive big bundles of documents for the mediation. Why not use AI to scan them for us? Lawyers are already using AI for document review and to prepare bundles from the vast amounts of digital information which they need to deal with by way of disclosure. Perhaps it will help us find the important documents if we can identify the keywords.

In practice mediation bundles are now slimmer as part of the general streamlining of the mediation process when it takes place online. Lawyers will able to use AI to scan and summarise pages of documents,, generate schdules and chronologies. This should make mediation bundles even slimmer and more useful. Good news for mediators.

One of the document summary programs that is being used by mediators is Humata. It is free for the basic version up to 60 pages. Or you can pay $14.99 a month for the upgrade. You can ask questions about your document. It is useful but not essential. At least not yet for most types of mediations.

Go to their website https://www.humata.ai/. Try it out.

You have to convert your documents into a PDF. If you know how to do that follow these steps

1 Select the file tab.

2 Click Save

3 If the file was previously saved, select File > Save a Copy. If the file is unsaved, select File > Save As.

4 Select Browse to choose the location on your computer where you want to save the file.

5 In the drop-down list, select PDF.

6 Select Save.

So document review is something that AI can help mediators with. What about researching for information?

Is AI a quicker and more user-friendly way of researching for information – just finding out stuff? For example, you come across an initial or an acronym. What does it mean?

You can go into Google, which is what we do now, or you can click on ChatGPT. Which is better? I found that ChatGPT gives you more context. You have to do a little less work as the searcher. Will it replace Google? Who knows? Some mediators say that they have given up Google and just use ChatGPT. Google have recently announced that they are building ChatGPT into their search engines.(see **Chapter 5**).

Let us look at some examples.

Say, you are not just finding out a fact but are trying to establish some common ground of information. For example, the value of the property that everyone is arguing about. How often at mediations do people say: 'We've got a valuation but it's two years old.' or 'All that I could get from the agents was a drive-by valuation'. At the moment what people in the UK do at mediations is use Zoopla.

Can you use ChatGPT instead? Try it. Here is what happened when I tried.

Question: What is the current value of the property 25 Townshend Road Richmond Surrey TW9 1XH?

Response

6.06

'As an AI language model, I do not have access to real-time property market data or property valuation tools. The value of a property is influenced by various factors such as location, size, condition, and current market conditions. The best way to get an accurate valuation of a property is to consult a professional appraiser or real estate agent who can provide you with a comprehensive report of the property's value based on its unique characteristics and current market conditions.'

Comment

6.07 Not at all helpful.

Or you can try slightly more complicated valuation questions which crop up at mediations. For example, how do you value a company with an EBITDA of £2 million in the care home industry in the UK in 2023. By way of experiment, I asked that question. Here is the response.

Question What is the value of a company with an EBITDA of £2 million in the UK care home sector?

Response

6.08

'The value of a company with an EBITDA of £2 million in the UK care home sector would depend on various factors such as the company's growth prospects, profitability, market share, assets, liabilities, and the prevailing market conditions.

Typically, valuing a company in the care home sector would involve analyzing factors such as the demand for care home services, competition, regulatory environment, staffing, and the quality of care provided by the company.

Valuation methods such as discounted cash flow analysis, comparable company analysis, and precedent transactions analysis could be used to determine the company's value. However, the accuracy of any valuation would depend on the quality of information available and the assumptions made about the future prospects of the company.

It's worth noting that valuations in the care home sector can vary significantly based on various factors. Therefore, it's always best to seek the advice of a professional business appraiser or investment banker who can provide a more accurate assessment of the company's value based on its unique characteristics and market conditions.'

Comment

6.09 Again, not very helpful.

Searches

6.10 Somebody at the mediation is trying to remember a case that they think is relevant to the discussion. As we know, it rarely is but sometimes it is. In any case if someone think it is relevant then it is relevant because it is influencing their thinking. Again, type into ChatGPT. It does help you with your searches. It is extraordinary.

6.11 *What can AI do for mediators?*

> **ALERT**
>
> As of September 2023, ChatGPT's cut-off date for information is September 2021 for the free version or January 2022 for the paid version.
>
> Always check the cut-off date.
>
> But although background information might be helpful. What really matters usually is foreground information. You have to think carefully how you prompt it (see **Chapter 5**).

Comment

6.11 Of limited value – good at what it can do but there is lots that it cannot do.

Analysis

Responses A and B, para 1

6.12 Both versions A and B say the AI can provide data analysis or data analytics.

As a general statement of functionality, we can accept that. But does it really help mediators at mediation? It might help in preparation, but this is really an extension of information gathering.

Comment

6.13 If you have a lot of documents – very extensive pleadings and reports – then in theory you could ask the software to summarise them for you. Prompt it to just to pick out the main points. You can see how that would be helpful. But in practice how many mega documents mediations are there? Not that many. And you can also see how it will be expensive.

Access

6.14 What access does the mediator have to the AI? This is an important consideration. Are mediators going to have to buy their own licenses? If they are this will add to the cost of being a mediator. Or will mediators be granted access to someone else's AI eg. the parties' AI programs. Or will mediation providers provide a service for their panel mediators to use?

> **ALERT**
>
> - Mediators will spend more on licenses and subscriptions for AI tools.
> - Update your business plan (see **Chapter 16**).

Reality Testing

6.15 Reality testing is something that mediators are trained and encouraged to do. Mediators vary in the way they do this. Some are very inquisitorial and claim 'to give the parties a hard time.' Others are more indirect. Whatever the style some discussion about how likely it is that the parties can achieve what they want either by negotiation or by litigation happens at all mediations.

In practice reality testing is a combination of:

- Asking tough questions.
- Identifying obvious problems in someone's position.
- Providing predictions about what's likely to happen at court in other words second-guessing judges.
- Going through the costs both direct and indirect of continuing with litigation. Encouraging the parties to consider what they would do with the costs saved ie no more lawyers' fees, the opportunity cost of not having to meet lawyers once a week but get on with their business.
- Challenging the completeness and accuracy of information provided. For example, exploring the assumptions behind valuations.
- Putting one side's questions and comments to the other side.
- Run reality checks.

Keeping it friendly

6.16 Experienced lawyers know that reality testing happens at mediations. They tell their clients and prepare them for it. At least they should do. Clients do not always absorb what their lawyers tell them. They can find reality testing hostile and unpleasant. When feeling under pressure they retaliate by accusing the mediator of bias. 'Well, you obviously made up your mind and you think the other side are right!'

As mediator you can deflect this accusation by saying,' Well I'm asking the other side tough questions as well.' Or 'Let's be realistic – any judge is going to ask this question.'

Would it be better if the mediator could say: 'Well I've run the information through the AI program and it has come up with these questions by way of analysis. They're not my questions. They are the computer's questions!'

Will that get over the problem of perceived bias? It might. But will the programs that can be used to interrogate information to generate these sorts of questions be available to mediators on the day of the mediation or as part of their preparation?

Will we be able to collaborate with ChatGPT? If mediators need to provide some fresh energy and momentum to the discussions, why not suggest 'Let's see what ChatGPT says.'

6.17 *What can AI do for mediators?*

There does seem to be a human tendency to want to believe the machine is smarter than them. Researchers refer to 'machine heuristics'.

For example researchers at the University of Georgia[1] found that when volunteers were asked to count the number of people in a photograph of a crowd and were supplied with suggestions that were generated by a group of other people and suggestions generated by an algorithm they chose the algorithm.

Researchers at the University of Pennsylvania found that people who trusted machines were significantly more likely to hand over their credit card numbers to a computerised travel agent than to a human travel agent.[2]

Comment

6.17 Yes, it could help mediators here.

Document preparation

Response A, paras 1, 4, Response B, para 1

At the start of the mediation

6.18 As we saw in **Chapter 5** it seems to be generally accepted that AI can do a lot of the work that is done by junior lawyers. One of these is preparing drafts. So, can lawyers use it to help them prepare their mediation statements? If they can might this mean that they are done more quickly and not sent to the mediator 24 hours before the mediation? More importantly will it free them up to spend more time about thinking about how a settlement could be structured?

Conclusion: Yes it could help here.

Could it help with research? Yes:

- by summarising articles.
- by searching for key words and highlighting relevant documents.
- beware of using it for legal research. Recall the New York lawyers at **Chapter 5**.

At the end of the mediation

6.19 Draft settlement agreements.

Please see this exchange with ChatGPT.

Question: Please draft a settlement agreement for use at mediation

1 Watson, Schecter and Bogert Scientific Reports, *Nature* 13 April 2021.
2 Sundar and Kim 7 May 2019.

Response

6.20

'[Disclaimer: This is a general template and may need to be modified to fit your specific situation. It is recommended that you consult with a legal professional before using this agreement.]'

Settlement agreement

6.21

'This Settlement Agreement (the 'Agreement') is made and entered into on [date], by and between [party 1 name] ('Party 1') and [party 2 name] ('Party 2') (collectively referred to as the 'Parties').'

Recitals

6.22

'WHEREAS, the Parties are involved in a dispute (the 'Dispute') regarding [briefly describe the nature of the Dispute];

WHEREAS, the Parties have participated in mediation and have agreed to resolve the Dispute through settlement; and

WHEREAS, the Parties desire to enter into this Agreement to document the terms of their settlement and to resolve the Dispute.

NOW, THEREFORE, in consideration of the mutual promises and covenants contained herein, the Parties agree as follows:

1. Payment

   Party 1 agrees to pay Party 2 the sum of [dollar amount] as full and final settlement of the Dispute. Payment shall be made by [method of payment] no later than [date].

2. Release of Claims

   Party 1 and Party 2 hereby release each other from any and all claims, demands, causes of action, suits, debts, obligations, damages, and liabilities, whether known or unknown, arising from or relating to the Dispute. This release is intended to be a full and final release of all claims and liabilities, and each Party represents that it has not assigned or transferred any claims or liabilities to any other person or entity.

3. Confidentiality

   The terms and existence of this Agreement shall be confidential and shall not be disclosed to any third party, except as required by law or as necessary to enforce the terms of this Agreement. Each Party agrees to maintain the confidentiality of this Agreement and to not disclose any information regarding the Dispute or the settlement to any third party, except as required by law.

4. Governing Law and Jurisdiction

   This Agreement shall be governed by and construed in accordance with the laws of [state]. Any action or proceeding arising from or relating to this Agreement shall be brought exclusively in the courts of [state], and the Parties submit to the exclusive jurisdiction of such courts.

5. Entire Agreement

   This Agreement constitutes the entire agreement between the Parties with respect to the Dispute and supersedes all prior negotiations, discussions, and agreements between the Parties, whether oral or written. This Agreement may not be amended except in writing signed by both Parties.

6. Counterparts

   This Agreement may be executed in counterparts, each of which shall be deemed an original, but all of which together shall constitute one and the same instrument.

7. Effective Date

   This Agreement shall be effective as of the date first written above.

IN WITNESS WHEREOF, the Parties have executed this Agreement as of the date first written above.

[Party 1 Name]

[Party 1 Signature]

[Party 2 Name]

[Party 2 Signature]'

Comment

6.23 This is a nice clear short settlement agreement. It is a template. There are lots of templates available on the Internet. The CEDR and the PLC ones in the UK have become industry standard. But as we know it still takes far too long at mediation for people to record the settlement. Are any of them really any better than this? And it was so easy to find. Less than 10 seconds.

This will be of value to those mediators who panic about drafting settlement agreements. Sometimes they have good reason to be anxious. They are not lawyers. They are not used to drafting agreements. But here is something that they could work with. All the parties can see that it is a standard template and not some clever wording produced by one side or the other or by the mediator. This should make it more acceptable to everyone and therefore easier to agree. Of course, you still have to insert the precise terms of the settlement. But it's a useful first step.

As I posted in LinkedIn in a commercial mediation a lawyer asked me if I had a precedent for a particular part of the settlement agreement. I didn't have one to hand because I only had my iPad with me and suggested that we try ChatGPT. There were eight people in the room and they all looked sceptical. I logged on to ChatGPT and typed in some prompts. Instantly a precedent appeared. Everybody was astounded. They all wanted to try with their own prompts. Drafting became a collaborative exercise with much enthusiasm and energy being generated. It eventually got everybody over the line.

At a subsequent mediation one room was drafting a settlement proposal which included a letter of apology from their client. They used ChatGPT to generate various versions. All done in seconds not minutes.

Presentation

6.24 This raises another potential advantage of AI; being the mediator's digital assistant (DA) who is accessible to all and is objective. The DA has not been appointed by anybody, has no prior dealings with anybody and is just there providing information. Can it act as an even more neutral third party? The question is: Will AI generated content be seen as more accurate and human work product than human work product?

Perhaps AI can help mediators mediate but could it mediate instead of mediators?

Worked examples

6.25 Let us see what ChatGPT says it would do if it had to mediate a small building dispute.

Question: In what ways could AI help mediate a dispute?

Response

6.26 AI can help mediate a dispute in several ways, including:

1 Providing neutral and unbiased analysis: AI algorithms can provide unbiased and neutral analysis of the dispute by evaluating the facts and data presented by both parties. This can help to identify the root cause of the dispute and highlight areas of agreement or disagreement.

2 Facilitating communication: AI chatbots can be used to facilitate communication between the parties in a dispute. These chatbots can provide automated responses to common questions and can guide the parties towards a resolution.

3 Predicting outcomes: AI algorithms can predict the potential outcomes of the dispute based on past cases and legal precedents. This can help the parties to make informed decisions and reach a resolution quickly.

4 Providing alternative solutions: AI can provide alternative solutions to the dispute that may not have been considered by the parties. For example, an AI algorithm could suggest a compromise solution that both parties may find acceptable.

5 Analysing emotions: AI can analyse the emotions and sentiments expressed by the parties during the mediation process. This can help to identify areas of high tension or conflict and help the mediator to address them effectively.

Overall, AI has the potential to provide valuable support in mediating disputes by providing impartial analysis, facilitating communication, predicting outcomes, suggesting alternative solutions, and analysing emotions. However, it is important to note that AI should not replace human mediators entirely and should be used in conjunction with human expertise and judgment.

Comment: another example of a general, uncontroversial – even trite – summary. Possibly useful for student essays. Not much use for mediators.

Question: Could AI mediate a dispute?

Response

6.27

> 'AI could potentially mediate a dispute, but it would depend on the specific circumstances and the complexity of the dispute. AI algorithms are currently capable of analyzing data and providing unbiased analysis, but they may not be equipped to handle the nuanced emotional and interpersonal dynamics that often arise in a dispute resolution process.
>
> In addition, the success of any mediation process depends on the willingness of the parties to participate and engage in good faith. It is not clear whether parties would be willing to engage in a dispute resolution process mediated entirely by AI, or whether they would prefer to have a human mediator who can offer more personalized and empathetic support.
>
> While AI could be a useful tool in facilitating a dispute resolution process, it is likely that human mediators will continue to play a crucial role in this area. Ultimately, the best approach would be to combine the strengths of both AI and human mediators to achieve the most effective and fair outcomes for all parties involved.'

Comment

6.28 What the response says is that it cannot mediate the dispute **yet**. It is not saying that it can **never** mediate it. What we have to realise is that the responses are based upon the information on which ChatGPT has been trained. This includes all the text written by mediators and commentators saying that AI could /should never replace the human touch of mediators. That's what mediators want to hear. A good example of confirmation bias perhaps?

Again of use to students studying mediation but not for mediators doing mediation.

What about this small building dispute?

Question: How would you mediate this dispute?

6.29

- Sam asks Pat to do install a new kitchen and patio. Pat agrees to do this and says it will take four weeks and cost £8K for the patio and £12K for the kitchen.
- Sam pays 50% in advance.

- After six weeks the job is not completed. Sam has no kitchen and tells Pat to leave.
- Sam gets Charlie in to finish the job and charges Sam £15K.
- Pat sues Sam for £10K and Sam counterclaims for £15K.

Response

6.30

> 'As an AI language model, I can provide some general suggestions for mediating the dispute between Sam and Pat in this building project, but it is important to note that every mediation is unique, and the best approach will depend on the specific circumstances and needs of the parties involved.
>
> Here are some steps that a mediator could take to help resolve this dispute:
>
> 1. Identify the key issues: The mediator would need to identify the key issues that are causing the dispute. In this case, the main issues appear to be the delay in completing the project, the additional cost incurred by Sam to hire a new contractor, and the quality of the work completed by Pat.
> 2. Gather information: The mediator would need to gather information about the project, including the contract between Sam and Pat, any correspondence between them, and any other relevant documentation or evidence. It may also be helpful to visit the site to assess the work completed by Pat and Charlie.
> 3. Listen to the parties: The mediator would need to listen to both parties' perspectives and concerns to gain an understanding of their positions and interests. They could do this through individual meetings or joint sessions.
> 4. Identify common ground: The mediator could identify areas of common ground between Sam and Pat and encourage them to focus on finding a mutually acceptable solution rather than simply arguing their positions.
> 5. Brainstorm solutions: The mediator could facilitate a brainstorming session where both parties can suggest potential solutions to the dispute. These solutions could include financial compensation, completion of the project, or other remedies that address the interests of both parties.
> 6. Negotiate a settlement: The mediator would then help the parties negotiate a settlement agreement that addresses their interests and resolves the dispute. The agreement should be fair, reasonable, and legally enforceable.
>
> In this case, the mediator would need to carefully consider the specific facts and circumstances of the dispute, including the contract terms, the quality of work completed by Pat, and the reasons for the delay. The mediator may need to engage in active problem-solving to help the parties reach a resolution that meets their needs and interests.'

Comment

6.31 Not much help at all. A poor outline for a student essay. Again, this is too general to be of any practical use at a mediation.

Let's try and delve a little deeper.

Question: Thank you but what would you do in this particular dispute?

Response

6.32

'As an AI language model, I am not able to provide a definitive solution to this specific dispute, as I do not have access to all of the relevant information and I am not a licensed mediator. However, based on the information provided, here are some general steps that a mediator could take to help resolve the dispute between Sam and Pat:

1. Review the contract: The mediator would need to review the contract between Sam and Pat to understand the terms of the agreement and the scope of work.
2. Identify the cause of the delay: The mediator would need to understand the cause of the delay in completing the project. This could include issues such as unforeseen circumstances, lack of communication, or failure to meet agreed-upon deadlines.
3. Assess the quality of work: The mediator would need to assess the quality of work completed by Pat and Charlie to understand whether Sam's counterclaim for £15K is justified. This could involve examining the work completed, consulting with experts, or conducting tests.
4. Facilitate communication: The mediator would need to facilitate communication between Sam and Pat to identify areas of common ground and potential solutions.
5. Explore potential solutions: The mediator could explore potential solutions to the dispute, such as allowing Pat to complete the project and compensate Sam for the delay or allowing Sam to keep the work completed by Charlie and compensate Pat for the work completed.
6. Negotiate a settlement: The mediator would help the parties negotiate a settlement that addresses their interests and resolves the dispute. This could involve financial compensation, completion of the project, or other remedies that meet the needs of both parties.

Overall, the mediator would need to use their judgement and expertise to help the parties reach a mutually acceptable solution that is fair, reasonable, and legally enforceable.'

Comment

6.33 This is better. A useful check list for an inexperienced or nervous mediator.

Let us prompt a little more.

Question: Thank you. What questions would you ask Sam and Pat to facilitate communication and explore potential solutions?

Response

6.34

'Here are some questions that a mediator could ask Sam and Pat to facilitate communication and explore potential solutions:

1. What are your main concerns about the project and the dispute?
2. What do you think caused the delay in completing the project?
3. How do you feel about the quality of work completed by Pat and Charlie?
4. What would be the ideal outcome for you in resolving this dispute?
5. What are your priorities in resolving this dispute?
6. What solutions have you considered to address the issues in the project and the dispute?
7. How can we work together to find a mutually acceptable solution to the dispute?
8. What are the key issues that need to be addressed in order to resolve the dispute?
9. What steps can we take to prevent similar disputes from arising in the future?
10. Is there anything else that you would like to share or discuss related to the project or the dispute?

These questions can help to open up communication between the parties, identify areas of common ground, and explore potential solutions that meet the needs of both parties. The mediator would need to listen carefully to the responses of both Sam and Pat and help them to work towards a resolution that is fair and reasonable for both parties.'

Comment

6.35 Useful on a training programme or at a simulated mediation. But would mediators need this in a real time mediation? I suspect not.

Question Thank you. What questions would you ask Pat when talking in private?

Response

6.36

As an AI language model, I do not have any information about the specific circumstances or dynamics of this dispute. However, in general, here are some questions that a mediator might ask Pat during a private conversation:

1. What were your expectations for the project when you agreed to take it on?
2. How did you communicate your expectations to Sam?
3. What challenges did you face during the project that led to the delay?
4. Did you communicate with Sam about the reasons for the delay?
5. What is your perspective on the quality of work completed by yourself and Charlie?
6. How do you think the dispute could be resolved fairly and reasonably for both parties?

7. Are there any concerns or issues that you would like to raise with me in confidence?

The mediator would use the information gathered from these questions to better understand Pat's perspective on the project and the dispute, and to help identify potential solutions that could be acceptable to both Pat and Sam. It is important for the mediator to maintain confidentiality and impartiality during private conversations with each party in order to facilitate an open and honest dialogue that can lead to a successful resolution of the dispute.

Comment

6.37 This is more useful. Possibly of use to a nervous newly accredited mediator or someone who is suffering from mediator's block.

But still only of limited use.

7 Prediction

Response B, para 4, response A, para 3

6.38 AI has been widely advertised as a useful tool to predict the outcomes of cases. So can this be of use to mediators?

Mediators help the parties to find the exit price – what each party to the dispute is prepared to contribute to the cost of getting out of the dispute. One thing is for sure whenever you are in a dispute it costs you money to get out. This applies whether you fight your way out or talk your way out. So, the question is: how much is each side prepared to contribute to the exit price?

One way of arriving at this is to carry out a two-part calculation:

- Price the risk of going to trial. That is litigation risk and litigation discount which lawyers advise about.
- Put a value on the benefit of settlement. This is for the clients. People in a dispute have all sorts of reasons to want to get out. Financial – no more lawyer's fees; commercial – it is interfering with my business; personal – it is interfering with my personal life, family, religious, social or political life and so on. If there is a benefit put a value on it.

Doing those two calculations helps you find the exit price. You could ask an AI system to do it for you. They may make a better job of it. This is not so much as making decisions as providing automated assessments. There are hurdles:

- It is all too complicated. You can do a simple cost benefit analysis without having to input lots of data into an expensive computer program.
- Algorithms are only as good as their assumptions. There has long been a phrase in computing: GIGO -garbage in garbage out. And we must not lose sight of it.
- Consumer resistance. Lawyers, especially English barristers, are reluctant to quantify their clients' chance of winning. They much prefer qualitative

evaluations – 'a strong case', 'a very strong case', 'as sure a thing as you can ever get at trial'. These phrases may convey something to them. Whether clients ever understand the words in the same way is another matter. But 50-50 is 50-50, ie the toss of a coin. A 75% chance of winning can be quantified into a price to pay either to buy off the risk or to justify further investment.

Even basic calculations based on summing the differences of expected values of different outcomes is usually resisted by qualitatively inclined lawyers. Surprisingly their clients are more interested in the figures and accept the implications of the calculations much more readily. After all, they are paying the legal bills.

Following the science, or going where the numbers take you, can provide a face-saving way of agreeing to a proposal. Clients often say: my head is telling me to accept this offer, but my heart is telling me not to. Your heart may be saying one thing, but your head has now got the edge. You may feel strongly. You may feel unjustly treated. But the figures show that a realistic financial outcome is X. If you can get X you have done well. If you can get above X so much the better.

And for the paying party, if you can pay below X, you have done well.

Comment

6.39

- When it comes to prediction, probability, and pricing algorithm-based systems could be of great help.
- One thing is for sure: all users of mediation need a working knowledge of them, so they appreciate the possible benefits to themselves.

Let us prompt a little more.

Question: Pat's lawyer has advised Pat that there is a 40% chance of winning. If the case goes to trial Pat's legal costs will be £6K and Sam's will be £4K – which Pat will have to pay if he loses. What offer to settle should Pat make?

Response

6.40

'As an AI language model, I cannot provide legal or financial advice. However, based on the information provided, here are some general considerations that a mediator or party in a dispute might take into account when making an offer to settle:

1. Strength of the case: The strength of each party's case can be a major factor in determining a settlement offer. Pat's lawyer has advised that there is a 40% chance of winning, which means that the case is not a slam dunk for either party.
2. Costs of litigation: The costs of litigation can be substantial, and both parties will incur legal fees if the case goes to trial. In this case, Pat's legal costs will be £6K, and he will have to pay Sam's legal costs of £4K if he loses.

3. Risk tolerance: Each party's willingness to take risks can be a factor in determining a settlement offer. Pat may be more risk-averse than Sam and may be willing to accept a lower settlement amount to avoid the risk of losing at trial and having to pay Sam's legal costs.
4. Desired outcome: Each party's desired outcome can also be a factor in determining a settlement offer. Pat may want to avoid the time and expense of a trial, while Sam may want to be compensated for the delays and additional costs he incurred due to the project not being completed on time.

Based on these factors, Pat may want to make a settlement offer that is lower than the potential damages or legal costs he could face if the case goes to trial. The specific amount will depend on the details of the case and the parties' negotiating positions. It may also be helpful for Pat to consult with his lawyer and/or a mediator to help determine an appropriate settlement offer.'

Comment

6.41 Again, just background information. We want more foreground.

Question: Thank you. Can you do an EV calculation based on Pat's position?

Response

6.42

'As an AI language model, I can provide a general overview of how to perform an Expected Value (EV) calculation, but I cannot perform one for this specific case as I don't have access to all the relevant details and figures. However, here is a general explanation of how an EV calculation works:

An EV calculation is a way of assessing the expected outcome of a situation based on probabilities and potential outcomes. In a legal dispute like the one between Pat and Sam, an EV calculation can be used to estimate the expected financial outcome of going to trial versus settling out of court.

To perform an EV calculation, you would need to consider the potential outcomes of going to trial and the probabilities of those outcomes occurring. For example, if Pat's lawyer has advised him that there is a 40% chance of winning the case, then you would assign a 40% probability to the outcome of winning and a 60% probability to the outcome of losing.

Next, you would need to estimate the potential damages or costs associated with each outcome. For example, if Pat wins the case, he may be awarded damages of £10K, while if he loses, he will need to pay Sam's legal costs of £4K, plus his own legal costs of £6K. These figures would be used to estimate the expected value of each outcome.

To calculate the EV of going to trial, you would multiply the probability of each outcome by its estimated value and add the results. For example, if the probability of winning is 40% and the damages awarded in that case would be £10K, then the expected value of winning would be £4K (0.4 × £10K). Similarly, if the probability of losing is 60% and the costs associated with that outcome would be £4K + £6K = £10K, then the expected value of losing would be -£6K (0.6 × -£10K).

Once you have estimated the expected values of each outcome, you can compare the EV of going to trial versus settling out of court. If the expected value of settling is higher than the expected value of going to trial, then it may be more advantageous for Pat to settle the case rather than risk going to trial. If the expected value of going to trial is higher than the expected value of settling, then it may be more advantageous for Pat to continue with the legal proceedings.

Again, please note that this is a general explanation of how an EV calculation works, and the specific figures and outcomes would depend on the details of the case. It is always advisable to consult with a qualified legal or financial professional when making important decisions related to a legal dispute.'

Comment

6.43 It is a standard explanation of how to do an EV calculation. Nothing wrong with it as general background.

Let us try and find out something specific that a mediator could use on the day.

Question: Thank you; so based on the EV's calculated above of winning £4K and losing £6k what is the overall EV of Pat's position?

Response

6.44

'The overall EV of Pat's position depends on the probability of winning the case. If Pat's lawyer has advised him that there is a 40% chance of winning, then we can use that probability to calculate the overall EV as follows:

Overall EV = (probability of winning × EV of winning) + (probability of losing × EV of losing) Overall EV = (0.4 × £4K) + (0.6 × -£6K) Overall EV = £1,600 – £3,600 Overall EV = -£2,000

This calculation suggests that Pat's overall expected value for going to trial is -£2,000, meaning that, on average, he can expect to lose money if he proceeds to trial. This would indicate that it may be more advantageous for Pat to consider settling the case out of court if he can negotiate a settlement that results in a higher expected value than -£2,000. However, please note that this calculation is based on the assumptions and figures provided and is not a guarantee of actual outcomes.'

Comment

6.45 Eureka! This could be very useful in helping the parties to think quantitatively.

ALERT

I could not help myself. I had to try and build rapport. A good example of the Eliza effect. This has dangers. See **Chapter 5** and below.

Thank you Chat. This is very helpful. Stephen

You're welcome, Stephen! If you have any further questions, feel free to ask.

'Thank you for listening'. These were the words of the defendant in a bitter and protracted neighbourhood dispute that eventually went to mediation four weeks before trial. It didn't settle. But at least one of the neighbours felt better. Mediators are trained to listen and to let people think that they have been heard. To demonstrate active listening mediators, summarise, reframe and play back words that they have been told.

See below the exchange between a computer program and a person. All that is happening is that the program is feeding the person's responses back to them. The text is from studies carried out by Joseph Weizenbaum.

This is what is happening with computers using generative AI. And it can be misleading. We end up crediting the program with far more ability and intelligence that it can ever have. This is over-attribution bias. We have to be aware of it.

Would the participant in the neighbour dispute have been just as happy with such an exchange? That really will be both a challenge and a help to mediators if ChatGPT can do effective active listening.

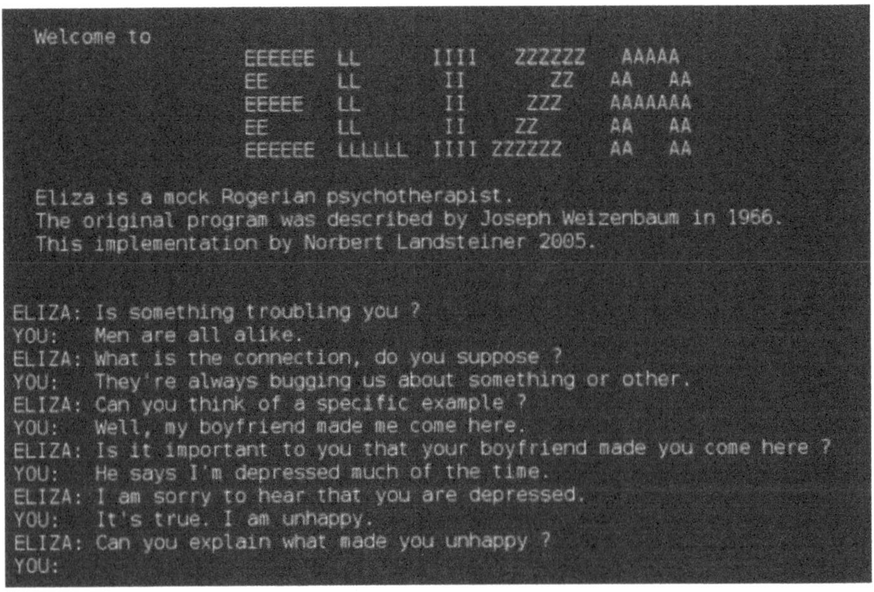

Psychological

Reading emotions

6.46 What about emotional AI (EAI)? This is technology that can sense and interact with human emotions.

This is billed as the next big thing. Yes, yet another next big thing and it is set to be **the** dominant application of machine learning. Look at what is happening.

Zoom is introducing Zoom IQ, which will provide users with real-time analysis of emotions and engagement during virtual meetings.

Smart Eyes a Swedish company has acquired Affectiva, the MIT Media Lab spinoff that developed the SoundNet neural network- an algorithm that classifies emotions such as anger from audio samples in less than 1.2 seconds.

This story is from *WIRED World in 2023*. Chatbots are getting better at closely mimicking human emotions so they create more empathetic connections with users in banking, education, and health care. Microsoft's China based chatbot Xiaoice has passed the Turing test, with the users failing to recognize it as a bot for 10 minutes.

Juniper Research Consultancy reports that chatbot interactions in health care will rise by almost 167% from 2018, to reach 2.8 billion annual interactions in 2023. The perceived benefit is that save medical staff's time and therefore a great deal of money.

But there are red flags. Criticise say that most EAI is based on flawed science. It uses algorithms that reduce facial and tonal expressions to an emotion without taking into account a person's social and cultural background and the situation that they are in at that moment. A scowling face doesn't always mean that a person is angry but an algorithm is likely to conclude that it does. We all display our emotions in ways that accord with our social and cultural norms. These may reflect our inner states. Our expressions of emotion may be learned responses to meet expectations of how we should behave.

The big fear is that such EAI technologies that make assumptions about emotional states will aggravate social, gender and racial inequalities. This is a form of stereotyping and will perpetuate power imbalances. Which is one the things that mediators are enjoined to address at mediations.

Would mediators find useful if their computer screen analysed the behaviour of the parties round the table whether in person or online? By analysing their facial gestures, breathing patterns, choice of words, tone of their voice and the rate of speech they could predict whether the person was stressed and whether they were stressed because they were lying. See **Chapter 3**.

Personally, I would find it very useful. I realise that this may sound creepy but is it in fact any different from what we do anyway. Is a computer-based data driven analysis any more objectionable, or creepier, than our own instinctive assessment?

Taking decisions

6.47 Even an AI enthusiast like the Master of the Rolls is very cautious and guarded about predicting when AI will take decisions instead of human judges. But since mediation is not about taking decisions – only about exploring options for settlement – will there be the same reluctance to replace human mediators with automated ones?

I suspect that there will not be the same judicial reluctance. In January 2023 Josh Glancy reported in the *Sunday Times* about the work at the Institute of Ethics in AI at the University of Oxford. He referred to a conference that took place chaired by Lord Neuberger. While acknowledging the judges may have an intuition to spot a lying witness and an obligation to explain and account for their decisions, which are things that machines at the moment cannot do, he says the case 'for at least partially integrating them into the justice system remains quite strong.' And went on to say that 'one suggestion is that litigants might have the option to submit to an AI mediation before entering a human court room.'

You can see how that might appeal to the judiciary: retaining their own jobs and putting their competitors out of business. Mediators, on the other hand, might think the better solution is to submit to human mediation before entering an AI court.

Digital dilemmas

6.48 The use of AI as a predictive tool raises interesting questions.

1 What if AI's prediction is different from everybody else's including the mediator's EV calculation. As has been noted in **1.03** there is a trend in the UK for commercial mediators to be more evaluative. They are often asked to give a view or even make a recommendation. What happens if the recommendation or view differs from the one produced by ChatGPT.

2 Will this undermine the mediator's credibility? Will the parties lose confidence in the mediator even if what ChatGPT says favours that party?

3 What will their lawyers' position be if they go against AI's view or recommendation? Will they be negligent? After all AI is supposed to be better than humans at prediction.

4 If lawyers and their clients start using AI to prepare for mediatons by gaming different settlement and negotiation scenarios, will this make them less flexible? What if the computer has told them what steps to take, what responses to make and when to stop the mediation? Will they exercise any manual override or will they just follow the computer generated flight plan?

5 How do mediators reality test computer generated scenarios? Obviously they can examine assumptions. Will they need to be able to generate their own alternative scenarios for comparison?

6 Are we going to see the emergence of the satyr mediator- a human working symbiotically and seamlessly with a machine – their Digital Assistant powered by Generative AI? My guess? Sooner than you think but probably not within three years.

Communication/natural language

6.49 I see the use of chatbots for mediators as limited. Although some counsel's Chambers, for example Clerksroom, say they use a chatbot – Billybot – as part of their clerking and administrative function mediators are not in a big enough way of business to justify that. In any case, mediators want to have as much human contact with their potential clients as possible. I would not even use a chatbot to answer the phone.

Quants

6.50 Mediators, advisors and clients all have different approaches to quantification. Some people love following the numbers. They have Excel spreadsheets on their screens and constantly update them.

Others are figures averse. How many advisors do you hear at mediations say: 'I prefer not to give a percentage chance of winning, but I am very confident that we're going to succeed.' Or just 'Oh, I don't believe in quantification.'

If you like figures you will find ChatGPT and AI helpful.

- You can use it to open an Excel spreadsheet.
- You can use that to do your discounted flow calculations or to show the change in settlement values by applying different interest rates.
- You can use it for EV calculations or decision trees.

I suspect that sooner rather than later most mediators will be using ChatGPT and have it on their devices. In this sense all mediations will become co-mediations because every mediator will have ChatGPT open and available to help them at mediations.

I already have and it worked. I was discussing pricing up risk in one room. Their barrister was taking us through his probability calculations. None of us was really following. I suggested we ask ChatGPT. Everyone laughed and said 'Yes, Let's go for it.'

Here is the result.

Question

6.51 'In a court case in order to win I have to prove my opponent was negligent, that the negligence caused the loss, and my loss was £1million. I have a 60% chance of proving they were negligent, and 80% chance of showing that it caused the loss and a 50% chance of showing that the amount of my loss was £1 million. Please calculate my overall chances of winning £1m'

6.52 *What can AI do for mediators?*

Response

6.52

> 'To calculate your overall chances of winning, we can multiply the individual probabilities together.
>
> The probability of proving negligence is 60% or 0.6. The probability of showing that negligence caused the loss is 80% or 0.8. The probability of showing that the amount of loss was $1 million is 50% or 0.5.
>
> To find the overall probability, multiply these three probabilities together:
>
> 0.6 * 0.8 * 0.5 = 0.24
>
> Therefore, your overall chances of winning the court case are 24% or 0.24, based on the given probabilities.'

This took less than 90 seconds.

Question

6.53 'I have a court case. I have three possible defences. On defence one, I have a 60% chance of winning. On defence two, I have an 80% chance of winning. On defence three, I have a 50% chance of winning. I only have to establish one of these defences to win. What are my overall chances of winning?'

Response

6.54

> 'To calculate your overall chances of winning, we need to consider the probabilities of winning on each defence and determine the probability of winning at least one of them.
>
> Let's calculate the probability of not winning on each defence:
>
> - Defence one: 100% – 60% = 40%
> - Defence two: 100% – 80% = 20%
> - Defence three: 100% – 50% = 50%
>
> To find the probability of not winning on any defence, we multiply the probabilities of not winning on each defence:
>
> 0.4 * 0.2 * 0.5 = 0.04
>
> The probability of not winning on any defence is 0.04 or 4%.
>
> Therefore, the probability of winning at least one defence is the complement of the probability of not winning on any defence:
>
> 1 – 0.04 = 0.96
>
> Your overall chances of winning the court case, considering the three defences, are 96% or 0.96.

> In the given example, we calculated the probability of not winning on any defence, which represents the complement of winning at least one defence. To find the probability of winning at least one defence, we subtract the probability of not winning (0.04 or 4%) from 1.
>
> By subtracting the probability of the complement from 1, we ensure that the sum of the probabilities of both the event and its complement adds up to 1, as required by probability theory.
>
> Did they accept what ChatGPT said? No, it was not what they were expecting. What did they do? They signed up for ChatGPT there and then and did it themselves. What happened then? We settled.'

What about other technologies? Can they be of use to mediators.

Blockchain

6.55 What is it? Let's ask those who are using it and advising on how to use it.

According to Deloittes, 'Blockchain technology is a new approach to recording, sharing information on the members of the community. Instead of relying on a central party, community members can directly run networks and host data that represents anything from payments to carbon credits.' Originally it was used as a system for recording digital payments. Each event and overall balances were logged on a digital ledger that is replicated across a distributed network of computers.

Bitcoin is one of its best examples but it is a technology that enables members to agree on a single record of events. All the information is encrypted and secured. Tampering and amendment is said to be impossible.

It can be used in healthcare where patients' encrypted records could be shared securely, or for voting systems.

According to PwC

> 'From a business perspective, it's helpful to think of blockchain technology as a type of next-generation business process improvement software. Collaborative technology, such as blockchain, promises the ability to improve the business processes that occur *between* companies, radically lowering the 'cost of trust.'

Financial institutions are exploring how they could also use blockchain technology to upend everything from clearing and settlement to insurance. '

This technology facilitates the work of groups who are operating collaboratively towards a common goal using decentralised autonomous organisations (DAO's). In the words of Raam Chandrasekharan – DAO Contributor & Strategist – these are a new form of open and transparent organisational structure underpinned by Blockchain. For example, a participant could put forward a proposal. If the proposal is passed self-enforcing digital agreement smart contracts can execute the agreed actions autonomously. This speeds up decision-making and improves aligning strategic decisions with members' interests.

Kleros

6.56 What is it? The name derives from the Ancient Greek word for casting a lot. It is a decentralised dispute resolution platform built on blockchain technology. It is not mediation. It is adjudicative although the decision is not made by a single person or body but by a randomly chosen group of jurors.

The methodology combines blockchain, crowdsourcing and game theory principles. Every step in the arbitration process – securing evidence, selecting juries, recording, and enforcing decisions is automated.

Jurors receive the evidence, review it and make a decision. If they vote with the majority, they are rewarded. If they vote with the minority, they are penalised. They are rewarded by an increase in the value of their Kleros tokens (or PNKs) which they buy to qualify as a juror. They are punished by losing some of the value of the Kleros token.

The decision is not binding on the parties: they can appeal. When they appeal the process is repeated. And they can appeal multiple times. The charging system discourages multiple appeals. If the jury's decision is not appealed, it is incorporated into a smart contract.

The methodology is based on game theory and in particular the work of Thomas Shelling.

His work was on how to find solutions when people have to coordinate their behaviour in the absence of communication. They tend to behave in a way that seems natural or relevant to them.

The system can also be used where communication is possible, but no party can provide the other with a reason to believe that what they say is true. In other words, it works on focal points ie each person's expectation of what the other expects him to be expected to do.

The example that Schelling used was:' Tomorrow you have to meet a stranger in New York City. Where and when do you meet them?' You could choose anywhere. The most common answer, is 'The information booth at Grand Central Terminal.' It's a traditional place to meet and therefore is a natural focal point.

What are you doing is not trying to find the truth. You are trying to predict what most of the people will decide is the answer.

It is fascinating and innovative and you can see a marketplace for those who use smart contracts as the ordinary way of carrying on business.

What can it do for mediation? Nothing.

Is it a challenge to mediators in 2023? Not really. Will it ever be? Doubtful. Will it become a challenge to the other adjudicative processes or even early neutral evaluations? Very possibly.

For more information go to https://blog.kleros.io/the-kleros-juror-starter-kit/

Crypto currency

6.57 A cryptocurrency, eg Ethereum or Bitcoin, is a medium of exchange, such as the Euro, but is digital and uses cryptographic techniques and its protocol to verify the transfer of funds and control the creation of monetary units. The network is decentralised. It has no intrinsic value or physical form. Its supply is not determined by a central bank but by the protocol.

A crypto protocol is a set of rules and procedures governing participants' behaviour in a decentralised network that uses cryptography to secure its operations. Crypto protocols are usually open-source and transparent, allowing anyone to examine and verify the underlying code.

Does this have relevance for the mediator?

Crypto currency has already led to litigation. There are disputes, there will be more regulation, this will mean more work for lawyers and mediators. The real question is whether those who use crypto currency will feel more comfortable using a Kleros type mediation than the conventional dispute resolution models on offer at the moment.

Smart Contracts

6.58 According to IBM

> 'Smart contracts are simply programs stored on a blockchain that run when predetermined conditions are met. They typically are used to automate the execution of an agreement so that all participants can be immediately certain of the outcome, without any intermediary's involvement or time loss. They can also automate a workflow, triggering the next action when conditions are met.'

Siri

6.59 Let's not forget Siri which has been available since 2010. It's a basic digital assistant which supports a wide range of user commands such as checking basic information, scheduling events, searching on the Internet, et cetera.

Are any of the above technologies relevant to mediators?

6.60 They are a potential source of work for mediators. Inevitably, there will be disputes arising out of the use of them. Some of those disputes will come to mediation. There has already been a significant amount of litigation about crypto assets.

If there is one thing that differentiates digital exiles from digital natives it is Siri. At a recent commercial mediation we needed to convert US dollars and euros into sterling. The age range of the room was from twenties to sixties. The 20-year-old just spoke to Siri. Back came the answer while everybody else was still fumbling with their iPads and calculators.

Can we use any of this technology to improve what we do?

6.61 That is far more problematic. It may be that in time readily available systems for arranging appointments, storing documents, and making payments will become available at a low cost. In September 2023 for most mediators there is not any immediately apparent application..

In a nutshell

6.62 In time ADR may come to mean **Automated** Dispute Resolution. Soon, it will come to mean **Augmented** Dispute Resolution.

AI could help mediators with:

- Brainstorm generating ideas. ChatGPT can be seen as an objective source of suggestions.
- Generating questions. Not all mediators will welcome this. Will Gerry O'Sullivan's book *The Mediator's toolkit: formulating and asking questions for successful outcomes* have to be remaindered? Probably not. You may need to re-read it to judge the quality of the questions which ChatGPT is generating.
- Prediction.
- EV calculations.
- Mediators will need to have ChatGPT on their iPads or iPhones at mediations – online or in-person.

Part B

OLM: First choice or second best?

Chapter 7

Why don't we like OLM?

In this chapter you will learn about:

1 Techno angst

2 Messing up

3 Rapport

4 Body language

5 Emotion

6 Loss of control/support

7 Back channels

8 Tiredness/ Energy exchange

9 Confidentiality/privacy

10 Tempo

11 Documents

12 Magic

13 Philosophy

General dislike

7.01 Many mediators merely tolerate online mediation (see the remarks of Ethelwald Mendes in **4.15**). As we saw in **Chapter 1** Lockdown meant they had to adopt it. Many have been quick to abandon it and prefer in-person mediation.

As the well-known and successful English mediator, Amanda Bucklow, said in her contribution to a book *Commercial Mediation in the Digital Era* (2022) says: 'Mediation has always been an in-person experience. Replicating that experience remotely seems unlikely.'

On 31 March 2020 CMC published a letter to its members discussing the future of online mediation. Sir David Foskett, chair of the CMC highlighted what he considered to be some of the challenges.

7.02 *Why don't we like OLM?*

> 'From the mediators' point of view, the lack of immediate personal contact with the participants. The training of mediators until recently has always involved training face-to-face with real people. Much of the mediator's art is to 'read' the parties and react to the way the participants themselves are speaking and behaving during the mediation. That is so much easier in person than via Zoom or other similar virtual meeting. As I have said, I am not suggesting that mediation via that medium does not work – it does – but I think most mediators would prefer the face-to-face contact, certainly in very difficult cases'.

We have seen from the quotation from Paul Sills in **Chapter 1** that it's almost like two definitive groups; the online camp and not-online camp.

He was frank about his preference: 'I certainly felt that when I was in mediation during Covid, online, it was with one hand tied behind my back.'

As David Sixsmith concluded in his survey: 'This study suggests it [online mediation] has been used during the pandemic primarily as a means to an end with reversion to the familiarity of face -to-face mediation now social restrictions have been removed. However, the data suggests that a step towards normalisation has been achieved. Remote mediation occupies a much more viable option available to the parties than it did prior to the pandemic.'

He warns 'It Is important to remember that this study only concerned the perceptions of the mediators themselves, however, and this this must be taken into account when attaching weight to the conclusions drawn.'

Is this general suspicion about online mediation justified? Is it a diluted version of the real thing? The results of the 2023 CEDR Audit suggests that it is not, given that 64% of commercial mediations were conducted online.

What needs to be acknowledged is that the interests and preferences of mediators, representatives/lawyers, and client might not be always aligned.

Let's look at the most common dislikes about OLM.

Techno-angst

7.02 'Your Internet connection is unstable'. We have all been on the screen when these dread five words flash up. The next thing is buffering and your vision and sound fade. Sometimes the whole thing just stops.

What to do? You end up logging out and logging back in. Or trying to boost the connection to your computer by using the hotspot on your phone and so on. All very worrying and wearing.

The main worry is weak broadband. Your connection drops. If you are working from home, you will be on a domestic broadband. This means using a shared line. Depending on how many other people are using it the strength will go up and down during the day. That is a fact. A quick improvement is to use an ethernet cable, but it is not a complete solution (see **Chapter 11**).

But don't panic even if your internet connection becomes unstable, Go to Plan B. Continue with the online mediation via your iPad or your smartphone which probably has a different connectivity.

Chapter 11 shows you what to do when preparing for a Zoom mediation to reduce the load on your broadband and to give yourself the best chance of the connection staying stable throughout the day.

ALERT

If the technology fails the mediation fails. You are only as good as your broadband. This is why it is essential to have the best technical equipment you can afford (see **Chapter 11**).

Reverb

Reverb can be a problem. The solution is simple. Turn mics and speakers down or turn them off when you are not speaking. Remember to deal with both the mics and the speakers. Most people only mute their mic (see **Chapter 11**).

Amanda Bucklow said: 'However the initial anxiety about using video has been supplanted by fatigue from the time spent in remote meetings.'

Comment

I think that she is right about the initial anxiety having dissipated. I think she is wrong about the fatigue (see **Chapter 14**).

Messing up

7.03 Apart from unstable broadband connections people angst about messing up the technology on the day. We have all been there: you cannot log onto Zoom. It says you need a password or a meeting ID. What are they? Where do I find them?

As for logging in, clients should not have to worry at all. The mediator acts as host. They set up the meeting by sending you a zoom link. It gives the time and place. You just click on it.

If you have difficulty logging in on the day email or text the mediator. They can invite you direct into a live session.

As a mediator you worry about putting people in the wrong room. Or you cannot stop people moving from room to room. Will they be able to eavesdrop? In practice these worries are exaggerated.

> **TOP TIP**
>
> What you do is:
>
> Explain the code of conduct to the participants.
>
> - If anyone find themselves in the wrong room, own up immediately.
> - Tell the mediator.
> - Don't just sit there.
>
> You can do this when you have your dummy run. See below.

How to lower anxiety levels

7.04 Have a dummy run before the mediation. Any problems can be identified. You can practise using the system. This lowers angst levels both for you and for your clients (see **Chapter 8**).You get to show how it all works in a live setting. Your confidence increases. They get to see that you can make it all work. They have confidence in your competence.

Mediators online have a higher level of responsibility as host than at in-person mediations. As the host you are in charge of the tech. You have the controls. Make sure that you are fully familiar with the system. You must be able to display competence and confidence in the tech. If you don't you could undermine the participant's confidence in the whole mediation process.

> **TOP TIP**
>
> 1. Go on a course and get trained by a mediator who uses Zoom.
> 2. Practise with family and friends.

Let's not forget that acting as mediator at an in-person mediation is not responsibility-free. You may not be the host in the sense of being charge of the venue. But you are in charge of the process. Once you are in the venue you need to make sure that everybody:

- knows where they are going and how to find their rooms
- knows where the toilets and the refreshments are
- is comfortable with the temperature and their Wi-Fi connections.

You need to display competence and confidence in the process. People quickly pick up on someone else's anxieties. You are in charge of the process. Just as you are you are when online.

There is a risk that you will mess up. Manage it by using checklists (see **Chapter 11**) and keeping calm (see **Chapter 14**).

Rapport building

7.05

- 'There is just something extra when you are all in the same place.'
- 'You need to see the whites of their eyes.'
- 'I'm a people person and I want to read their body language.'
- 'If it's a big case with lots of money, or personal issues are involved it has to be in person.'

The above quotes are from clients and lawyers at recent mediations. Mediators put their objection differently. They say it is harder to establish rapport online. And add that you miss out on the body language.

Mediators are trained in rapport building. It is a highly valued competency and crucially important in the mediation process. You need to build rapport with the parties and their advisors to be able to mediate at all. The conventional view is that you can only really build rapport if you are physically present with people.

What is it about rapport building that is so important? What does it mean anyway?

In essence it is getting along with people and winning their trust. Showing that you are warm and accessible at a mediation is seen as essential. Although it has to be acknowledged that not all mediators are warm and accessible. Some of them still manage to be effective. Sitting and having some small talk about what the journey was like; making sure people have a cup of tea; handing them a plate of biscuits and so on can be really useful. At least it breaks the ice. Don't forget that at in-person mediations this is often the first time the mediator is meeting the parties.

Who wants to be physically in the same room?

- Mediators are particularly keen.
- Advocates are fairly keen.
- Clients usually do not care one way or the other.

In fact, clients often don't want to be physically present with the other parties. They do not want to meet them or see them, let alone talk to them. Sometimes they don't even want to be the same building, let alone in the same room.

It can be just the opposite. Some clients want to physically confront the other side. Not in a violent way but to tell them exactly what they think. Many parties feel so upset, let down or outraged that they want to explain that to the other side.

They want the other party to be exposed to how bad the dispute has been. Lives have been wrecked. Homes have been lost. Marriages broken. Health ruined. They are usually appealing to the other side's sense of fairness or humanity. They want to load them up with guilt. This may be because this type of appeal is all they have. They don't have strong legal arguments and may not have much financial leverage either. Appeals to someone's better nature and to fairness often amount to throwing themselves on the mercy of the other side. It works more often than you might think. But not as often as most people hope.

Or they want to challenge the other side to tell their side of the story. 'They won't dare lie in public'. Ah! This is not always the case. People do lie in court. Sometimes those lies are accepted by judges as credible evidence.

Over a run of months and mediations the number of times when this sort of personal interaction is essential is very few.

You can build rapport online, but you might have do things differently. Thomas Gaultier, an experienced mediator, lawyer and commentator based in Portugal reported: 'What I have noted when mediating online is an increased need for me to share personal aspects of myself as a mediator, to help a party relate to me, and trust in me. As such, I have found myself talking about my family and my experience as a mediator or as a professional much more than I would in an in-person mediation.

This makes sense to some extent, as mediators expect parties to open up in an online setting, and opening up themselves is a good way of leading by example.'

Another experienced mediator and commentator, John Sturrock, reported how he picks up visual cues from the participants' backgrounds. He wrote in his Kluwer blog how he had noticed one of the lawyers had a collection of vinyl LPs. They started talking about Pink Floyd. And this led to a rapport-building interchange.

'It's hard to beat Dark Side of the Moon' he said. 'What a piece of music.' I agreed: 'Did you ever see Pink Floyd play Dark Side live? I recall being at Earls Court in 1994.' 'I was there too!' he exclaimed. For a moment or two, we reflected on the album's seemingly relevant song titles, like 'Us and Them'.

It is about being opportunistic – really paying attention to what you can hear and see and picking your moment to identify a link and build on it. I could not have done what John Sturrock did because I loathe Pink Floyd. But the approach could be a good one.

I have also found paradoxically that being online can lead to a freer exchange of personal information. People can feel safer in their own environment and less inhibited (see **7.10**).

Body language

7.06 What is body language? Are we talking about our own body language or other peoples'? In reality, how many of us can use it either to read other people or to send a message ourselves?

Mediators and therapists stress the importance of body language. You need to be able to see people and interpret their facial and bodily gestures. Otherwise, how will you understand their hidden needs? They complain that when mediating online body language is pretty much irrelevant. You cannot see very much. You can see someone's face and eyes if they are on an individual screen although even then you cannot usually see them clearly or in close-up.

'You need to be able to see the whites of their eyes'.

7.07 This is the phrase used most often when discussing the pros and cons of online mediation. And it is nearly always lawyers who say it. Sometimes clients do but they are more likely to talk about being 'a people person' and preferring face to face contact.

In the mediation context it is a strange phrase to use. It comes from an order given by an American officer William Prescott at the Battle of Bunker Hill who told his men 'Don't fire until you can see the whites of their eyes.' We don't go to mediation to make war: we go there to make peace. When someone talks about seeing whites of eyes, do they actually mean you need to look into their eyes or is it just a shorthand expression for being close to somebody?

Is it just a metaphor?

7.08 How important is the sclera? This is the tough fibrous exterior coating of the eye. It protects the interior components from injury. It forms the entire visible white exterior of the eye. The iris is the coloured portion inside the anterior chamber of the eye. Is it important that we can see people's eyes? Well, it might be.

Humans are the only animals with visible eye whites and with an iris that is more prominent and therefore readable. You can tell where someone is looking and sometimes what someone is thinking by looking at their irises. Eyes are not just for seeing; they are also for communicating.

The Theory of the Mind (TOM) is a key concept not just in psychology but in mediation. It is the principle of understanding (or not) that others may have a different perspective from us. Humans show a much more developed ability to understand someone else's perspective than animals. Chimpanzees can do it better than most other animals but not nearly as well as humans can. Conspicuous irises can show where someone is looking. That can help us understand what is of interest to them. In other words, to read their minds.

You can use eyes to miscommunicate and to provide inaccurate as well as accurate information. You can pretend to look at something because it is of interest when it is the exact opposite. Football fans know the expression 'giving the goalkeeper the eye'. That is when the penalty taker looks one way and kicks the ball the other.

Poker players are always trying to manipulate the other players' mental state. They might just pretend to be interested in something, look away or even put dark glasses on. As Professor Nicholas Haslam of the University of Melbourne said 'perhaps humans evolved visible sclera because our much more developed Theory of Mind makes conveying and reading others' gaze direction and emotional expressions much more important for our social intelligence.' It's not just a metaphor.

7.09 *Why don't we like OLM?*

So, seeing people's eyes is important. But do you have to be physically with them to do this?

Check whether you can see the whites of someone's eyes more clearly across a table than on screen. You might be surprised. Don't assume that people cannot read your face, or you cannot read theirs because you are online. In fact, how you compose your face is even more important online (see **Chapter 12**).

If you switch to speaker view on Zoom you can see people's eyes, faces and shoulders. But that is pretty much it. Some mediators – for example Graham Ross – advise the parties to sit further back from the camera so that he can see their hands. Frankly this is a waste of time. Hands tell you very little. It is the feet, which you cannot see online, that betray hidden tension or cognitive dissonance. But at in-person mediations feet are usually under a table hidden from view. It is the faces and shoulders that you want to see. The voices that you want to hear. Eyes and voice are more important than hands and feet as indicators of what someone is thinking and feeling (see **Chapter 12**).

When mediating from someone's office online several people may be in the same room and using a wall mounted screen. Can you mediate better if you can see their bodies? Sometimes yes. You can see how engaged in the process they are. Are they slumped in their chair, leaning back or forward? But often, it is far more difficult to read people when they are using a wall mounted screen than when they are using individual screens on their laptops. Why? They are usually sitting too far from the camera or at an awkward angle. You can see their body shape but not their faces (see **Chapters 1** and **10**).

TOP TIP

- If you can't scan the room and talk to the camera at the same time – use your observer. Ask them to note reactions to what you were saying.
- When you can look at someone watch out for their shoulders. You can always see them. Hunched up equals tension. Slumped equals tiredness or boredom.

In practice how useful is body language?

Other people's body language

7.09 Always believing what people tell you is neither possible nor sensible. Is body language a tool for finding out what people really feel and think? Yes, body language can help you double-check what you are being told.

The difficulties are:

- Being able to reliably interpret body language takes a great deal of training and practice. Take one of the tests available on YouTube. Interpreting facial expression is much more difficult than you might think.
- Signals are ambiguous. People may scratch because they have an itch not because they are lying.

- Different people interpret the same signals differently.

See Chapter 8 of my book *Mediation Behaviour.*

Your own body language

7.10 Is body language a science? Perhaps not exactly a science in the same way physics is but researchers have come up with interesting results. One is the importance of mimicry.

- Researchers in Holland found that waitresses who repeated word for word the customer's order received 70% bigger tips than waitresses who paraphrased the order.
- Humans seem to have an inbuilt tendency to mimic others. This probably evolved as a survival strategy when we needed to know who we could trust.
- One way of to mimic is to match or mirror behaviour.

Mediators are taught the importance of mirroring behaviour. You can do this in person.

Try following this three-stage process:

1 Observe

  Pay attention to what the other person is doing. Are they crossing their legs or arms, leaning backwards or forwards?

2 Pause

  Do not immediately copy the behaviour. Pause for 20 seconds. Then imitate the behaviour. So, if they lean forward, you lean forward.

3 Relax

  When you start imitating you will be very conscious of what you are doing. With practise, it becomes instinctive. In fact, you are probably imitating people all day long without realising. Try looking at other people to see how they interact with each other and note how much mimicry goes on.

Remember:

- Don't overdo it. You don't want to appear fake and manipulative.
- Imitation is often said to be the sincerest form of flattery. And as all mediators know flattery is a very useful tool at mediations.

Researchers at the University of Sussex have found that the following tips are useful in controlling the mood of a meeting:

- Keep hands above the table.
- Use palm up batoning to encourage.
- Lean forward to encourage.
- Lean back during drama.

7.11 *Why don't we like OLM?*

Can you do it online? You can (see **Chapter 12**).It is more difficult. But you can still lean forward, smile -especially smile-nod and make a note. This shows empathy and engagement.

TOP TIP

- The standard trio of behaviours will still see you through online: smiling, nodding and eye contact.
- Practise them in front of the mirror.

Can you deal with emotions online?

7.11 No, say many mediators. People cannot express them: mediators cannot interpret them.

But online you can see faces. We all communicate whether we want to or not. You need to be able to recognise emotions. We tell ourselves that it is vital especially when working out whether someone is lying or not. To learn more about this read Chapter 3 and para 14.17 in my book *Mediation Behaviour.*

Recognising emotions is one thing, expressing them and dealing with them is another. At a recent international conference on mediation in February 2023 a well-known mediator who is listed in the WWL Global Thought Leaders categorically said: 'You can't deal with emotions online. I refuse to do online mediation.'

They are not a lawyer and come from a background in the construction industry. Their mediation approach is based on uncovering emotions and dealing with them as the way of finding solutions to all sorts of disputes including commercial ones. So it is not just therapists, counsellors and mediators with a psychological background who believe that online mediation is not appropriate because it prevents the proper expression and interpretation of emotion.

Paradoxically another participant at a different mediation conference reported that they had found it easier to discuss a particularly sensitive and personal matter with the mediator because they were on screen and not physically in the same room.

People can feel protected and liberated on screen. They can become disinhibited and more outspoken on screen than they would in person. They can also behave better because of the constraints of the system and the way in which you can express yourself. As explained in **8.33** banging tables and swearing on screen doesn't have the same effect that it has across the table in person.

Loss of control

7.12 Lawyers and mediators identify this as a disadvantage of online mediation (see **Chapter 4**).

Mediators worry about their loss of control and ability to influence the participants, The Sixsmith Survey gives several examples from respondents.

> 'my preference is for face-to-face mediation as it is easier to control the environment and the participants and...influence the parties as the mediator moves towards persuading the parties to close the gaps in difference between the parties.'
>
> Another said 'remote mediation is a harder to move parties past the 'sticking points', partly because the pressure of being in the same physical space is lessened.'
>
> 'The mediation that failed to settle did not achieve resolution because as mediator I could not convince both parties that their approach was over-confident to the legal position that they were clearly being advised to maintain. Had this been a face-to-face mediation it would have been possible to exert greater influence on the parties.'

Lack of personal investment in the mediation

7.13 Mediators also fear that being online and therefore remote from the physical presence of everyone else including the mediator makes clients less committed to the process and they are more likely to leave.

Anybody can click Leave Meeting and they are gone. They can do this without warning or giving any reason. Getting them back is difficult. You cannot chase after them. You can try and contact them by WhatsApp, text message or phone but if they are not answering there is not much you can do. Mediators tell each other stories about how this has happened to them. In nearly every case after prolonged telephone negotiation the mediation was resumed online but not always. It is a risk.

Is clicking Leave Meeting a greater risk than people physically walking out of an in-person mediation? That happens as well. Usually, they do it with advance warning as a threat or ultimatum. The mediator can see them before they have left the building and try to persuade them back into the mediation. But again, not always. Sometimes people just put on their coats and go.

In practice, leaving a mediation without warning whether online or in person is rare. It is dramatic when it happens, but it doesn't happen very often.

Lawyers who are not physically present with their clients express concerns that they will not be able to support their clients properly. What do they mean by support? Do they in fact mean control?

Many lawyers and advocates think a big part of their job at mediation is to control their client. That is why they don't allow them to speak at Joint Opening Sessions or in extreme cases even in caucuses or private sessions. They like to do all the talking on behalf of their client. This is understandable because that is what they have been hired to do – represent the client and advocate on their behalf.

Mediators hate this sort of censorship. It is frustrating when everything goes through the advocate. This doesn't help build or maintain settlement momentum.

In practice, during the mediation even the most assertive lawyer tends to become less assertive and the most diffident of clients become more self-assertive and speak up for themselves. But again, not always. Plenty of times mediators are in breakout rooms where the clients are in different locations from their lawyers and are on mute. And they stay on mute until the mediator speaks to them directly.

What about controlling the mediator? Can you do this online? One barrister who is also a mediator reported that he thought his room found it easier to ask the mediator to leave them to have private discussions when they were online. They were all gathered around a boardroom table with a wall mounted screen. The mediator appeared larger-than-life on screen. But they felt no hesitation in asking them to leave the breakout room,

At an in-person mediation the client, who was a professional used to dealing with people and persuading them to do things, said that they had wanted an in-person mediation so that they could control the mediator better. They said it with a smile, but they were not joking.

As a mediator do you allow yourself to be manipulated? People, especially lawyers, try. How often do they succeed? One of the great mediation unknowables. But as mediator you act as host on Zoom. You have all the controls – a useful protection against manipulation.

Lack of back channels

7.14 What is a back channel? It is a way of communicating directly with someone outside the formal setting. At in-person mediations this means accidentally on purpose bumping into somebody on the way to the coffee machine or the toilet and having a quick private discussion. Or just doing it more overtly by the mediator asking if they could have a private word with one of the lawyers. Most mediators will tell you that these back channels or informal off-grid discussions are invaluable. Especially when you are trying to unlock a stalled mediation or to negotiate a way through an impasse.

The very fact of mediators hanging out in the reception area and not being in their own room gives participants more access to them. Often clients seek out the mediator. They want to know how the mediator thinks it is all going. Is there a chance of a settlement? Are their lawyers doing the right thing? Even more surprisingly clients will confide in mediators that they have doubts about the way their team is handling the mediation. Sometimes they explain that they want to do something, but their lawyers are advising them not to do it and they seek help and advice from the mediator.

Is this more difficult online?

7.15 In some ways it clearly is. There are no coffee machines to linger by. People go to their own toilet in their own house.

But as the mediator you can still make yourself accessible. Give all participants your mobile number as well as your email address. That means they can email,

WhatsApp, text or call you privately. This does happen. Usually, it is the lawyers who send a message saying they would like a private word. Most takes place over the phone. Sometimes they ask to be put into a breakout room with the mediator. These private chats work. Not many mediations last all day without there being some sort of private communication between the representatives and the mediator. It happens but it is rare.

Making direct contact with a client in this way is more difficult for a mediator. You must observe the professional etiquette. You don't want to undermine the lawyer's position. That risks destroying their faith in you as the mediator and damage your credibility.

Don't be afraid of making direct contact. How and when you do it will depend on the sort of relationship you have with the representative. You may have worked with them before. If so, it is easy to suggest or initiate a call. Or you may have had a constructive conversation with them before the mediation. Again, as a mediator you can build on that. If you have not had prior contact, work on establishing a relationship of trust and openness with the representative during the private sessions.

TOP TIP

- Tell everybody that if they want to have a private discussion of the sort that they have at in-person mediations, they can.
- Make sure they have your mobile number and tell them to just call.

Lawyers have developed coping strategies to overcome the difficulties of offering support or exercising control over their clients when not physically in their presence. Some agree safe words with their clients.

If the client is feeling uncomfortable and wants time out but feels reluctant to say so in front of the mediator, they just use a phrase or word and the lawyer asks for a time out or a private session. It's the mediation equivalent of asking 'Is Angela working tonight?' Or, if the lawyer thinks that the client is going off piste, they can do the same. Some mediators even work out their own safe words for participants to use.

This seems overly subtle. In practice, either the client or the lawyer can simply say they would like a time out. That's it. The mediator leaves the room. They message the mediator when they are ready to resume their private session. Asking for a timeout is not difficult. It is not rude or disrespectful and it is not obstructive. In fact, it is constructive. You don't want people talking themselves into dead ends or just going round in circles. That dissipates energy and purpose.

Tiredness/energy exchange

7.16 Being 'Zoomed out' was one the early and frequent complaints about online mediation. Why did this happen?

7.17 *Why don't we like OLM?*

- Seeing yourself. One of the reasons often cited for Zoom tiredness is seeing yourself on the screen the whole time. But you can now use the hide self-view function on Zoom (see **Chapter 11**).
- Less energy exchange. You are not bouncing in and out of the room energising them in the same way. But there is less energy expenditure – there is no travel.
- Sitting all day can be more tiring online – looking at yourself and squinting at others.

  Take breaks. Stand up. Stretch.

  Better time management is one of the advantages of online mediation. When the mediator is not with you, you can go off screen and do other work. The temptation is to do that without giving yourself a break. At in-person mediations when the mediator has left the room you can get up and walk round to the coffee machine. Stretch your legs. Make a phone call. If you are at home on your computer screen you can easily just keep on working. Make yourself take breaks. Set your alarm to remind you.

The mid-afternoon slump is well recognised. Blood sugar, concentration and energy all drop while frustration, boredom and fatigue rise. In fact, there are some mediation users who think that people at mediation only agree to settle when they have been worn down by the day. They are fed up, tired, hungry and want to go home. This attritional approach is sometimes tried at in-person mediations. But of course, if you are already at home it won't work.

The key question is: do people do deals in their comfort zone or in their discomfort zone?

Read **Chapter 14** on **Wellbeing**.

Confidentiality/privacy

7.17 Can uninvited people join the mediation? Can recordings be made without permission?

Mediators can take steps to prevent this:

- They can lock the meeting once everybody has been admitted.
- They can disable the record function in their settings.
- They can stipulate in their mediation agreement that no one should make a recording of the session. Unauthorised recording is a potential problem given the ubiquity of smart phones. It is the same at in-person mediations. But in practice it has not been a problem.

It is true that you cannot police who is in the room if they are off camera. Usually, if there is someone present who is not on camera you sense their presence. You might hear them, see a movement, spot an exchange of glances. If you have any doubts, ask if anyone else is present. You might be lied to. But the chances of it happening are, in my experience, low. And when it comes down to it, does it matter for the conduct of the negotiations and the outcome whether a particular person is in the room? It might. But it will be rare.

Worries about confidentiality can affect participants' confidence and trust in the process. A mediator who took part in the Sixsmith research is reported as saying '... The parties were concerned about being overheard in the private discussions, so I have tended to close down and open a new zoom meeting for each dialogue session which works fine.' Completely unnecessary. Just use breakout rooms.

Hayden Wilson, a well-known New Zealand litigator and mediator, when commenting and lamenting upon the lack of water cooler moments and back channels asked 'How do you do that in an online zone? Just send a private chat. Inevitably, I'll send that chat to "everybody" and that puts the whole mediation at risk.'

The answer? Don't use the Chat function. Use your phone instead (see **Chapter 11**).

> **TOP TIP**
>
> Don't use Chat for anything.
>
> Use WhatsApp rather than email or text to send private messages.

GDPR

7.18 In the UK mediators have to have regard to the UK GDPR and the Data Protection Act 2018. Generally speaking if you check for viruses, email protection, passwords and so on you will comply with the requirements. It's a good idea to review your arrangements each year. Consult the ICO website.

Resource: See https://ico.org.uk/for-organisations/sme-web-hub/

Tempo

7.19 The tempo is different. Even with best VC systems there is a slight time lag between you speaking and what people hear. This has turned out to be an advantage (see **Chapters 3** and **12**).

- Conversations are slower.
- People speak more slowly and clearly because there is more chance of mis-hearing what is being said.
- Mediators re-cap more frequently.

Toggling in out and of rooms is clunkier and more time consuming than walking along the corridor and knocking on the door. But less time is spent in chatting to pass the time (see **Chapter 10**).

Documents

7.20 Traditionally before the mediation the parties agreed a bundle of documents and exchanged position statements. They then sent them to the mediator. Even before mediations went online because of Covid bundles of documents were being exchanged electronically anyway. The days of large parcels of lever arch files arriving have disappeared. One KC recently commented on LinkedIn that his clerk telling him that the papers had arrived was an exciting moment. This excitement cannot be replicated by an e-mail message saying: 'Please find the link to the bundle of documents.'

The technology has improved with hyperlinks and bookmarking. Bundles seem to be getting slimmer. What is more discernible is that position statements or mediation papers are now less common. Instead, people rely upon their Letters of Claim and Letters of Response or on the pleadings. From a mediator's point of view this is usually good enough. This is another illustration along with less small talk and smaller teams of how being online is streamlining the mediation process.

But there is a danger that preparation is less thorough and being left until the last moment. Receiving an email link with a large bundle of documents on a Friday afternoon is all too common. No need to make arrangements for the Post Room to send the packet of lever arch files instead email them just in time.

Producing the settlement document still causes problems. Digital signatures are not always available. Ideally the parties should have a printer so they can print out the settlement agreement, sign it and scan it back. The standard provisions in mediation agreements about there being no legally binding agreement until a document incorporating the terms of the settlement has been signed may have to be amended (see **Chapter 13**).

Producing and signing the settlement document is usually easier in person.

Magic

7.21 The magic of mediation is missing. Mediators talk a lot about the magic of mediation. What is it? It is the tipping point when antagonism changes into mutualism. People see that it is to their advantage to lower their distrust levels and work with the mediator and the other side to achieve a settlement.

But how often is there a 'gotcha' moment? Not very often in practice. There is more often a gradual dawning of realisation as options are explored, priorities weighed up and negotiation stratagems played out. The key point is that settlement rates are just as high online as in person.

The important question is: Do clients like online mediation? Most say they do. In fact, in my experience many seem to prefer it. See **Chapter 8** for some of the advantages.

Philosophy

7.22 For several years ODR has been described as the next big thing. Now the technology is robust and available, the political will is here, the legal requirements are in place and the commercial imperative is widely appreciated.

But the question is raised: is it really mediation? Many mediators say that it is not. It is simply claims or dispute settlement. Without the parties meeting and talking to each other face-to-face there cannot be a genuine exchange of perspectives and acknowledging of each other. You need the handshakes, the embraces, the tears and fist shaking, the walk-outs and the walk-back-ins. Without them there can be no real resolution. Possibly but there are thousands and thousands of disputes where this emotional interaction is not necessary for people to make an agreement with each other. See what was said about the new mandatory mediation scheme in **4.16**.

As discussed in **Chapter 1**, the traditional mediation model (TradMed) is already being reshaped. For the smaller, simpler disputes the process is likely to become more evaluative and less facilitative. Mediation will probably become more like adjudication, arbitration or ombudsman referrals where decisions are made and an outcome guaranteed.

In a nutshell

7.23

- Clients are the ones that count at mediations. They are the ones with the problem, they are paying and they make the decision.
- Always ask clients what they would prefer in person, hybrid or online. Give them the choice.
- Ask yourself if online mediation is suitable for overseas clients why isn't suitable for domestic clients? If it is good enough for someone in Santiago why isn't it good enough for someone in Billericay?

Chapter 8

Why we do like OLM

In this chapter you will learn about the advantages of OLM

1 Cost

2 Travel angst

3 Disruption

4 Intimidation/Power Imbalance

5 Stress

6 Vulnerable clients

7 Time management

8 Flexibility

9 Reconvening/scheduling/timetabling

10 Better access/participation

11 Visuals

12 Energy/efficiency

13 Eco

14 Access to Justice

15 Profitability

16 Work/life balance – wellbeing

17 Better communication

Cost

8.01 Saving money. This is something that we all want to do.

Post Covid, Brexit and the Ukraine situation, travel and accommodation costs in the UK like everything else have risen significantly over the last three years. Everybody involved in mediation can save money using online mediation.

- Mediators don't have to spend money on travel and overnight accommodation to make sure that they are on time at the mediation. Nor do clients and their lawyers.
- Clients don't have to pay for the venue. Even when a mediation is held in a barristers' chambers some are now making a charge despite a member of their own chambers being involved in the mediation.
- No one has to pay for overpriced and unhealthy food and drink. You will save pounds in both senses of the word. More pounds in your pocket and fewer around your waistline (see **Chapter 14**).
- Clients save on legal costs. Mediators usually charge a lower rate for online mediation because they save travel time and expense. Even now some mediators charge a subsistence rate on top of their fee for the mediation. Some charge at cost; others a flat fee, for example £250, for subsistence.
- And you should be able to negotiate a more flexible if not lower charge for their attendance at the mediation. The reason for this is better time management. See **8.12**.

Travel angst

8.02 Are the trains on time? What's the traffic like? Where is the venue for this mediation? These worries are a thing of the past when you mediate online. Nor do you have to worry about finishing late because of the last train or the long drive home.

Take these two recent examples:

From a solicitor:

> 'I did that mediation you missed out on last Friday. In Birmingham at Bloggins & Co. We signed off at 2.30 am on Saturday and I got home by Uber at 4.00 am.'

From a fellow mediator:

> 'I had a rather long (and testing) day mediating yesterday – got up at 03:58 and arrived home at about 02:45 today. VERY long story. My observer had to find a hotel for the night.'

There is a whiff of achievement as well as exasperation in these messages. But frankly it is a complete waste of time and totally unnecessary. At least the first one settled: the second one didn't.

And there will be the energy drain (see **8.26**). Just the hassle of travelling on the tube in rush-hour to attend a mediation in central London is draining. How much nicer and more productive to be able to take a walk round the block before sitting down at your screen in your own home. But techno angst has replaced travel angst. See **Chapter 7**. Perhaps we all need some angst in our lives?

Disruption

8.03 As explained in **Chapter 1** the TradMed model assumed that the mediation day was a big event. Clients were told that they could have their day in court without going to court. Lawyers prepared as though they were going to court. Unfortunately, many of them acted at mediation as though they were in court.

Clients had to travel to the venue and take a whole day out of their lives both professional and personal to attend the mediation. Many found this too disruptive. For lawyers disputes are their business. For clients disputes interfere with their business. For lawyers, litigation is uptime: for clients, it is downtime.

The TradMed model is becoming obsolete. Life goes on for clients even though they are at a mediation. It is no longer a case of 'Stop the world I've got a mediation today'. As explained in **1.06** and **8.12** if you are online you can dip in and out of the mediation.

Clients don't have to make special arrangements. They can mediate from their own home or office. There is less disruption.

If you have care responsibilities for family members or children, you don't have to turn your arrangements upside down to cope with going to mediation.

Anyone who has mobility issues will prefer not to have to travel to a mediation.

All of this is in a context of new working patterns. Home working during lockdown showed many people that it is easier to combine home life and work life than they had previously thought. WFH remains popular with many clients.

Intimidation

8.04 Many clients find online mediation less intense, less intimidating and more conducive to open discussion and thought.

In your own home you feel liberated, protected and just more relaxed. Take three examples:

- In a building dispute over high-end West End properties the construction director said at the end of the mediation that he liked being online. He would not have been as flexible in his approach if he had to be in the same building, not just the same room, as the disaffected clients.
- Many professionals – mediators as well as lawyers – underestimate how stressful the whole process is for clients. As a director in a recent online mediation said: 'I know that being at mediation is not the same as being in court but when you're in a lawyer's office surrounded by lawyers it feels awfully like it.'
- A director in a shareholders' dispute that was being held in person in their own solicitor's office said: 'I know this place. I've spent hours here. And I've still got

palpitations.' They said it with a smile but it wasn't a joke as we saw stress taking hold during the day and them ending up in tears. Not good!

Power imbalance

8.05 Mediators have to address power imbalance. Who says so? The CMC amongst others. They adopted the European Code of Conduct for Mediators.

Being online helps mediators do this. The medium itself is a great leveller.

- Everyone is sitting down. Everyone looks the same height. The psychological advantage of being tall is lost.
- Mediators are always urged to have a roundtable for joint sessions if they can. On screen you can. Being in Gallery View with everybody on screen is much like sitting at a round table.
- Status symbols are not so obviously deployed – the Rolex watches, Prada bags and Mont Blanc pens. They may still be there, but they cannot be seen so clearly.
- The venue. You are in your own home. The intimidation of the gleaming glass and steel palaces of justice that barristers and lawyers now occupy is all gone. There is no home ground advantage. Everybody has their own home ground advantage.
- Boardroom settings. Some of them may be designed to intimidate visitors but their effect is muted online.

Comfort zones

8.06 The psychology of hosting in-person mediations is complicated. Do you give the other side the best room or the worst room? Do you restrict the supply of refreshments, particularly late in the day as energy levels drop? You may think this is all underhand and unprincipled. You may be right. You would be wrong to think that it doesn't happen.

Online everyone can remain in their own comfort zones. And back to the question do you make better deals when you are in your comfort zone or you discomfort zone?

Appearance

8.07 Yes, you dress smartly. But online can anyone really tell whether your suit or outfit is Savile Row or M&S: Simone Rocha or TK Maxx?

Shoes

8.08 Shoe anxiety disappears. You don't have to choose whether to wear heels or not. Trainers or lace ups? You cannot tell whether they are Jimmy Choo, Louboutin, Lobb or Church's.

Appearances are now more much homogenised. Everyone appears like a passport photograph.

Stress/Mediation mindset

8.09 Getting into the mediation mindset is easier. The hassle and stress of travel has gone. The anxiety about being in an alien and possibly hostile environment is reduced. Just being in your own home or a familiar environment lowers stress levels.

Stress is one of the biggest obstacles to settlement at mediations. The mediator's job is to lower stress levels and increase trust levels.

A surprising number of clients worry at in-person mediations about seeing their opponents, let alone meeting or talking to them. Mediators are asked to scout whether the way is clear for them to go to the toilet without bumping into the other side. And it's not just unsophisticated nervous private individuals. Just because you are in a tough commercial dispute does not mean that you are a tough commercial person.

One of the biggest stressors is fear of the unknown. Most clients going to mediation have never been before and they will probably never go again. It is an alien experience, and they are worried about it. On top of that they have techno angst. The solution is dummy runs.

Dummy runs

8.10 Pre-mediation contact has become more important for online mediations and there is a lot more of it. With traditional in-person mediations mediators would have phone calls before the mediation. These were with the parties' representatives. They rarely talked to the parties themselves.

With online mediation mediators want to make sure that everybody is familiar with the technology and comfortable with the privacy and confidentiality of the platform being used. During lockdown we all became more familiar with Zoom. The number of Zoom users rose from 10 million a day in March 2019 to 350 million in December 2020. Most of them were using Zoom for social purposes. They used the free version. They had not used Zoom for mediations. (For more information about the different types of Zoom programs see **Chapter 11**.) Plenty of people had also used Teams for work related meetings but not for mediation.

Mediators quickly realised that having dummy runs gave them three things.

- Reassurance that the technology worked, and the system was secure.
- An opportunity to start rapport building before the mediation itself.
- An opportunity for the parties to raise any concerns about the process. Quite often this develops into a discussion about some aspects of the substance of the mediation. As a result, the parties feel much better prepared for the mediation

both psychologically and technically. This helps the mediation to get off to a flying start on the day.

This enhanced pre- mediation contact has proved to be a real benefit. Even when conducting in-person mediations more and more mediators try and arrange online pre-mediation chats with the parties and their advisors.

See **Chapters 7** and **11**.

Vulnerable clients

8.11 Some clients are vulnerable. Being in a dispute might be particularly upsetting for them. For example:

- They have been subjected to intimidation, threats or bullying. Understandably they will be reluctant attend an in-person mediation or a Joint Opening Session.
- They are so annoyed about what has happened they cannot trust themselves not to say or do something inappropriate. This can happen online as well. Recently at an online mediation a director being sued by the Liquidator of their company said: 'If I am in a meeting with them, I'll lose my temper.' So no Joint Opening Session.
- Their personality cannot cope with confrontation. They are nervous or prone to anxiety. This may be due to family, medical or behavioural issues. Sometimes they are on medication because of the stress induced by the dispute.
- Medical conditions such as diabetes mean they need to rest and eat at certain times. This is so much easier to handle if they are in their own home rather than in a lawyer's office.

The vulnerability could arise from completely different sources. For example, lower levels of digital literacy. By reason of age, background or location they don't habitually use computers or the Internet. Will they be at a disadvantage if they mediate online as opposed to being in person? Possibly. The way round this is to arrange a hybrid mediation as discussed in **Chapter 9**.

Time management

8.12 Time has always been a vital ingredient in mediations. How much do we have? When does it run out? It has never been a free good. You have always had to make the best use of the best hours.

Minimising downtime

8.13 Downtime is one of aspects of mediation that participants don't like. This is where clients are in their room with their solicitors and advisors waiting for the mediator. This is a particular problem in caucus-based mediations. And the predominant model of mediation in the UK for civil and commercial disputes is the caucus model. The alternative model of everybody sitting in joint session for most of the day is not popular with clients, lawyers, or mediators.

Neighbourhood, workplace, or family mediations use joint sessions more but even there the trend is toward some separate meetings.

When the mediator is not in their room what do they do? Traditionally mediators were trained to leave them with tasks – homework – things to do while the mediator was away. But this couldn't go on forever. And many were the complaints about having to sit in the same room (often without natural light) watching the sandwiches curl.

You can only talk about hobbies, horticulture and holidays for so long. Boredom sets in. Closely followed by frustration and impatience. Everybody becomes fed up and starts to disengage. Mediators would come back into the room and find them watching the news on their iPads or texting on their phones. They were not engaged in mediation-purposeful activity. They were engaged in distracting activity.

This is inevitable. No one can sustain their concentration on one subject for eight hours. Attention wanders. Energy levels drop. Boredom sets in as points are repeated. Frustration starts to takeover. There is a loss of interest and appetite for negotiation. All very dangerous (see **Chapter 9**).

With online mediation you don't have this. Or at least you can mitigate it. When the mediator is not with you can go off screen. Just click the Mute and Stop Video icons and nobody can see or hear you. You can get on with doing other things.

Is there a danger that when the mediator wants you to come back in you will have become distracted and lost momentum? Yes, there is. You will need to be brought up to speed. Losing momentum is a problem but much less of a problem than sinking into a frustrated torpor as happens at in-person mediations. The parties may have been applying their minds to something else but at least they have been applying their minds and not just talking about their last cruise.

Maximising time

8.14

- Participants can get on with other work. Clients say that being able to do other work and therefore not waste time is one of the biggest advantages of online mediation (see **Chapter 9**)
- In other words, they can earn money as well as participating in a mediation. That makes the whole idea of mediation more attractive. It is not all downtime, wasted expenditure and lost opportunity costs.
- At a recent mediation conducted online in-house counsel for the insurers asked how long I thought I would be with the other room. I replied about 30 minutes. He said that was fine he was going to go off screen to do something else. Would I let him know if I was going to be longer than 30 minutes?

> **TOP TIP**
>
> - Keep the sessions as short as possible.
> - You don't want to guillotine people or let make them feel them you don't have time for them. So, warn them.
> - Let them know that you have told the other room that you will be back with them in half an hour but that if it looks like you will be longer, you will need to text them to say so.
> - People rarely object if you say this.

More businesslike

Getting down to business quicker

8.15 There is less introductory chat and small talk in OLM. Participants want to get down to business more quickly. Why is this?

- They are often in their own office or home. This is where they live their lives and do their work. They have not been disrupted by going to a hotel or a barrister's chambers. They feel they are still leading their normal lives. They don't need to be told where the toilets are or how to get a cup of coffee.
- Having had a dummy run they are they don't need to be inducted into the process and the system.
- Chatting in a room with other people physically present is a different experience from doing it online. Some prefer it: others don't like it. Online, you have more control (see **Chapter 12** on **Communicating Online** and **Chapter 14** on **Wellbeing**).
- Mediators having spent some time in a dummy run are not meeting the participants cold. They don't need to start from scratch with rapport building. Also Zoom and humour don't mix. Jokes that would have had people falling out of their chairs at in-person mediations fall flat on screen.

Joint Opening Sessions

8.16 Joint Opening Sessions are becoming extinct. This reflects the more business-like approach to mediation and participants' desire to get on with things. The traditional Joint Opening Session much beloved of mediation trainers and theorists was falling out of fashion even before Covid and lockdown. Now they rarely take place online.,

The traditional model was that everybody gathered in the same room with the mediator. There were introductions. Sometimes the mediation agreement was passed round the table and physically signed there and then. The mediator made their opening remarks. These usually included a short description of themselves, an explanation of the purpose of mediation and the process to be followed.

Different mediators did it in different ways. But this took time and energy. For more information on this see my book *Mediation Advocacy.*

The mediator finished their remarks and invited the parties to say whatever they wanted. The lawyers on each side usually grabbed the chance to state their clients' position in the most positive and forceful way with the added benefit of attacking the other side's clients. Sometimes the lawyers became quite forensic and even theatrical in their presentations with finger waving, table banging and warnings to the other side's clients about how unpleasant cross-examination would be for them. Altogether a negative experience with everybody becoming more entrenched in their positions.

What was the reaction? Those being attacked simply went into defence mode. Both barriers and blood pressure went up.

Meet and greet sessions

8.17 These are replacing traditional Joint Opening Sessions. The mediator puts everybody together on screen and goes round asking them to say who they are and why they are at the mediation. They make some opening remarks about the purpose and process of mediation.

They move the participants back to their breakout rooms. No presentation of cases as there is in traditional Joint Opening Sessions.

Joint working sessions

8.18 These are common in all mediations – both online and in-person. The mediator gathers those members of each team who are needed to address a particular point and puts them together in a different breakout room from the one that their team is in. Usually, the mediator remains in the room during a joint working session but not always. The atmosphere is much more collaborative and less antagonistic than in the traditional joint opening session.

Flexibility

8.19 People don't have to stay in an office all day just to be at a mediation. The mediation can be spread over time. People can participate by email, messaging, smartphone etc as and when they choose. And there is 24/7 access to the process.

Asynchronous mediation can be an advantage when you have people in different time zones. For example, carrying out a mediation with a mediator in Europe, a claimant on the west coast of the US and a defendant in Australia creates a wide time spread. Having breaks and spaces in between discussions can give people the opportunity to be at their best. They don't have to respond immediately. They can take time out to think about things. They can rest. All very much less pressured.

8.20 *Why we do like OLM*

Fixing a date for the mediation is easier online. Not having to make special arrangements and travel frees up more dates in everyone's diaries. Rearranging or adding extra hours or sessions is much simpler.

Timetabling

8.20 Mediators know that timing can be everything. Information disclosed at one point during the day can have a completely different effect if disclosed earlier or later. When to make proposals can influence the whole mood of the day. Managing the disclosure of information – how much, what and when – is one of a mediator's most important functions.

Being able to schedule when key individuals join the mediation helps the strategic choreography of the negotiation dance. If the CEO is joining at 15:00, time manage the discussions accordingly. Whatever the CEO needs to know, discuss, or decide has to be ready by then.

Online this is much less of a problem. See the next section.

Reconvening

8.21 People are more inclined to reconvene.

With mediation now being less of a stand-alone, one-off event and more a stage in a process, participants are more willing to take time out, pause the mediation and schedule a later session. Say, they have run into a roadblock or stalemate – maybe there is some information which needs to be considered before people can move. An up-to-date report for example. Perhaps counsel's opinion or tax advice is needed. Whatever it is, is not available there and then.

At in-person mediations this could be fatal. Participants struggled on and did not come to an agreement because information or advice that they needed was not available and they left frustrated. Or if they did settle, the agreement became difficult to implement because it was not really the right deal, eg the tax structure was not optimal. So, people tried to renegotiate. The whole experience was unsatisfactory. And everyone was reluctant to have another go.

Breaking off and coming back

8.22 Online mediation gives you more flexibility when managing time and energy during the mediation. Traditionally you would travel to the mediation venue and spend the whole day there. That requires an investment of time, money, and energy. People didn't want to waste their investment, so they were committed to the process of trying to achieve a settlement. This was a positive, but there was a negative. Too often participants gave in to the temptation to carry on with the mediation late into the day. They got too tired. Bad deals were done. Or they just carried on talking even when there was no realistic prospect of the settlement on the day, because they had spent the money and the time to be there.

This is changing. Arranging sessions online is much easier so participants are taking the opportunity to call time outs. You have been mediating for five hours. No one can see any realistic prospect of concluding a deal that day.

Why not pause the mediation? 'Let's call it a day now and come back again when we've had chance to think about things or to checkout some important information.' After all clients pay for eight hours they might as well use the eight hours.

Experience shows that when parties do pause mediations in this way, they nearly always conclude a deal at the resumed session.

Half day mediations with optional extras

8.23 Half day mediations have become more popular. This is a result of:

- the more business-like approach to mediations.
- the sense of it being more of a process then a full day's event.
- the ability to stay in your own environment and work on other things.
- the greater flexibility in arranging sessions.

If you do arrange a four-hour mediation and are starting to run out of time you can easily add another two or three hours either on the day or on another occasion.

Better participation

8.24 Who should attend the mediation? That is an important question for all types of mediation.

For an in-person mediation you need to assemble everybody physically in the same place at the same time. Five or six people would turn up at in-person mediations. They had all had to put the date in their diary and make the commitment. This is why it took so long to arrange mediation dates. There were so many different diaries to coordinate.

Online you can avoid this congestion. You can turn up when you are needed. Even at in-person mediations not all members of the team needed to be there for the whole mediation. Quite often some people would be there just to deal with specific areas of the dispute or discussion. For example, you don't always need your expert there all the time. Or you might not need your tax advisor present until the outlines of the deal have become clearer. They can be available online as and when they are needed. They don't have to devote a whole day out of their diaries to attend the mediation.

Timetabling participation in this way provides a better structure for the day. If the boss, who by definition is a busy person, is going to be on screen in 30 minutes you are less likely to spend yet more time going around the same point. Which as all mediators know is one of the abiding sins of mediation advocates. The more senior members of staff who are needed to take the decisions or to increase the mandate for negotiation can be more easily involved online than in person.

Often people come to mediations confirming that they have authority to settle but only up to a point. They may have to ask for an extension of the authority or obtain sign off. This is common where insurers are involved and the case handler is not at the mediation. Or where the Finance Director needs to be involved before the final figure is agreed. Being online makes all this much easier to arrange.

During the mediation day, because they are in their own environment participants can access information more easily. If it is paper based, it will be to hand. If it's on computer, they will not have to rely upon their laptop or iPad. They will have scanners and printers on tap. No one takes their heavy-duty computers to mediation. Other members of their staff or family who they might need to check information with will be nearby.

There is a paradox. The teams attending online mediation are getting smaller Although fewer people attend the mediation at the start online more people participate during the day.

Visuals

8.25 For some mediators, flipcharts are essential. Others make no use of flipcharts at all. Online you can use flipcharts with Zoom. You cannot if you mediate by phone or email. Most AC systems have a document sharing facility and a whiteboard. You share your screen and people can see the documents you create.

It is much like using a flipchart. You can allow the participants to annotate or change what you have written. This is much the same as handing someone the marker and asking them to write on the flipchart. The impact is effective. But drawing on the screen is not as engaging as standing in front of people writing on a flipchart. And it is usually slower. In practice whiteboards are not used much at online mediations.

Screen Sharing is now used more as people have become familiar with it. Using a screen online has advantages. You can share visuals and images. For example, plans, drawings and photographs often look better and clearer on a computer screen than they do in a photocopied hardcopy. So, take the opportunity to think more creatively about using visuals and images in mediation. Have them prepared in advance. This applies to both mediators and advocates (see **Chapter 10**).

Laurence Boule a well-known Australian mediator and author has written about how he has 'developed a whole set of documents, cartoons, photographs, charts, quotations and the like that I could keep in my favourite toolbox and use when appropriate. I have a couple of favourite cartoons that seem to lighten up people's attitudes: one is of two people building an old-fashioned bridge with stones, and the other is more accusatory with pointing fingers. Each provides a useful metaphor for mediation use.'

> **ALERT**
>
> Resist PowerPoint. Keeping an audience engaged in the flesh is difficult enough if you are taking them through a set of slides. This is especially true if you just read out what is on the screen. It is even worse doing it online.

Energy/efficiency

8.26 Mediation whether online or in-person is tiring. Clients, advisors, and mediators all say this. Physical, emotional, and mental tiredness sets in. 15.30 is the usual low point. Certainly, it is evident at the end of the day and on the next day. Energy is used up. You will have to replenish it some time.

So, energy conservation is important. Although mediations are traditionally eight hours these are not eight equal hours. People's energy levels go up and down. They become bored and distracted. You need to make the best use of the best hours.

If you mediate online, you avoid the strain and hassle of simply getting to the venue. Energy has been saved. You don't start frazzled. You don't have to decompress after the journey to the venue. You are all ready to go as soon as you switch on your computer. This helps explain one of the differences between online and in person mediation, namely that people are more business-like and want to get down to business sooner. There are fewer preliminaries while people recover from their journey to the venue (see **Chapter 7**).

By being able to take breaks more easily you can top up your energy levels during the day. You will not be reliant upon sandwiches and chocolate biscuits to do this. You can go for a walk and eat some healthier more energy-sustaining food.

You can even have a rest. It has been known for people to have a snooze at mediations. Probably better not to do this one on screen. Power naps of anything between 5 and 20 minutes are now recommended as a way of staying healthy generally and more energised during the day. So, what is wrong with clicking Mute and Stop Video, setting your alarm and having a 10-minute snooze if everybody else is doing something which does not require your presence? (See **Chapter 14**.)

Eco

8.27 Let's not forget the eco argument. We are all encouraged to save the environment – quite rightly – so why travel when you don't have to? Driving to mediations instead of taking public transport has always been questionable to say the least. Now it is positively undesirable.

Protecting the environment is something we all need to do now. Mediators sign up to the Mediators' Green Pledge. (Although some of them still fly to international mediations and conferences!).

8.28 *Why we do like OLM*

Mediating online is obviously more environmentally friendly. DM can operate with less infrastructure. This again is a saving – no capital costs such as court buildings or mediation suites.

This raises the interesting ethical question: should mediators even offer in-person mediations anymore?

Access to justice

8.28 Online mediation provides greater access to justice. For Sir Geoffrey Vos and Richard Susskind this is one of the main advantages and objectives of DM.

- People with claims which are too low in value to justify them incurring conventional legal/mediation costs in pursuing them, can now do it.
- It removes geographical barriers. Someone who had purchased a pair of trainers in Milan might find it too difficult to sue the manufacture in Slovakia. Not with OLM.

Profitability

Online mediation opens up more markets

8.29 Mediators can be situated anywhere in the world and so can the parties. Cross-border mediation becomes much easier. Both the markets for the supply of mediators and for the type of mediations is wide open.

Get more bookings

8.30 The greater flexibility about scheduling helps mediators make better use of the diary. Having no travel frees up time. If you do have to travel overnight for a mediation, that prevents that day being available for mediation. If you have a stretched day, for example going past midnight, the next day will be a write-off.

Travelling from one in-person mediation to another and staying overnight in hotels is hard. It is not impossible, but it is very tiring. And can also cause high levels of logistical stress.

Mediating online frees up dates.

Say you are asked to mediate in person on Tuesday. You live in London and the mediation is in Norwich. You will have to travel up the night before. That means you can't mediate either online or in person on the Monday. If you are mediating online on Tuesday, in theory you could also mediate online on Monday and Wednesday. So instead of having two days available for mediation you have three.

Let us take the worst example: you travel up one night and it overruns to the next day. That takes three days out of your diary in a five-day week. Contrast that with online. To be sure, if you overrun the next day will be affected but you will only be taking two days instead of three days out of your diary.

As a matter of good practice some mediators never do back-to-back mediations. That is highly desirable. It is not always practical because dates get shifted at short notice.

Also, many mediators will gladly do back-to-back mediations. You can see plenty of examples of mediators posting and boasting about how many mediations in a week that they have done, drawing attention to some of them being back-to-back. Indeed, one well-known mediator was recently boasting of having done five mediations in a week. I am glad that I was not attending their Friday mediation.

Be aware of burnout. Your reputation will suffer if you start nodding off at mediation or look worn out before you start. This is easier to avoid online (see **Chapter 14**).

Lower operating costs

8.31 The cost savings that clients as well as lawyers and mediators enjoy through no travel and hotel and venue hire have already been mentioned. In addition, lawyers and mediators who might otherwise operate out of an office don't need to if they are mediating from home.

You can save on work apparel. **Chapter 12** shows how appearance on screen still matters. However, you don't need the same number of smart suits. If one of them has worn elbows, it doesn't matter. You can still wear the jacket on screen because people don't see your elbows.

Work life balance

8.32 Covid and lockdown forced people to work from home. Many still prefer to do that. Employers and recruiters complain about the difficulty in attracting people back into working at central office locations.

Generation Z, ie those born between 1997 and 2013, have become used to the greater flexibility in managing the competing priorities of family personal and work. Anybody with a young family can now do the school run and participate in bath time in a way that you cannot if you are attending in-person mediations.

Better communication

8.33 Traditional mediation advocacy does not work on screen. Everything is more muted. Pointing fingers in the same dramatic way on screen as advocates do at in person mediations doesn't work. There just is not the space. Especially not in gallery view where everybody is on screen with a small tile showing their head and shoulders.

8.34 *Why we do like OLM*

The sound quality even with professional mics and speakers is not as good as being in a room with each other. Words can get lost or misheard. In most systems there is a gap between the person speaking and the listener hearing what has been said (see **Chapter 7**).The gap may only be slight, but it is there.

The pace of conversation is slower on screen than in person. That is not a bad thing. In fact, it is usually a good thing. This is discussed in more detail in **Chapter 12** on Communicating online. People are better at turn taking on screen. There is less talking over each other. Partly this is because of the gap between the words being spoken and being heard and because talking over other people is much more difficult to cope with on screen then in person. As a result, people are more considerate of each other and more considered in their responses. In this sense the quality of conversational exchange is better on-screen than in-person.

There is a little more conversation and a lot less argument. More dialogue and less speechifying (see **Chapter 9**).

Information exchange

8.34 Exchange of information happens at every mediation. Often these exchanges take place in a piecemeal fashion. Someone asks a question. The other room gives the answer. Then the questioner asks more questions and so on. You can spend a lot of time gathering and exchanging information. Sometimes this is important, but more often information requests are a displacement activity, a pressure tactic or just part of the settling- in process.

When the information is not available, and it could have been, frustration and irritation take over. 'Are these people really serious about trying to settle?' Sometimes, they have just forgotten it. Sometimes, they have deliberately left it behind. At in-person mediations they have an excuse: 'Sorry didn't realise it would be important. Left it at home.' Online they are in the home or their office on their computer and don't have that excuse.

Accessing information which is not in the mediation bundle is easier online. As one insurance executive said 'I was able to do my calculations of loss much more easily because I was on my desktop linked to the office system rather than on my laptop which I take to in-person mediation.'

Offers

8.35 The information that everyone wants to receive at mediations is the other side's offer. Traditionally at in-person mediations mediators receive details of the offer, write them down and take them to the other room. They read them out and everybody in the offeree room writes them down. There was plenty of opportunity for confusion and omission.

At one mediation a very well-known KC mediator brought his stiff-backed notebook into the room and with great gravitas read out the offer. He left the room to allow the offer to be digested. Within 15 minutes he was back looking slightly flustered to say that he had got the offer wrong.

That can be avoided at in-person mediations by asking the parties to write down the offer. There are lots of good reasons for doing that – greater precision and commitment to something written. But often lawyers and clients are reluctant to do this. 'We'll just read it out to you'.

Online, parties email their offers. This saves time, helps crystallise the offeror's thinking and reduces the risk of confusion or mistake. Indeed, one experienced mediation advocate sends their offers – including their first offer – in the form of a draft settlement agreement.

In any negotiation taking the initiative and setting the agenda can give you an edge. Formulating your offer in the format of a settlement agreement does that. You control the drafting. But there are those who disagree. They don't want to start drafting a settlement agreement too early because it may be interpreted a sign of weakness. This approach can be seen at both in person and online mediations.

Is early drafting a sign of weakness or an expression of serious intent? If you are mediating online the sooner you have a working draft settlement agreement the better. As explained in **Chapter 7** it always takes longer to agree and sign the document online.

In a nutshell

8.36

- Online mediation is not a replication of in-person mediation.
- Online is a different way of doing mediation.
- You can compare them by looking at process, outcome, and experience.
- Process is much the same only the medium is different.
- Outcome measured by assessment rate is much the same.
- The experience is different. Mediators tend to prefer in-person, lawyers seem to be evenly split, and clients seem to prefer online.

Chapter 9

How to choose

In this chapter you will learn

- The three key questions to ask when choosing.
- The Franklin method for balancing pros and cons.

We have gone through the advantages and disadvantages of online mediation and how it works in practice. So, how do you decide what's best for your dispute?

Online, hybrid or in- person mediation. What's the right choice?

To help you decide

9.01 First ask these three questions.

1 Is it a multi-party mediation? The more parties there are the more down time there is – just waiting for the mediator to come and see you. Time management is a lot easier online. People can do other work while off screen waiting for the mediator (see **Chapter 9**). **Online** might be the better option.

2 Is the dispute emotionally charged?

A dispute about your water bill is different from a dispute over your mother's will. Some people think that to vent your emotions you must be in-person (see **Chapters 8** and **9**).Paradoxically I have found that people feel safer online in their own environment and can express their emotions more freely.

You know your clients so go with your instinct but remember your job is to keep their stress levels down. **Hybrid** is a good safe bet.

3 Finally, What's your mediation approach?

Do you need to see the whites of the other side's eyes? Do you need to smell their fear? (See **Chapter 8.**) If you do, tick **in-person**.

But remember even at in-person mediations the other side don't have to meet you if they don't want to. Sometimes at in-person mediations not only do the clients never see each other, neither do their lawyers. Why hold the mediation in person at all? A good question. But, these mediations still result in settlements.

9.01 *How to choose*

If you still need to examine the choices more closely try this technique. Benjamin Franklin (1706-1790) inventor of the lightning rod and bifocals devised it! Known as the First American he knew about making decisions. He called it a Pros & Cons list. More ambitiously renamed by Irving Janis (1918-1990) (famous for his theory of groupthink)-and Leon Mann as 'a decisional balance sheet.'

Go through the following questions. See the table below. Put a tick in the columns which best apply to your mediation.

The one with the most ticks is your best option.

Here are the questions?

1 Is your client vulnerable?

If yes, tick **hybrid** or **online**.

2 Do they need support from family members or advisers?

If yes, tick **online** or **hybrid**.

3. Will they feel safer in their own homes?

If yes, tick **online**.

4 Do your clients want to avoid conflict and confrontation?

If they want to avoid, tick **online** or **hybrid**.

5 Do they want to engage with it as part of the mediation process?

If they want to engage, tick **in-person**.

6 Are there mobility or care issues?

If there are, tick **online**.

7 Are there any health issues?

If there are tick **online**.

8 Is your client tech savvy?

If they are not, tick **in-person** or **hybrid**.

9 Do they have a good enough broadband connection?

If not, tick **in-person** or **hybrid**.

10 Are the parties geographically miles apart- in different countries?

If yes, tick **online**.

	Questions	**Online**	**In-person**	**Hybrid**	**Total**
1	Is your client vulnerable?				
2	Does your client need support from family members or advisers?				

	Questions	**Online**	**In-person**	**Hybrid**	**Total**
3	Will your client feel safer in their own home?				
4	Does your client want to avoid confrontation?				
5	Do your clients want to engage with confrontation?				
6	Are there mobility or care issues?				
7	Are there any health issues?				
8	Is your client tech savvy?				
9	Does your client have reliable broadband?				
10	Are the participants far apart geographically?				
	Total				

Ask others.

9.02 A director of a major litigation funder posted:

> 'Over our 11 years of operation, mediation has emerged as our preferred route to settle legal disputes. The evolution of the court process and the legal landscape has highlighted the importance of embracing ADR.'

Traditionally, mediation involves physical meetings in neutral environments. However, the landscape change drastically with the onset of Covid-19. Online mediation became a necessity and is here to stay. It provides a secure videoconferencing platform, replicating the traditional mediation experience while saving time and energy.

Based on our experiences here are some tips for successful online mediation.

- Choose an experienced online mediator: **4.21**
- Familiarise yourself with the platform and test IT equipment: **Chapter 10**
- Establish effective communication channels: **11.12**
- Plan for breaks, as online mediation can be tiring: **11.13.**
- Have settlement documentation ready in advance: **13.21**
- Consider a half-day mediation for quicker resolutions: **8.23**

In a nutshell

9.03

- Always ask your clients what they prefer.
- Go through the pros and cons with them.
- Resist the temptation to have power struggles with the other side over whether to mediate online or in-person.
- Remember whatever type of mediation you chose – you are there to make peace not war.

Part C

Getting OLM right

Chapter 10

Zoom: gloom, doom or boom?

In this chapter you will learn

- What Zoom is
- What Zoom does
- How to make the best use of Zoom

Remember March 2020? Lockdowns announced all over the world. In the mediation world, everywhere is doom and gloom.

Then along came Zoom

Zoom

10.01 All mediators owe a great debt of gratitude to Eric Yuan. In 2011 he founded the California based company and two years later the software was launched.

Covid and lockdown boosted its business. Daily meeting participants rose from about 10 million in December 2019 to over 300 million in April 2020. Amazing. It is the best system available but there are others such as Microsoft Teams, Skype, Bluejeans and many others.

Richard Susskind concludes that Zoom was not a paradigm shift. He might be right but it certainly was a big change. And the effects of the Zoom way of mediating via VC has been transformational in many ways for mediators.

What is Zoom?

10.02 It is a platform for video telephony and online chat services. It's stylised as 'Zoom' but its full name is Zoom Video Communications Inc – Zoom for short.

Zoom has become the industry standard for mediators. It is designed for social and business users, not specifically for mediation. You can find mediation-specific software, for example Just Act, Cerillion.com, progressmediation.co.uk etc. They often incorporate Zoom or some of its functions or similar software but offer other features such as scheduling, uploading documents and technical support during the mediation. Their value proposition is that you can have an integrated suite of apps and functions – all in one place. They can be useful but perhaps the price or specification are too high for most mediators working solo in the gig economy.

As of May 2023, there were several versions of Zoom. For mediators the two relevant versions are Zoom Pro and Business. The main features of them are summarised here.

Basic

10.03 It is free.

- You can hold meetings of up to 40 minutes with up to 100 participants.
- You can have Screen Sharing and three editable whiteboards.
- Includes a team chat where participants can collaborate and file share.
- Includes Mail and Calendar
- You can join from your mobile, on your desktop, or your iPad.

TOP TIP

- Download the basic version of Zoom. It is free.
- It allows you to practise.
- It is a useful short-term backup if your main version goes down.

Zoom Pro

10.04

- This costs £149.90 a year per user.
- The differences between this and the basic version are that meetings can last up to 30 hours. That's long enough for any mediation.
- You also have 100 attendees.
- Includes three whiteboards, team chat and email and calendar functions.
- In addition, you have 5GB of cloud storage.

Business

10.05

- This costs £159.90 a year per user.
- The same as Zoom basic except that you can have 300 attendees per meeting.
- Includes extras such as simplified sign on – SSO managed domains and company branding

For full up-to-date information visit their website zoom.us.

What do you need to do?

10.06 Get trained on it. This is not difficult or expensive.

Training

10.07 You have three options:

1 Go on the Zoom website and watch their educational videos: zoom-learn.us.

The videos are clear and comprehensive. They are not aimed at mediators. This is the cheapest and quickest way of training. You can also find some good videos on linkedin.com.

2 Attend a course given by trainers who use Zoom but don't mediate.

All courses cost money. The going rate is between £400 and £600 (ex VAT) a day. The advantage of trainers who use Zoom but not do not mediate is that there are more of them. They will know a lot about Zoom but very little if anything about mediation.

3 Attend a course given by mediators who use Zoom.

This is your best option. You have someone who is regularly using Zoom in mediations. They will be able to share what the experience is like both for the mediator and for the parties and their lawyers. They can tell you what goes wrong at mediations and how to cope with it. You will be able to ask them questions about Zoom in the mediation context. These courses are usually given by mediation providers such as the ADR Group (see **Chapter 7**).

What features of Zoom are particularly useful for mediators?

10.08 The Zoom menu bar appears at the bottom of the Zoom window once the meeting begins. If you don't see the menu bar, move your mouse slightly and the bar will appear. (The bar disappears after a few seconds when in full-screen mode.)

The Zoom rooms

10.09 Zoom allows participants to have private and joint sessions. There are three spaces on Zoom: the main session, waiting rooms and breakout rooms.

Main session

10.10 When you are in the main session you can see and hear everybody else in the main session. Usually, you are on gallery view. You see a screen full of small tiles of heads and shoulders.

Waiting room

10.11 The waiting room is the opposite. When you are in waiting room, you are on your own. You cannot be seen or heard by anybody else. The mediator as host cannot come into your waiting room.

They are not used very much at mediation. Some mediators claim to have used them for crowd control – if someone has been misbehaving, they put them into a waiting room to cool down.

Breakout rooms

10.12 Breakout rooms are different again. There are used all the time at mediations. When you are in a breakout room you can see and hear everybody else who is in the same breakout room as you even though you are physically in different locations. You cannot see or hear anybody who is not in the same breakout room and they cannot see or hear you. The mediator can come into the breakout room.

The mediator sets up the breakout rooms and assigns participants to a breakout room as they join the main session.

Security

10.13 Confidentiality and security are concerns at every type of mediation. All online communications including telephones, email, and video conferencing have potential vulnerabilities. Sending emails by unencrypted methods has been likened to sending a postcard.

At the start of lockdown in 2020 there were lots of negative comments about Zoom security. Many of them were unwarranted. Some were deliberately misleading. In any case three years of using Zoom for video conferencing and for mediations has shown that there are no real concerns that should worry mediators and those attending mediation. Of course, if the subject matter of the dispute is ultra-sensitive, for example a matter of national security (and there have been mediations like this) there might be a different set of considerations. But those are extremely rare.

Here are the main features in Zoom which when used should provide all participants with adequate reassurance that the discussions will be confidential and secure.

Lock meeting

10.14 Once the participants have been admitted into the mediation session the mediator locks the session. That means that nobody who is not on the invite list can join the session.

Click the Security Icon. Click Lock meeting in the drop-down menu.

Turn off record

10.15 Zoom allows you to record sessions. Most mediation agreements stipulate that there should be no recording of any part of the mediation. The host can disable that function.

- Sign in to the Zoom web portal.
- In the navigation menu, click Settings.
- Click Recording.
- Click the Automatic Recording toggle to disable it.
- If the Verification dialog appears, click Disable to verify the change.
- If you want to enable the automatic recording, do the same thing except click Enable instead of Disable.

See **Chapter 7**.

Screen share

10.16 All participants can use Screen Share if the function is turned on. The host controls that. Screen share can be useful but is used less than you might imagine. It is most often used when drafting.

You

- Click the Share Screen icon in the toolbar.
- Click the option that you prefer in the drop-down menu.
- If you are Screen Sharing and want to stop Screen Share, click the orange tab at the top of the screen.

Whiteboard

10.17 The whiteboard is like a flipchart on screen. Some mediators use it a lot. Others hardly at all. In practice, whiteboard is not used very much either by mediators, clients or their lawyers.

To use it, you:

- Click the whiteboard icon in the toolbar.
- Click advanced whiteboard sharing options.
- Make your choices.

Closed caption

10.18 This is a useful feature that the mediator can enable. Your spoken words appear as text on the screen. This is particularly useful for people who are hard of hearing.

To enable automated captions for mediations

- Sign into the Zoom web portal as an admin with the privilege to edit account settings.
- In the Navigation menu, click Account Management then Account Settings.
- Click the Meeting tab.
- Under in the Meeting (Advanced), click the Automated captions toggle to Enable or Disable.
- If the Verification dialog appears, click Enable or Disable to verify the change.

Mute

10.19 People can mute themselves by clicking the Mute icon in the toolbar at the bottom of the screen. When you do this, you cannot be heard but you can still hear others.

The mediator can mute anybody. This is useful if people are misbehaving.

Stop Video

10.20 You can do the same thing with the Stop Video icon Just click it. You cannot be seen. You can still hear others.

How to set up Zoom

10.21 When you install your Zoom app you need to set it up. The best way to do this is to have a look at the current Zoom videos. Zoom updates all the time and you want to be sure that you are looking at the right video for the version you have. Go to supportzoom.us.

CHECKLIST TO SET UP ZOOM

10.22 What you do is:

- In your Internet browser enter Zoom.us.

- In the top right -hand corner click Resources.
- Then click download Zoom Client.
- Under Zoom Client for meetings click the download button.
- Complete the installation process.
- Double click the Zoom desktop icon to begin using Zoom.

CHECKLIST: HOW TO SCHEDULE YOUR FIRST MEETING

10.23

- Sign in to Zoom.
- You will see a page with four buttons on it.
- Click Schedule.
- Choose the date and time for your meeting.
- Choose the calendar from the options shown.
- Click save. You will then be moved to your calendar which will show a panel. Click invitees and type in the email addresses or names of the people that you want to invite.
- When you have done that click Send.
- Click Save.

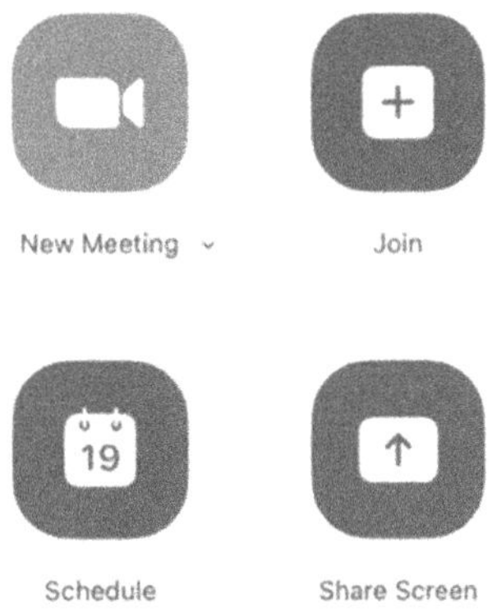

There are two other platforms that mediators use.

Teams

10.24 This is the Microsoft videoconferencing workplace chat software. To find it, go to support.microsoft.com.

10.25 *Zoom: gloom, doom or boom?*

At the start of lockdown, it had less functionality for mediators than Zoom. Over the last three years it has improved. For example, it now has a breakout room function.

Zoom v Teams: Which should mediators choose?

10.25 Choosing between Zoom and Microsoft Teams depends on what your priorities are. Here are the main differences:

- Zoom is primarily a video conferencing tool.
- Teams is an all-in-one tool that combines video conferencing with team chat and other productivity features. Zoom is better for external meetings; Teams is better for internal meetings.
- It's easy for external participants to join a Zoom meeting from anywhere on any device – all you need is a link. To join Teams, you need the app or to be on Microsoft Edge or Chrome to join via the web. It's more restrictive.
- Zoom copes better with larger meetings and slow Internet.

Google Meet

10.26 This is a video communication service developed by Google. While Zoom has largely taken over the video conferencing space, Google Meet (formerly Google Hangouts) is a good video conferencing platform and Zoom alternative.

Zoom v Google Meet

10.27 Generally speaking:

- Google Meet is best for small organisations and individuals who want a user-friendly video conferencing solution that is already integrated with Google Drive.
- Zoom is the better option for larger organizations with stricter security expectations that need to accommodate more people and provide hosts with advanced controls.

All the platforms are developing all the time. They leapfrog each other with new features. Keeping up is a bit hard to do. Try some of the comparison websites such as Zapier.com, trusted advisors.com or crazyegg.com.

Google Meet is not used much for mediations.

Technical dominance (TD)

10.28 Mediating online means that you need to have good infrastructure, ie good broadband connectivity and good equipment.

Broadband

10.29 Recall what was said in **7.02**: as an online mediator you are only as good as your broadband. Remember there are two elements: speed and stability. Don't rely upon using the domestic broadband that most of us have for our ordinary residential use. Spend some money on an upgrade.

If you don't, you will be liable to experience interruptions during mediation. The dread phrase: 'Your Internet connection is unstable' flashes up. This is never good news. Connection is lost and conversation is interrupted. Result – unease and frustration all round.

You can boost by plugging into your smart phone and using your G4 network or you can connect an ethernet cable.

Better to use one of the upgraded systems or even rent a dedicated business line. That is what you would have if you were working from your office. If your home has become your office why not treat it accordingly and invest the money.

It will cost you more money – possibly as much as 10 times as ordinary domestic broadband – but it is much better.

Think about using cableco.uk broadband checker to find the best broadband deal for your area. Remember you want both speed and stability. In practice stability is more important.

Camera

10.30 Built-in cameras are acceptable but external cameras give a much better performance. They are not expensive. I use the Logitech Brio. Go on to their website where you can buy a good quality external camera for £150 (April 2023). Logitech.com.>en_gb>products>webcams.

The trick with cameras is to remember to look at them when you are talking to someone on screen. The temptation is to look at the person that you are talking to. That is fine if there is only one person on screen. If you are talking to several people for example in gallery view with five or six different tiles on display, you need to look at all of them. The only way to do that is by looking at the camera. If you look at one tile you are looking at that tile but not at all the others. See **Chapter 12**.

One way to cope with this is to use a device such as PlexiCam.

10.31 *Zoom: gloom, doom or boom?*

PlexiCam

10.31 This is a simple fast device which hooks onto your laptop and your camera and allows you to put your camera whatever you want it on the screen. They also supply a list of accessories such as LED light, extension, phone holders, etc. Have a look at the websiteplexikam.com.

See more about cameras in **Chapter 12** on Communicating Online.

Microphones

10.32 Sound is just as important as image. In fact, in many ways, it is more important. Research shows that viewers on YouTube are turned off more quickly by poor sound quality than by poor image quality.

You can engage in the process even if you cannot see the others very well, provided that you can hear them properly. In fact, that is often what happens online where for example one group is in a boardroom. You may not be able to see them very clearly, but you can usually hear them well enough.

- As with cameras don't rely upon the internal mic. Although they have improved and become more directional to cut out background noise, they are not the same quality as an external one. Upgrade.
- You can get much better ones quite cheaply. For example, the Yeti Blue. You can buy much more expensive ones and some mediators treat themselves. They post images of their set-ups on LinkedIn and some of them look like a BBC studio. To get a flavour scroll down LinkedIn Posts and observe competitive boys' toys posts with images of 40" curved screens and multiple ring lights.
- One well known mediator spent over £800 on a Sennheiser MKH 8050. They loved it explaining that it made them feel they were on TV! You will find a lot of frustrated wannabe TV celebrities amongst mediators.

TOP TIP

- Try noise suppression software.
- KRISP is reliable, easy to install and good value. Go onto the website krisp.ai.

Speakers

10.33 You can use external speakers. They are nice to have but not essential. External mics and cameras are.

Resource: If you are interested in external speakers go to techradar.com/uk.

Backgrounds

10.34 Backgrounds – or do you have a green screen or not? Do you have a plain background? Do you have it blurred or clear? Some people think plain or blurred backgrounds are more professional. Others think they are rather sterile and inhibit rapport building. Why not show a bit of yourself by having your actual background? Usually, this is a background of books.

Artificial backgrounds were in vogue. People appeared on screen lying on beaches under palm trees or sitting in the Vatican library. That has faded. With good reason. The images always look fake and rarely appealed.

Some mediators use their background as a visual cue just to set the mood. Amanda Bucklow prefers to have 'a generic but interesting background rather than a personal photo'. She says: 'sometimes I choose something calming or uplifting. Pictures of the sea or mountains are known to be psychologically beneficial. A view or horizon help support the idea of what lies beyond the present.'

ALERT

Your backgrounds give visual cues. Research has shown that:

- Blurred backgrounds arouse suspicion – what are you hiding?
- Plain backgrounds were less popular with customers – they don't say anything about you.
- Viewers preferred to interact with people who used a revealing background.

Why? They trusted them because they prepared to disclose something about themselves. Blurred or plain screens suggested that you have something to hide.

Screens

10.35 How many screens do you need? If you have a big screen for your desktop computer, say 38 inch you can have split screens on it with ease. Most people don't. Remember you know that you are on a big screen, those watching won't. They will see their own screen.

Big screens are cumbersome. They take up a lot of space and you cannot pack them into your bag when you are going elsewhere.

One well-known mediator based in the Midlands was mediating in person in Scotland and had an online mediation the next day. They realised that they would not be able to get back home to do the online mediation. So, they booked an extra day in the hotel and carried out the online mediation from their room. They packed their 38-inch curved screen into the back of the car and took it with them along with their external lights, mic and camera. Devotion to the cause of duty or disproportionate investment of time, money, and energy?

In practice for most mediations, you need three devices.

- One for Zoom where you are conducting the mediation.

- A second to display the documents.
- A third open all the time for emails and messages. As explained in **7.15** there can be quite a lot of email, text, and WhatsApp traffic during mediation. You can't just rely upon your smart phone.

See this advice from a barrister who is an experienced user of online mediation:

> '3 screens are a joy. One 32" flanked by two 28" either side.
>
> 32" adorned by a Benq desk lamp, which cradles on top of screen. Desk lamp beautifully designed.
>
> Have tons of space. 4th screen requirements seem unlikely unless you are moving into air traffic control.'

Comment

10.36 This is the gold standard.

Headsets

10.37 Should you wear them? Only if you want to look like Mr Spock or an air traffic controller. Unless of course you are unfortunate enough to be working in an open plan office. You do not have any choice. You must use them. Many find headsets alienating. They don't help you establish rapport or build intimacy.

If you use headsets, be careful which ones you choose. Better not to use the ones you use for gaming. They can also give the message that you are a gamer or a bit immature. Dred Beats could be off-putting.

Earbuds are also an alternative. Air Pods seem to be the favourite. Clients can get away with wearing what they like. There is more latitude for lawyers then there is for mediators. And don't forget as the mediator you are going to be seen and heard by more people than anybody else at the mediation.

But more important than all that is the quality of your mic. If you have upgraded your mic to the best that you can afford you should not need headsets. The only exception is if you are mediating in a room surrounded by others. That raises the bigger question: should you be mediating at all in a room surrounded by others. The answer is no. You do you want some privacy if possible. Which it usually is.

Board room mediations

10.38 These are used when there is a hybrid mediation. Just to recap, hybrid mediation is where some of the parties are physically together in one location but communicate with the other parties and the mediator by Zoom.

Very rarely does the technology work well. This is mainly because the venues which are often solicitors' offices or barristers' chambers have not invested in high quality audio-visual equipment. What you usually have is a large TV screen on a wall. That is linked to someone's laptop. They have a good image of you. You see less clear images of them. The camera is usually too far away. The sound is often sub-optimal. Nearly always someone from IT has to come in at some time to try and sort it out. But people persist in using them. As a mediator you just have to put up with it.

If you are using the boardroom, have your individual laptops to hand. You can then switch to using those and have a better interaction with the mediator than by sitting looking at the big screen.

An alternative is to use NEAT bars and Owl cameras which focus on the speaker. They do work. Sadly, in practice they often don't work very well.

As mentioned in **7.02**, if you have several laptops open in the same room, you may have a problem with reverb – where you can hear the echo of people speaking. The way around this is to have those who are not speaking turn their mics and speakers to mute.

Mobile phones

10.39 Make sure that everyone has their mobile phones near them and charged. You can use them for private messaging. The parties or the lawyers can use them to send texts or WhatsApps to the mediator saying they would like to join them. This is an alternative to the chat function or help button on Zoom. It is outside the Zoom system so if anybody is worried about confidentiality and privacy, they can be reassured.

Also, as mediator, using your mobile phone rather than Chat or Help buttons means you can move away from the screen. If you have taken an offer into one room and they have asked for a few minutes to discuss it, you can click Mute and Stop Video, walk away from the screen make yourself a cup of tea but still be in touch. When they are ready to see you again, they send you a text or WhatsApp and you rejoin. All very straightforward.

Mobile phones are also back-up if the Zoom system falters. You can join Zoom from your mobile phone. Also, you can plug your mobile phone into your iPad or your laptop and use the 4G system if your Internet has gone down.

Finally, you can sign documents electronically on your mobile. See below.

Updating and keeping in the loop

10.40 Recall what was said about time management in **Chapter 8**. For clients one of the worst things about mediation is the downtime and not knowing what's happening (if anything) when the mediator is not with you (see **Chapter 8**).

Time seems to drag more slowly on Zoom. Mediators need to keep sessions shorter.

10.41 *Zoom: gloom, doom or boom?*

More importantly, keep people in the loop. Use your mobile to send a text or a WhatsApp just keeping them posted about what you are doing. You take one room's offer into the other room and are then asked to step out while they consider it. Text the offeror room to say what is happening. eg 'Proposal delivered. They are thinking about it. Have been asked to go back in 15 minutes.'

Electronic signatures

10.41 There are several ways in which electronic documents can be added to signatures.

Most businesses now have the software that allows that to be done as a matter of course. Private clients and mediators may not use it. Consider buying one of the programs that let you do this. DocuSign is industry standard along with Adobe. Or try Markup on Apple.

Here is how you do it. Check the website: support.apple.com.

Use Markup on your iPhone, iPad or iPod touch.

With Markup, you can edit screenshots and photos, select different opacity and font thickness, and even add a signature to a PDF document.

Mayday

10.42 If you are a client or adviser and your Internet connection becomes unstable and throws you out of the mediation session don't panic. Just text or WhatsApp or even phone the mediator. They can come out of their private session in a breakout room, return to the main session, let you back in and return you to your breakout room.

You will have to do this if the mediator has remembered, as they always should, to lock the meeting once everybody has arrived and the mediation is underway.

Door knocks

10.43 This means how you let someone in a breakout room know that you would like to come into their room. Don't bother with digital door knocks. Use your mobile to send a WhatsApp or text. Don't use the Chat or Help buttons.

Lighting

10.44 LED lights give a more reliable light.

Ring lights. They provide a full 360° of light. This is good for facial lighting. Place directly in front of you with the light in line with your face. This means the ring light will not be positioned too high or too low. That will avoid unflattering shadows across your face.

Your angles. Keep the camera directly in front of your face.

Using a backlight can give more depth to your image on the screen. I use a directional floor-placed one angled upwards. I only use it when the light is fading, and it is getting too dark to see without a light. I don't want use an overhead ceiling light at all.

There is a huge range of options. The technology keeps on changing and improving. To keep up to date look at the comparison websites such as bestproductsreviews.co.uk.

TOP TIP

If you wear glasses, try this.

- Make sure you are lit from the front or the side. The easiest way to achieve this is to set your desk up to look out of the window.
- Turn down your monitor's brightness. You may forget, but your monitor is also a light source.
- Use a large soft light rather than a simple bare bulb.

In a nutshell

10.45

- Use Zoom- it's the industry standard.
- Upgrade your broadband.
- Use external mics and cameras – they are much better.
- Have your mobile to hand and use it.
- Have shorter sessions.
- Keep people in the loop with text or WhatsApp.

Chapter 11

How to run a Zoom mediation

In this chapter you will learn how to set up a Zoom mediation:

- What to do before the mediation
- What to do during the mediation
- What to do after the mediation

Before the mediation

11.01 You have acquired all your equipment (see **Chapter 10**). Now you need a suite of letters that you can send out to clients. Here are some examples.

You have been appointed mediator.

You need to issue your paperwork – your mediation agreement (see **Chapter 13**) and your invoices (see **Chapter 15**).

Letter 1 – Mediation Agreement

11.02

> 'Dear Both
>
> I attach the draft mediation agreement.
>
> Please could you liaise with each other about any amendments and about the definition of Dispute in clause 1.3.
>
> When you are happy with the agreement, please could you have it signed by all members of your team who will be participating in the mediation and return it to me.
>
> If there are any problems, please let me know.
>
> The invoices will be sent separately.
>
> Regards'

Make contact and sort out the logistics.

11.03 Ask them when they will be sending you the documents. Sort out both a dummy run with clients and lawyers and a private pre-mediation chat with the lawyers.

Letter 2 – Logistics

11.04

'Dear Both

I write about the mediation on XXX 2023

4 things

1. Is there any material that you would like me to read before the mediation? If there is, when do you think that you will be able to send it to me? I am happy to receive material by email to this address.
2. As the mediation is online, I like to have a dummy run on Zoom with each team separately. This is to make sure that the technology works and that those who have not used breakout rooms before are comfortable with the privacy and confidentiality of the system.

   If you would like a dummy run, let me know when would be convenient. I can offer.......
3. I also like to have private word before the mediation. Could each of you let me know a convenient time for me to call you? We could combine this with the dummy run if you prefer.
4. What is your preferred start time?

Regards'

Set up the dummy run.

11.05 The dummy run is to check the tech and to make sure that everyone is happy with the confidentiality of the system. But it is also to meet the clients before the mediation. This is so valuable if you can organise it (see **Chapters 3** and **7**).

Check list for dummy run

11.06

- Send out invite for dummy run.
- Logon five minutes before the appointed time.
- Admit participants to the main session.
- Explain how Zoom works. (See **Chapter 11**.)
  - Main session
  - Waiting room
  - Breakout room

- Demonstrate how each of them works.
- Show them the icons for Stop Video and Mute. Explain this is how you can take a break. (See **Chapter 9**.)
- Explain how you will use text or WhatsApp to communicate during the mediation. Warn them off using the Chat or Help functions. (See **Chapter 10**.)
- Remind them
  - to speak more clearly and
  - to wait until the person before them has finished speaking before they start. Otherwise, you over talk or click the end of each other's sentences. This is more difficult to cope with on Zoom. (See **Chapter 12**.)
- Ask about process – do they want a Joint Opening Session? (See **Chapter 8**.) Explain the difference between a traditional joint opening session, a Meet and Greet and joint working session.
- Refer them to your website for further information about online mediation. Make sure you have some content on there about online mediation – either a blog or a video. (See **Chapters 17** and **18.**)
- Explain about the three screens that you use:
  - the main screen or which you conduct the mediation.
  - the second screen which is displaying your documents.
  - the third screen which is open for emails, text notifications and WhatsApp.
  - Reassure them that if you glance away from screen one you will be looking at either 2 or 3 and are not being distracted by something that is nothing to do with the mediation.
  - Confirm the names of the attendees.
  - Confirm the start time.
- (See **Chapters 11** and **??**).

TOP TIP

Signs

Make sure you have your signs to hand. You can hold them up to the camera if the audio fails.

Make a series of them, as follows:

1. 'Please Unmute.'

Please unmute

2. 'Can you hear me?'

Can you hear me?

3. 'I can't hear you.'

I can't hear you

4. 'Try pressing F12.'

Try pressing F12

5. 'My mobile is 07770 875681.'

My mobile phone is 07770 875681

6. 'What is your mobile?'

What is your mobile?

7. 'I will phone you.'

I will
phone you

8. 'Log off and log back on.'

Log off
and
log back on

9. 'Will close meeting and send fresh link.'

Will close
meeting
and send
fresh link

11.07

4 One or two days before the mediation schedule the meeting (see **Chapter 11**). Send the Zoom invite and the confirmatory email.

Letter 3 – Zoom invites

11.08

'Dear Both

I have sent the Zoom invites. Please check that all members of your team have received theirs.

The start time is 09.00. I shall log on at 08.30 in case anyone wants to log on early to check their connections or to have a private word in their breakout rooms.

The mobile numbers that we will be using tomorrow for backup are:

Main xx

Reserve yy

If there is a complete mobile meltdown the landline is zz.

Please could you also check that all members of your team have signed and returned the mediation agreement to me.

Regards'

On day of the mediation

Early pre -mediation check list

Check

11.09

- Your Internet connection is working.
- All your devices are charged.
- Your mic is switched on and working and your camera is switched on and working.
- Your mobile phones are charged and to hand.
- Your iPad switched on to 'Never' in Auto-Lock so that the screen is visible all the time.
- The documents are loaded onto screen two.
- Your screen share is blank.
- Your background is uncluttered (see **Chapter 12**).
- All your notifications have been set to silent and you have quit as many notifications as possible (see **Chapter 11**).

- All the mediation agreements have been returned signed to you. If they have not email reminders.
- You have a comb, tissues and water and lozenges to hand. If you are a mediator who needs lipstick or nail files, make sure you have those to hand as well.

Tune your voice and do some stretches. You are in for a long day (see **Chapters 12** and **14**).

60 minutes checklist

11.10 In your notebook list attendees. Allocate them to their team's breakout room.

- Log on 30 minutes early.
- Wait for the participants to log on.
- A message will appear on your screen giving the name of the person who is in the waiting room.
- Click Admit. Admit attendees one at a time. You can then:
  - Verify who they are and which to which team they belong.
  - Tick them off your list of attendees.
- Set up the breakout rooms.
  - Click Breakout rooms icon in the tool bar.
  - You will see a dropdown menu.
  - Scroll to the number of rooms you want to open.

TOP TIP

- Always set up rooms twice the number of teams +2 extra.
- Why? You will have one breakout room for each team. Then have your 3 breakout rooms plus some spares for parallel breakout meetings.
- Leave a gap between the rooms for each team on the dropdown menu.

Say you have two teams.

Assign Claimant to Room 1 and Defendant to Room 3. Chose Room 5 for yourself.

Leaving a gap between Rooms reduces the risk of you clicking the wrong button later in the day when you are moving people around or joining meetings.

- Click the assign manually button.
- Click Create.

A second dropdown menu will appear.

- Click assign. A list of participants who have joined the meeting will appear. Click their name against the room you want to assign them to.
- Open All Rooms.
- Messages will appear on screens inviting them to join their assigned room.
- Ask them to click Join.

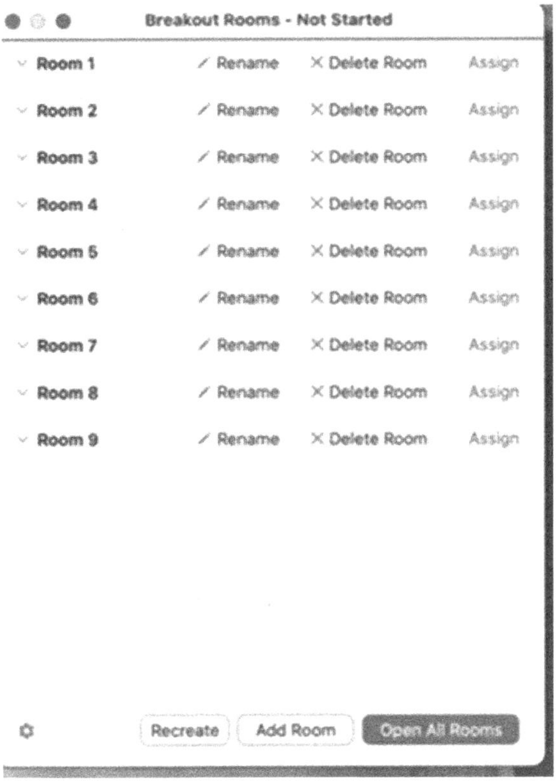

TOP TIP

- Assign yourself to a separate breakout room. No-one else can come into it. If you stay in the Main Session others can leave their breakout room and suddenly join you without notice.
- Also, when you join a breakout room from the Main Session you are automatically on mute. You can easily forget to unmute yourself. When you move from one breakout room to another you are not automatically on mute.

When everyone has logged on and are in their assigned breakout rooms lock the meeting.

- Go to the Security icon in the tool bar.
- Click Lock meeting.
- No one can now join the meeting even if they have the meeting ID and the passcode.

TOP TIP

- Send a test text or WhatsApp to each room to make sure that the comms are working.
- Often, they don't respond. Their phones are not to hand, or they are not checking them as they are talking to their clients.
- Ring them – often their phone is on voicemail with a message that they are at mediation.
- You will just have to join the breakout room unannounced. Make sure that you are not on mute and say clearly 'Can I join you?'
- Ask if your messages were not coming through.

Check with all teams whether they want a Joint Opening Session or not? Often you will be asked what you think would be best.

It is a matter of individual mediator style whether or not they encourage joint opening sessions of the traditional type or not. I found that they were going out of fashion even before lockdown. Since lockdown and we have been doing mediations online they have become almost extinct (see **8.16**). Even now in September 2023 with more mediations being done in person a traditional JOS is the exception not the rule.

I tell the parties that I take my cue from them. If anybody is reluctant to have a Joint Opening Session then we don't have one. I explain that mediation is quite stressful enough. I have found over the years that one of the main obstacles to mediation is high stress levels. The last thing we want to do is to increase them further.

I suggest a Meet and Greet as an alternative.

I also reassure them that we can always have joint working sessions later in the day.

If one team particularly want a Joint Opening Session and the other side doesn't really mind or is mildly opposed to it, I explain that if one team really wants a JOS and the request is refused this can build up to a ball of frustration. That can get in the way of constructive thoughts about the future because they are smarting about the rejection.

CHECKLIST: JOINT OPENING SESSION ON ZOOM

11.11

- Choose a spare breakout room.
- Join it first.
- Move each attendee into it one by one.
- You will all appear on screen in thumbnail tiles.
- Say who you are and say you will go round the screen asking people who they are and why they are at the mediation.
- Ask them to put themselves on mute if they are not talking.

Say whether this is a traditional JOS or a Meet and Greet (see **Chapter 18**).

- Then go round the screen asking each person by name to introduce themselves.
- After that make your opening statement (see Checklist below).
- After?If it is Meet and Greet return everyone to their rooms one by one. Say out loud which room you are returning them to. This helps prevent mistakes.
- If it is a traditional JOS invite whoever wants to go first to speak. Ask people to stay on mute while the speaker is talking. Put yourself on mute.
- As each speaker finishes, unmute yourself, thank them and invite the next speaker to start.
- When they have all finished return them to their rooms saying which room you will join first. Ask how long they would like before you join.

ALERT

- Joint Opening Sessions tend to be shorter online.
- Be prepared to intervene if someone tries to interrupt the speaker. If they persist put them on Mute.

Mediator's opening remarks

11.12 Thank attendees for their introductions.

Ask them if everyone can agree the code of conduct – i.e. if you end up in the wrong room, speak up, don't just sit there eavesdropping.

Set the scene for the mediation in your own way. For detailed guidance on this, see **Chapter 14.13** of my book *Mediation Advocacy.*

CHECKLIST OF POINTS TO COVER

11.13 The purpose of mediation is settlement.

1 For this you need three things

  a. Authority – ask each team if they have to consult with anyone else.

  b. Mindset – be flexible.

  c. Confidence – to know that if you are prepared to think flexibly and you don't settle, it will not be referred to later. Everything is both confidential and without prejudice.

2 The Mediator's role is not as a decision maker or adjudicator. 'I am here to find out what the obstacles to settlement are and help the parties to get over or around them.'

3 Say that you will invite the parties to say anything, bearing in mind that everyone has read the position papers and correspondence and that we are here to settle.

4 Outline the code of conduct, ie if you find yourself in the wrong room speak up.

5 If you want to Screen Share, tell me as the host and I will enable it.

6 If you are thrown out of the meeting by your Internet connection becoming unstable text me and I will unlock the meeting so you can logon again.

7 If anyone wants to contact me or speak privately – text or WhatsApp me.

When the speakers have all finished return them to their rooms.

During the mediation

Time

11.14

- Needs managing more carefully online (see **Chapter 8**).
- Note the time that you join a breakout room and leave it. Say it out loud as you write it down.
- Remember to click your timer on as you enter and leave.
- Try and keep sessions to 25-30 minutes (see **Chapter 8**).
- Text/WhatsApp the parties to keep them in the loop. For example, if you take an offer into one room and they ask you to give them 10 minutes while they consider, text the other room to say that is what is happening.

- Take notes at the end of each session before you leave.
- Ask the parties, 'Can I just make a note of that'. Don't take notes while they are talking on screen. Look at the camera. They want to see how you are receiving what they're saying.
- Summarise and recap more frequently during sessions.
- If you are reading a document, say 'I'm looking at it on the other screen' or if you have a physical piece of paper hold it up so they can see that you're reading it. This is a bit of theatre, but it emphasises engagement.

> **TOP TIP**
>
> - Give a time estimate of how long you will be away before you see them again.
> - Invite them to take breaks.

Breaks

11.15

- Reassure them that anyone can take a break any time that they want to. Remind them how to do it by clicking the Stop Video and Mute icons.
- Suggest that they keep their phone with them in case you need to get in touch.
- Agree lunch breaks. If no one is suggesting taking a break, you suggest it. Don't be heroic. You need to refresh and eat. Remember you are the one who cannot flag. You need to keep your energy levels higher than anyone else's (see **Chapter 14**).
- Decompress. After each session stand up and move away from the screen. Make sure you have clicked Stop Video and Mute. Then there is no chance of you being seen or overheard by anyone. The participants should not be able to come into your breakout room, but you may have put yourself in the main session by mistake. And they can come into that.

Offers

11.16

- Ask them to email offers to you. Explain that this reduces the risk of confusion from people not hearing what is being said if it is read out, and it can be forwarded, and everybody is clear.
- Keep an offer log i.e. the time that each party makes an offer and a brief note of the key terms.

After the mediation

11.17 If the mediation settles and you have overrun send them an invoice for your overtime.

If the mediation did not settle:

- Write a joint letter to the solicitors summarising where the mediation got to.
- If offers were made and left on the table summarise those and specify the conditions for acceptance.
- Tell them that you will stay in contact. Either suggest a time that you will call them or invite them to contact you if they think there is anything you can do to bridge the gap.
- Send an invoice for any overtime.

In a nutshell

11.18

- Use checklists.
- Double check everything no matter how many mediations you have done.
- Have your signs to hand in case the sound goes.
- Log on 30 minutes before the start time.

Chapter 12

Communicating online: what do you say, what do you wear?

Communicating online is different from communicating in person. What are the differences? Let's look at these:

Getting your message across when you are on screen

- how do you communicate?
- what do you say?
- how do you use your voice?
- what do you wear?

Getting your message across online

12.01 You communicate by how you look, what you say and how you say it .What is your look?

What do I wear?

12.02 Appearances matter. We are visual beings. As Professor Steven Pinker of Harvard says 'visual things stay put whereas sounds fade.'

How you look will influence how you feel and how others respond to you. When you are communicating, you need to feel confident. Confidence is infectious.

TOP TIP

If you act confident you will feel confident, and others will start to feel confident about you.

Let us start with clothes. Clothes can make you feel confident. This equally true for men and women. The fashion industry knows this and makes a fortune as a result. What you wear also affects your mood and your mood affects what you wear. If you are feeling fed up and down, you wear a hoodie and tracksuit bottoms. If you are feeling energetic and proactive, you dress differently.

What about online?

12.03 Clothes still matter at online mediations. Deciding what to wear on screen causes angst and generates torrents of advice both online and in print. Choice of clothes is a matter of individual taste. It is down to what image you want to project. Bear in mind that on screen you have fewer tools at your disposal for your image management.

We are talking about attending online mediations or mediation-related events such as webinars or conferences. Do you wear formal clothes or not?

At in-person mediations most people, certainly advocates and mediators, dress formally. Not all the men wear waistcoats and ties. But they don't often turn up in shorts and hoodies. Nor do the women. People do online. Wearing T-shirts might make you feel more comfortable. But it will not make others feel more comfortable about you.

As a rule, women dress more formally on screen anyway. Men need to decide whether to wear a jacket and/or tie. Ask yourself if I am mediating in-person do I dress formally or not? If the answer is that you do dress formally when in-person – why be different on screen? After all you are trying to do the same thing whether you are there as a mediator, advocate or client. That is to help the other side take a decision that they didn't want to make when they got up in the morning.

You don't want your clothes to give a negative impression, to generate the wrong vibes or to become a barrier to acceptance. If people react unfavourably to your appearance, they tend to react unfavourably to you and what you say. This can happen at in-person mediations as well. Because of the more limited range of non-verbal cues online the visual cues become even more important on screen.

Your clothes and appearance are most influential at the start of the mediation. We all know that first impressions matter. Sitting there in a pizza-stained T-shirt might make you look like a tech bro but is that what the other participants at the mediation are expecting to see? If it is not, then think twice. Defying people's expectations makes them feel uncomfortable.

The dress code varies.

- Clients have the most latitude in deciding what to wear.
- Advocates have slightly less.
- Mediators have very little. Not many mediators just turn up in hoodies and T-shirts to mediations even in the most cutting-edge dynamic youthful industry disputes.

Plenty of research shows that people accept someone has authority if they dress authoritatively, which means a suit and tie for men.* They can also appear easier to talk to and more capable. People standing by the road waiting for the traffic like to change are more likely to cross on red when they follow a man in a suit than someone who is dressed in a hoodie.

*Furnham, Chan and Wilson. J Appl Soc Psychol.2013 Sep, 43(9) 1838-1850

As a mediator you want to display confidence and competence. How you are dressed can help you do that. The same with advocates. They also need to build credibility with the mediator and the other side. So do their clients. Will your credibility be undermined if you turn up in a hoody? Some people react negatively. They think you are not taking the occasion seriously. It is back to this point: would you turn up dressed like this if you were meeting in person? If you wouldn't, why do it online?

In the early days of online mediation and court appearances LinkedIn was awash with images of people wearing jackets and ties with flip-flops and shorts. All highly amusing. But be careful when you are online and during the mediation you have to stand up when the doorbell rings or you spill your coffee. Your carefully curated image with your formal top half will be undermined by your hairy knees and toenails or pyjama bottoms and fluffy slippers.

TOP TIP

Always check how you look on screen before you start the mediation session. Both when standing and sitting.

So yes, dress to impress but don't overdo it. In fact, it is harder to overdo the logos and designer labels online than it is in person. The trustee in bankruptcy who turned up at in-person mediation wearing a mink stole did not create a favourable impression. Even her own counsel advised her to take it off when having a joint session with the bankrupt's wife who was facing losing her home.

The impact of the mink stole would have been lost on the screen. As discussed in **Chapter 9**, online mediation is a more level playing field than in-person. Power imbalances are alleviated.

ALERT

Microphones are very sensitive. Be careful about wearing clunky bracelets or cufflinks near your keyboard.

Bill Wood, a well-known and successful commercial mediator, posted on LinkedIn about how at one of his mediations someone asked what the jingling noise was. Eventually they worked out it was the brass buttons on Bill's blazer. He put tape over the buttons. Problem solved.

Not quite – when he attended an in-person mediation wearing the same blazer one of the clients asked why he had tape over his buttons.

TOP TIP

- Avoid blazers and brass buttons at all times. For acoustic and aesthetic reasons.

Smiles

12.04

'A smile is the best make up any girl can wear' (Marilyn Monroe)

'Peace begins with a smile.' (Mother Teresa)

Two very different women who were world leaders in their chosen fields. And both advocate smiling.

The importance of smiling in human communication cannot be overestimated. Please see 8.038.05 in my book *Mediation Behaviour*.

In online communication where you focus on people's faces smiling is even more important. Remember the three types of smile:

- Genuine smile or Duchenne smile. You can tell this when the mouth curls and the skin crinkles around the eyes.
- The fake smile or 'say cheese' smile. Try and avoid in case it is misinterpreted as sarcasm.
- The Mona Lisa smile. That's the enigmatic half smile that we've all seen. Very useful as a resting state.

Smiling energises you and others. It lightens and brightens the mood. All very useful things to be doing at Mediation. Look at yourself in the mirror. **Practise** your smiles. Work out your best look and adopt it.

TOP TIP

- Smile when talking on the phone.
- People can hear the smile in your voice. No it's not just a cliché. Try it you'll see that it was true.

What about how you sound?

Voice

12.05 Sounds – the voice- are just as important as the visuals. You need to concentrate on your own and other people's.

OLM includes telephone mediations as well as AV mediations as explained in **Chapter 3**.

Telephone

12.06 When speaking on the phone you can't rely upon your body language as much to convey your message. Nor can you observe others' body language to help you relate to what they are saying.

Relying on your voice alone without any input from body language means you have to work harder. The core elements of phone conversations are:

- Time
- Tone of voice
- Empathy/Emotion
- Rate of speaking
- Choice of words

This is sometimes referred to as paralanguage.

ALERT

Be careful not be confused by the Mehrabian Myth. Professor Albert Mehrabian pioneered research into the relative importance of verbal and non-verbal messages His two main conclusions were:

1 Any face-to-face communication has three elements:

- words
- tone of voice (tonality)
- non-verbal behaviour, eg facial expressions.

2 Non-verbal elements are particularly important for communicating feelings and attitudes. They are especially important if there is a discrepancy with what is being said, ie the words spoken, and the non-verbal behaviour or the tone of voice. When this happens, the listener is more likely to believe the tonality and non-verbal behaviour.

In these circumstances Mehrabian concluded that:

- 55% of the impact is non-verbal or visual.
- 38% of the impact is vocal, such as voice tone and inflection.
- 7% of the impact is verbal, ie the meaning of the words actually used.

This gave rise to the Mehrabian Myth that the 7/38/55 rule applies to all verbal communications. Professor Mehrabian expressly states on his website that this is wrong: 'Unless a communicator is talking about their feelings or attitudes these equations are not applicable' (www.kadji.com/psy).

Further research has shown that when:

- judging the speaker's ability rather than how they were feeling, the verbal element is more important, ie are they competent or not.
- judging whether the speaker was honest or not, the non-verbal element is the most important, ie are they trustworthy or not.

TOP TIP

- Choose your words carefully.
- Make sure that **the way** in which you are expressing yourself syncs with **the words** that you are using.

Rate of speaking

12.07 Your rate of speaking is more important online than when face-to-face.

This doesn't just mean not speaking too fast for people to understand or too slowly to retain their attention. Both are to be avoided. Matching your rate of speaking to that of the other person helps you build rapport. You cannot engage in matching body language. Instead, you can match voice speed and tone.

Tone

12.08 Tone, which includes pitch and inflection, is crucial. Where you put the emphasis in a sentence can radically change its meaning. For example:

- He is asking me to leave?
- He is asking *me* to leave!
- *He* is asking *me* to leave!

So, watch where you put your emphasis.

Empathy

12.09 Persuasion has been defined as a combination of empathy and sincerity. Conveying empathy and sincerity with words is easier when you can also use body language and gesture. On the phone it is more difficult. But smiling can help.

Try this:

12.10 Put a big cheesy grin on your face. Pick up the telephone and pretend to have an angry conversation.

Difficult?

12.11 It cannot be done. Researchers have found that emotions follow facial expressions. In other words, people can make themselves feel happy by smiling.

Observations of skilled telephone negotiators show that they use a lot of facial and hand gestures while speaking on the telephone. They do this even though the listener cannot see them. It still helps them convey their message's emotional content. Less experienced telephone negotiators feel self-conscious doing this. Just practise. Make sure that you do it in front of a mirror. You will feel self-conscious, but you will notice things you have been unaware of. You will improve. You will be more confident.

TOP TIP

- The best mediations are like a conversation.
- Conversations conducted in a deadpan monotone go nowhere.

Matching tone, vocabulary, and tempo matters when speaking on the phone, in person or online. Don't overlook the power of mimicry and matching. Paradoxically this is even more important on screen. This is for two reasons:

1 It is harder to hear each other on most AV systems than it is when you are in the same room in person, even on the phone. The sound quality is just not as good. There is usually a delay between what the speaker says and what the listeners hear (see **Chapter 8**).

2 Focus on articulating more clearly. Speak more slowly and pause. Conversations can be more stilted and less free flowing. So, make your words count. Think more about the order of your words. Use fewer of them. Structure what you say better.

TOP TIP

- Be a little more deliberate. It is not as easy as you may think. Practise.
- Record yourself on Zoom. See how you look and sound.
- Remember the Three Ss: Speak shortly, slowly and sweetly (with a smile).

Listening

12.12 Effective talking requires effort. So does effective listening. Your main source of information about what people are thinking is what they are saying and how they say it. Online you have much less non-verbal information. Really concentrate. You need to process properly what people are saying to you.

Take more frequent and longer breaks in between caucus sessions. Work through what is being said. Look for word patterns. Recall the hesitations, repetitions, and deviations. Check what was said and what was not said.

Ask yourself what was the tone? Was it flat and monotone or lively and upbeat? Who was doing the talking? What are other members of the team doing? When people are in their own home they behave differently from when they are in someone else's office. They feel that they can be more themselves.

12.13 *Communicating online: what do you say, what do you wear?*

Clients sometimes leave their barrister to do all the talking. They turn side on and tune out so that you cannot see their face, just their profile. They don't do this as much when you are all physically in the same room. If this happens, tell them that you cannot see or hear them very well. Suggest that they move the camera.

If the client is in profile, it is harder for you to look at them and direct your question to them. If you ask a question you need to preface it with: 'Can I ask Simon/Jane?' Otherwise, their advocate will assume you are talking to them and answer for their client.

Turn taking

12.13 You can improve your listening skills by better turn taking. In other words wait until someone has finished before you start talking. Don't interrupt or talk over people.

Of course in a lively fast-flowing conversation people do chip in as soon as they have something to add. Online this is much more difficult to cope with. So, remember to make sure that the person who is speaking has actually finished before you start speaking.

Not only does turn taking increase the chances of you hearing what is being said, it also shows respect. People do not like being cut off before they have finished.

People have learned this lesson from mediating online and turn taking has improved. Some of this has carried over to in-person mediations but not as much as maybe it should have done.

Prepare your voice

12.14 There are three types of voice.

- The head voice. High pitched and can be jerky. A good area of the voice to excite an audience into taking action. Often used by children who are trying to distract adults. It can sound nagging and weak.
- The heart or chest voice. This resonates and is warm.
- The stomach or warrior voice. This is the voice of credibility. This area of the voice builds status and authority and will make your audience feel calm and secure.

If your breathing pattern is vertical your breath is trapped. If your pattern is horizontal, it engages the diaphragm. This will release your breath and you will appear calmer and more open and direct.

There are exercises that you can do to free up your voice before you do any sort of advocacy even if it's just walking into a drinks reception.

CHECKLIST FOR VOICE WARM UP

12.15 Try this, if you only have few moments:

- Breathe in on count of four.
- Hold your breath on count of four.
- Breathe out on count of four.

Do this four times. You will feel better.

If you cannot be overheard:

- Hum to yourself-making a MMM sound for 30 seconds. Repeat.
- Do the same making a ZZZ sound.

If you cannot be seen:

- Raise and drop your shoulders slowly three times.

Try it now. There you are. You're ready to go!

TOP TIP

- Whether standing or sitting, always lean forward before you speak. Take an inward breath through a gap between your teeth, not through your nose. This engages your audience.
- When speaking, always go to the end of the line. Most people fall away at the end of the line. Remember that in most sentences the most important information is in the last three or four words.
- Don't drop your eye line. Maintain eye contact.
- If you ask a question, rhetorical or not, pause. Let it sink in.

Posture

12.16 You send a message by the way that you hold yourself. Relaxed, confident and approachable is how you want people to see you. Posture matters, whether you are standing or sitting. If online, you will be sitting most of the time. But remember you can stand – buy an adjustable stand for your laptop or an adjustable desk. I use the Fellowes Lotus LT Height Adjustable Sit Stand Desk Convertor with Gas Spring.

12.17 *Communicating online: what do you say, what do you wear?*

When standing

12.17 Try this:

- *Knees*: Unlock your knees. Flex them slightly. You will feel more relaxed.
- *Feet*: Put your weight on the balls of your feet not on your heels.

  Never stand pigeon-toed.
- *Head*: Hold your head level. Most of us tend to lower it. Imagine a thread running from the middle of the crown of your head, through the back of your neck and down your spine to its base. Stand so the Golden Thread is straight.
- *Hands and arms*: Arms by your side if you are not holding anything. Never cross your hands in front of your genitals.
- Posture: Have a look at Professor Amy Cundy's TED Talk. She explains the science behind the Power Pose. It's not nearly as cheesy as it sounds. And it works. Perhaps surprisingly but it does.

And always smile. Always. Smiling relaxes and energises you. People respond to a smile. You are on your way (see **12.04**).

Resource: To learn more about this go to http://www.sylviacohencommunication.com/about/ *and watch the videos.*

When seated

12.18 Maintaining a good posture is harder when sitting down. Try this:

1 Sit on the edge of your chair. This forces your back to engage and keep your posture upright.

2 Sitting forward communicates engagement.

3 At all times put both feet flat on the floor. Don't cross your legs or ankles. Or wrap them around the chair.

4 Be careful about swivel chairs. Fixed ones are a safer bet. If you do use a swivel double check the lock is on.

5 Sit up straight in your chair. Make sure your back is straight. Imagine a string pulling you forward from your navel. Sit on the front of your seat bones.

6 Make sure your shoulders are back and down. Don't hunch forward.

7 Make sure that your head and neck are straight up and down. Nervous speakers often tilt their heads slightly back. They are certainly pulling away from the audience.

8 Square your shoulders to the screen.

9 'Untense' yourself. Researchers who studied presidential debates in the US found that 'power and credibility correlate with greater relaxation and poise'.

10 Remember to use open not closed body language.

   a Open body language uses postures like uncrossed arms, uncrossed legs and relaxed visible arms and hands.

b Closed body language has crossed arms and legs, a hunched over posture and hands in pockets or behind your back.

c Closed body language does not enhance your credibility. You appear defensive and insecure.

11 Avoid self-focused gestures like touching your hair or face. These suggest that you are more interested in how you look than? what you are saying.

12 Keep your hands on the table or on your lap unless you are using them to gesture. Keeping your hands still is much harder than it appears. Practise it.

13 Increase your hand gestures. They may not be able to see your hand gestures, but they will affect body language and the set of your shoulders.

14 Use eye contact as you would if you were standing. Make a connection with everybody on screen.

15 Breathe fully and deeply. Your upright posture helps this.

16 Move if you can. Even sitting in a chair, you can turn your upper body to face people, lean into make a point.

17 The key is to know where your camera is and look directly at it.

You can stand at mediations. Adjust your monitor so that the camera remains as high-level. Usually, the viewers cannot tell whether you are sitting or standing. Just remember to change the angles.

Presenting yourself

12.19 The key is to appear confident. As we saw in the section on clothes people are attracted to people who appear confident. Nervousness unsettles them.

What do you do? First, sort out your breathing. Why? To demonstrate confidence.

> **TOP TIP**
>
> - Next time you are in a group of people look at their pattern of breathing.
> - The most dominant people in a group have the slowest breathing patterns.

Get rid of tension

12.20 Of course, you might be nervous, but tension is the first thing that people notice about you. They pick up on it within the first 15 seconds or so. They can lose their confidence in you straightaway if you appear nervous and tense. Also, when you are tense you talk faster and lose clarity.

Any audience responds to your breathing, language, tonality and resonance. It doesn't matter if you are talking to a room of 20, 200 or just to one person.

TOP TIP

- Use short sentences.
- Use punctuation when you speak.
- Avoid rambling sentences.
- Don't join sentences together with 'and'.
- Pause between sentences. This adds impact. It helps people stay engaged.
- Make sure that your facial expressions sync with what you are saying and with your body posture.

In a nutshell

12.21

- Speak more slowly and clearly.
- Have shorter sessions.
- Your voice – its tonality and inflexion is more imporatnt online.
- Have more recaps.

Appendix 2

Breathing exercises

1 Stretch and breath: voice modifications

12.20 Start your routine by spending a couple of minutes in the Golden String position. Imagine that there is a golden string running vertically from the crown of your head down through your neck, and spine to your coccyx.

Focus on having:

- Your feet grounded.
- Your pelvis balanced.
- Your spine elongated.
- Your head balanced on the neck.
- Start to think of a small gap developing between your teeth.

Staying in that position start to release your jaw:

- Gentle pitter-patter your face with your fingertips.
- Then massage your face gently with your fingertips.
- Then stroke the muscles of the jaw (the challenge here is to keep the release in the jaw after the stroke).

Now do shoulder releases. Lift your shoulders up and let them drop.

- Forward release,
- Back release,
- Centre release

2 Twisting side to side with your hands on your hips

12.21 Change the position of your hands so that they are on the bottom of the ribcage. Make sure you are doing this with dropped and relaxed shoulders.

As you breathe in and twist feel the ribcage expanding. As you breathe out and twist feel the ribcage shrinking.

Incorporate this with the movement (don't try and make anything happen just be aware of the movement starting to get bigger in the ribs and the breath getting slightly longer).

12.22

3 Stretching the right hand up and bending slightly over to the left (so that there is a stretch on the right side of the body)

12.22 This position actually stretches and opens up the ribcage.

1st Stretch. Breathe in as you gently rub around the ribcage to wake it up. Continue rubbing as you breathe out.

Be aware of the movement in the ribcage (repeat on the other side.)

2nd Stretch. On the inward breath pat around the ribcage reaching around as much of the ribcage as possible. Do the same on the outward breath. Repeat on the other side.

3rd Stretch. Repeat above. This time release the breath on ***Sh*** sound keeping the jaw released. Repeat on the other side.

4 Stretching up to the ceiling

12.23 Do this with the head balanced on the neck, eye line level and forward and the jaw released.

1 Stretch up. Notice the breath moving to the tummy on the inward breath and the tummy contracting on the outward breath.

2 Stretch up and breathe into the tummy. Release the breath on a ***shhhh*** sound. (Do as ??is comfortable).

3 Repeat stretch. Do the ***shhh*** sound in three stages so ***Sh Sh shhh*** on one breath. Do this 2–5 times.

4 When you feel ready to move on to sequential counting 1,12,123,1234. Make sure that your jaw stays released.

5 Direct the spoken numbers to the farthest point in the room or to a point outside the window.

5 Spinal rolls against a wall to warm up the voice (if you have the time and space)

12.24

- Stand with your back against the wall.
- Feet hip width apart.
- Breathe in.

As you breathe out (go down)

1 Bring the chin to the chest.

2 Flop your shoulders forward.

3 Peel the top part of your spine off the wall.

As you breathe in (come back up):

1 Feel each vertebra of the spine make contact with the wall as you stack the spine back up.

2 Let the shoulders fall back into their sockets.

3 Head comes up last balanced on the neck.

Repeat this exercise.

- 7 times breathing out on the ***S*** sound.
- 7 times on a ***Z***.
- 7 times humming on the ***Mmm*** sound (keep your jaw and throat relaxed!).

Intone part of your speech or the days of the week. Speak what you have intoned. Notice the difference in your voice. For more help go to http://www.sylviacohencommunication.com/.

Chapter 13

Agreements

Mediation

13.01 Your standard terms need to be amended for online mediations. Below is a template of a mediation agreement for online mediation. Most of the clauses are the same for an in-person mediation.

Where something is different because it is an online mediation there is a commentary highlighting it. For a full commentary see **Chapter 16** in my book *Mediation Advocacy.*

Mediation Agreement Online: Mediation [*Reference number*]

13.02 THE FOLLOWING PARTIES:

1. XXXX represented by xxxxx
2. XXXX represented by xxxxx

the Parties hereby agree to appoint [*Insert Name*] to be the mediator in the online mediation of the Dispute on the following terms and conditions:

Definitions

13.03

The Parties:	**The parties named above.**
The Mediator:	
The Mediation Date:	
The Venue:	**Online**
Scheduled Period:	**4/8 hours**
Start Time:	**am**
The Deposit:	£
The Additional Hourly Rate:	£
The Agreement:	**This agreement.**
The Dispute:	**The matters in dispute as defined in clause 1.3**

1 Mediation procedures

13.04

1.1 The online mediation shall be held and conducted according to the Agreement.

1.2 The Mediator's standard Terms and Conditions as specified on the Mediator's website [insert website address] are incorporated into the Agreement. Where there is any conflict between them and the Agreement, the terms of the Agreement shall prevail.

1.3 The Dispute shall mean [all matters in dispute between the Parties arising out of]

1.4 Any settlement reached in the Mediation will not be legally binding until it has been reduced to writing and signed by or on behalf of the Parties. For the purpose of the Agreement, it shall be sufficient if

1.4.1 The Parties print out a copy of the settlement agreement sign it and scan it back to each other and the Mediator.

Or

1.4.2 The Parties sign the settlement agreement using an electronic signature.

Or

1.4.3 The Parties confirm by email to which the settlement agreement is attached that the email may be accepted as their signature.

1.5 For the avoidance of doubt, it is not necessary for all the Parties to sign the same document. They can each sign a copy of the settlement agreement and exchange their signed parts.

Commentary

13.05 Clauses 1.4–1.5 are included to address the problems of obtaining signatures. You need signatures for both the mediation agreement and the settlement agreement.

The mediation agreement provides that there is no legally binding settlement until the settlement document has been signed by or on behalf of all parties. It would be very unwise for a mediator to commence the mediation unless all attendees attending either in person or online had signed the mediation agreement.

Clauses 1.4–1.5 taken together provide that the parties may sign the settlement agreement in 1 of 3 ways:

- with a physical signature and the signature page is scanned back,
- with an electronic signature, or
- by confirmatory email attached to the agreement.

They do not have to sign the same copy of the settlement agreement.

2 Mediator

13.06

2.1 The Parties agree that [Insert name] will be the Mediator.

2.2 The Parties confirm that they shall not bring any claim against the Mediator for breach of contract, breach of duty or negligence unless the Mediator has acted dishonestly towards them

Commentary

13.07

- Whether or not mediators should include a limitation/exclusion of liability clause in their mediation agreements is a recurrent topic amongst mediators.

Some take the view that:

- they are probably unenforceable.
- the risk is low.
- not having one is a useful selling point.

Others take the more traditional view that it is better to have an agreement clause available about whether or not liabilities are excluded. Everybody is becoming more litigious and that includes clients at mediations.

> **TOP TIP**
>
> If you prefer not to include a limitation of liability clause check with your professional indemnity insurers that they are content.

3 Mediation fees

13.08

3.1 All sums referred to in this Agreement are exclusive of Value Added Tax.

3.2 The Mediation Fee consists of the Deposit and if the Mediation exceeds the Scheduled Period the additional sum calculated at the Additional Hourly Rate for any time up to 12 midnight and at the rate of £900 for each hour (or part thereof) after then.

3.3 The Deposit includes all preparation and travel time and expense, unless otherwise stipulated.

3.4 Invoices are payable on the date shown on the invoice and in any event before the date of the Mediation.

3.5 The Mediation Fee shall be borne equally between the Parties, unless as a result of a mediated settlement it is agreed otherwise. This provision shall not disentitle any Party from recovering the costs of the Mediation in any subsequent assessment of costs whether or not there has been a concluded settlement of the Dispute.

3.6 The Parties are required to inform the Mediator, either before or during the Mediation, if they do not wish to exceed the Scheduled Period.

3.7 Interest at the prevailing judgment rate will be charged on overdue amounts.

4 Consulting with legal advisors

13.09

4.1 A Party does not require legal representatives to participate in the Mediation but is free to choose whatever representation they wish.

4.2 If a Party is not legally represented, they are advised to obtain independent legal advice before, during and after the Mediation and before finalising any agreement reached at the Mediation.

4.3 The Parties recognise that the Mediator does not offer legal advice or act as a legal advisor for any of the Parties nor will he be obliged to protect any Party's position or rights.

Commentary

13.10 Increasingly parties to a dispute are attending mediations without their legal advisors being present. They are available either on the telephone or by Zoom to be consulted or even to join the mediation later in the day.

Mediators need to make sure that any late joiners sign the mediation agreement.

5 Each of the parties warrants that they will:

13.11

5.1 Tell the Mediator and the other Parties of any person who they wish to participate in the Mediation by any means before the start of the Mediation and confirm at the start of the Mediation who is participating or will participate during the Mediation.

5.2 For the avoidance of doubt this includes any person who may be off-camera or on any shared telephone or computer link.

5.3 Not make any recording any medium, digital, electronic or otherwise, of the Mediation or any part of it without the prior written approval of the Mediator.

5.4 Make themselves available for a private and confidential online session with the Mediator before the Mediation to allow the equipment and system to be used for the Mediation to be tried out.

5.5 Ensure that they will have sufficient computer and/or telephone links available throughout the entire duration of the Mediation.

5.6 Procure that they or their representatives will have full authority to negotiate and enter into a legally binding settlement agreement disposing of the dispute at the Mediation.

Commentary

13.12 Clause 5 is included to address two particular problems that can arise at online Mediations.

Who is participating?

13.13 See **Chapter 11**.

People can be physically present in online mediations but if they are not on camera they may not be seen. They may be participating by video link without necessarily being in the mediation session.

Also, that can be a problem when people login to join the mediation. Surprisingly often their names are not shown accurately on the name tag by their image. They may be using someone else's computer. They may be using a computer they also use for quizzes and have unusual names.

You need to have a list of attendees so that you can check who is coming into the mediation. Should they be admitted at all? If they are, to which room should the mediator be assigning them? You don't want to put the wrong people in the wrong breakout room at the start of the mediation. If you do that, participants will start wondering if you know what you are doing.

Techno angst

13.14 See **Chapter 7**. If the technology doesn't work, then the mediation doesn't work. All participants need to make sure that they have appropriate equipment and bandwidth to be able to participate in the mediation. Of course, supplies fail. Connections go down. You just have to go with it. That is all part of the fun.

Have Plan B ready.

- Transfer to mobile phones.
- Switch to Teams.

6 Private sessions

13.15

6.1 The Mediator may hold private sessions with one Party at a time. These private sessions are designed to improve the Mediator's understanding of the Party's position and to facilitate the Mediator in expressing each Party's viewpoint to the other side.

6.2 Information given to the Mediator in such a session is confidential unless (a) it is in any event publicly available or (b) the Mediator is authorised by that Party to disclose it.

7 Confidentiality

13.16

7.1 The Parties recognise that the Mediation is for the purpose of attempting to achieve a negotiated settlement and as such all information provided during the Mediation is without prejudice and will be inadmissible in any litigation or arbitration of the Dispute unless it would otherwise be admissible. Evidence which is otherwise admissible, shall not be rendered inadmissible as a result of its use in the Mediation.

7.2 The Parties will not issue a witness summons or otherwise require the Mediator or any other person attending the Mediation under the auspices of the Mediator to testify or produce records, notes or any other information or material whatsoever in any future or continuing proceedings.

7.3 All documents, statements, information and other material produced prior to or during the course of the Mediation, save to the extent that these documents have been disclosed already and are in the domain of the litigation, whether in writing or orally, shall be held in confidence by the Parties and shall be used solely for the purposes of the Mediation.

7.4 Any communication by or through the Mediator before the commencement of the Mediation or after its termination shall, unless expressly agreed in writing by the Parties, be subject to the same confidentiality provisions as set out in this Agreement.

7.5 No recording or transcript of any of the sessions whether private or joint sessions during the Mediation shall be made by any means by any person, including the Mediator, without the express prior consent of all the Parties and the Mediator.

7.6 The Parties undertake that they will immediately inform the Mediator if any other person who was not identified as participating in the Mediation at the start of the Mediation joins the Mediation by any means (including but not limited to by an online link) or enters the room in which the Party is situated.

Commentary

13.17 Clause 7.5 can give rise to some debate. It is standard practice in the UK for there to be no recordings of sessions – either of joint sessions or private sessions – at mediations. Being online makes this much more difficult to supervise. That is why the clause is there.

Also, with improved keyboard skills there is a tendency for one member of the legal team, usually the most junior member, to be typing away while meetings are in session. They type so fast it could be a full record tantamount to a transcript. Or it could just be their notes which they prefer to type rather than write by hand. But it is as well to be clear what is happening.

If this happens at a Joint Opening Session the other side may object. If it happens during a private session or caucus the mediator should ask why they are doing this.

Clause 7.6 is included to make sure, as best you can, that any late participants in the mediation are identified. As the mediator you can then make sure that they have signed the mediation agreement.

8 Termination of the mediation

13.18 Either of the Parties or the Mediator shall be entitled, in their absolute discretion, to terminate the Mediation at any time without giving a reason. Any Party wishing to so terminate will give the Mediator not less than 10 minutes notice of their intention to so do.

9 Signature of this agreement

13.19

9.1 This Agreement is to be signed by the instructed legal representative of each Party attending the Mediation (if represented) on behalf of that Party. It shall be sufficient if

9.1.1 The Parties print out a copy of the mediation agreement, sign it and scan it back to each other and the Mediator.

Or

9.1 2 The Parties sign the mediation agreement using an electronic signature.

Or

9.1.3 The Parties confirm by email to which the mediation agreement is attached that the email may be accepted as their signature.

9.1.4 For the avoidance of doubt, it is not necessary for all the Parties to sign the same document. They can each sign a copy of the mediation agreement and exchange their signed parts.

9.2 The legal representative is liable for the Mediation Fees referred to clause 3 in the same way as they are liable for disbursements incurred in the course of litigation.

9.3 The legal representatives warrant they have carried out all necessary checks to verify the identity of their client and any person attending the mediation on behalf of their client.

Commentary

13.20 Clauses 9.1.1–9.1.5 track the language of Clause 1.4–1.5 to cope with the practical difficulties of obtaining everyone's signature if they are physically in different places.

XXX	represented by XXX
Signed	Signed ....
	Representative
Name	Name ....
XXX	represented by XXX
Signed	Signed ....
	Representative
Name	Name ....

Accepted to act as **Mediator** as provided for:

Date..

Signed...................................... ("the Mediator")

Stephen Walker

Observer

Signed ....

Name ....

Other Attendees

.... Name..	Who sign only for the purposes of confirming their agreement to be bound by the provisions of Clause 7.

....

Name..

....

Name..

....

Name..

....

Name..

....

....

....

Settlement Agreements

13.21 As mentioned in **Chapter 8** drafting and signing the mediation agreement takes twice as long online as it does in person. Instead of the drafters sitting next to each other and marking up the amendments as they agree them they are emailed backwards and forwards. Eventually common sense breaks out and they have a meeting either in a breakout room or on the telephone to sort out any remaining issues – screen sharing can be useful. The mediator should be asked to enable it.

It saves a lot of time if amendments are made in track change and the various versions are numbered V1, V2 etc.

The settlement terms in a settlement reached online are the same as when reached in person. For a full explanation of settlement agreements please see Chapter 14 of my book *Mediation Advocacy*

Draft a template on screen. Complete it as far as you can before the mediation. Save it. Enter the details of the settlement as you reach agreement.

Don't leave it until the end of the negotiation to start drafting.

Drafting as you go saves time and energy. It also helps to avoid overlooking points of detail. As we all know, when you write something down you think more closely and you can see where the devils are hiding as the details emerge.

Resource: There is a wide range of templates available online. The PLC settlement agreement has become a standard. The latest CEDR suite of documents issued in February 2023 is very helpful. cedr.com>Commercial Mediation.

Also see the short form produced by ChatGPT in **Chapter 5** and the consumer dispute template in **Chapter 3.**

Chapter 14

Looking after yourself – wellbeing

In this chapter you will learn:

- What are the personal challenges of WFH and OLM.
- How to cope with them.
- How to manage stress
- How to manage energy

Strain

14.01 Online working means you are connected 24/7. WFH has blurred work/life boundaries. Mediators have found this to be less of a problem because they have always tended to work from home. But you still have to watch out. You will receive emails outside your normal working hours. Do you respond or wait until 09.00 the next day?

Watch out for overload. As a rule of thumb, for every day spent mediating there is another day spent on ancillary activity – travelling, preparing, and administration. In fact, for each day you spend mediating there could be two other days: one on ancillary activities and the other in recuperation.

Some mediators limit themselves to two mediations a week. Others will never ever mediate back-to-back no matter what the circumstances. As well as saving time travelling when mediating online you also save spend energy. Mediators are keen on energy conservation. Mediating is tiring. As a mediator you are involved in the whole process for the whole day. You need to stay focused, remember what people have said and plan the next steps. On top of this, you absorb other people's stress and anxiety. You need to recover.

Be aware of burnout. Your reputation will suffer if you start nodding off at mediations or looked worn out before you start. Burnout is easier to avoid online.

De-stress

Be kind!

14.02 Be kinder to others and be kind to ourselves. This is the slogan of the moment.

How does it apply to online mediations?

We are not talking about a life plan. We are talking about a day plan for online mediation. If it is all getting a bit too much and you need to de-stress quickly try

- A hug. Do you have someone to hug? If you do, ask them for one.
- At online mediations you are usually on your own so give yourself a hug. This releases oxytocin and will make you feel better. It is amazing how it works. But it does.
- Stroking your arms, face, hands or feet. According to Jacqueline Carson, a clinical psychotherapist, stroking 'is a particularly good way of soothing yourself because it calms the reflexes in your body.'
- A head massage. This is a great stress reliever. Psychologists at the University of Konstanz in Germany found that a 10-minute head massage helps the body to tap into its parasympathetic resting state. Don't worry if you don't have a head masseuse on tap. Most of us don't.
- Resting your head on the table for 10 minutes is an effective alternative to a massage.

Breathing

14.03 (See **Chapter 12**.)

Of course, you want to make sure that you keep breathing. Just as important is how you breathe. Recall the advice in **Chapter 12** on how to communicate online and the importance of breathing properly and voice production.

Breathing properly also helps your mood and energy levels. If you start to feel stressed just start breathing deeply.

Try this.

- breathe in on the count of seven.
- hold for the count of seven.
- breathe out on for a count of 11.

What you are doing is breathing from your belly, filling your lungs and emptying your lungs of stale air. This is important because when we meet a stressful situation our flight, fight or freeze response is triggered. We start taking rapid shallow breaths and even without realising it hold our breath. Breathing from the stomach helps prevent your shoulders from rising and falling which signals stress.

Just to calm your nervous system try what psychotherapist Lee Pycroft recommends: 'a psychological sigh – a long inhalation followed by short inhalation then a long exhalation.

This works whether you are under acute stress, eg when someone's just called you a liar, or chronic stress when you are getting tired because of the constant passive aggression of one of the lawyers. Or the Internet connection keeps going down! Remember **Chapter 11**.

ALERT

Always bear in mind that as mediator your job is to remain the calm centre of the storm.

Everybody else may be getting overexcited, even out of control and abusive but you are there to lead them along the winding, bumpy, uphill path to the calm plateau of settlement.

TOP TIP

- Don't be afraid to use the mute button. Participants can see that you have muted someone. It shows that you are directing the process. That is what they paid you for. The muted person may object but they will probably realise that they are overstepping the mark and rarely object to being muted.
- If they do, your response will be: 'I'm sorry if you feel like that. But we did agree that one person at a time talks, and we wouldn't interrupt each other.'

Sleep

14.04 We are bombarded with the message: have more and better sleep. Poor sleep is always a health disbenefit. So, let yourself sleep properly. Not during the mediation perhaps but before it.

I find that I always awake extra early when I have a mediation. I have also probably been thinking about it in my dreams without realising it. Sometimes I do realise it and recall missed trains and lost bags. Anyway, I wake up with an extra spring in my step on the day of a mediation.

You don't want to look and feel tired. Yor job is to bring energy and direction to the process. That is what people hire you to do. They can start to flag. You can't. You have to generate settlement momentum and keep it going (see the advice on appearance in **Chapter 12**).

Getting a good night's sleep

14.05 Search for tips on how to have a good night's sleep and you will be overwhelmed. What they boil down to is:

- Keep to a regular routine.
- Wind down before you go to sleep. 30 minutes minimum.
- Turn off all bright lights including phones and iPads.

- Keep your room cool rather than warm.
- Don't go to bed hungry or hangry.
- Avoid booze. Have a milky drink instead.

Not had a good night sleep before a mediation?

14.06 Don't panic.

- Get up as soon as the alarm goes. Get as much natural light as early as you can. If you cannot go for a walk just sit by the window. The light will tell your body that it is time to wake up.
- Have something to eat within 30 to 60 minutes of getting up. This tells your body that it is daytime. Get active. This helps regulate your blood sugar for the whole day.
- Stay away from sugary snacks. Instead go for nuts, veg sticks, apple or a tablespoon full of peanut butter. But watch the nuts – they are full of calories.
- Don't use caffeine as a crutch. The big problem about caffeine is that it is addictive. It does perk you up. But the more you drink the more you need to drink to get the same lift. So, restrict it to when you really need it – first thing in the morning and early afternoon. Otherwise drink tea or water. Dehydration is far more of a problem than people realise. Keeping properly hydrated will work wonders. It: keeps your energy levels up, stops you eating too much, and improves your mood. Fantastic stuff, H_2O.

TOP TIP

- Keep a bottle of water on your desk when mediating online.
- Use one with a valve.
- Keyboards don't suffer from dehydration. They don't like water or indeed any liquid.

Food

14.07 Food and drink influence our behaviour. We all know that. Mediators see how emotional and energy levels fluctuate during the mediation day. And particularly they see how people who feel hungry react negatively.

Studies suggest that low blood sugar levels increase impulsivity, anger and aggression. The reason seems to be ego depletion which makes us unable to exercise self-regulation and self-control. When our blood glucose levels are low, we are more likely to be aggressive and angry.

The original research has, of course, been criticised but we know from our own experience that people who are hungry tend to be less energetic and optimistic and more irritable and unfocused. We know it is because we feel it ourselves.

Therefore, don't let people become hangry at mediations. This applies as much online as in person.

Lunch

- The big advantage of mediating online if you are doing it from your own venue – your own office or house – is you can dictate what you eat and when.
- As a mediator I have never met much resistance when suggesting breaks for something to eat and drink during the day. Most people are too polite to ask about lunch or they don't want interrupt the process. They are grateful for the break. Most people return refreshed. See **Chapter 11**.
- At lunch avoid processed and sugary foods. Don't eat too much. Otherwise, you are likely to have a sugar crash which will make you feel even more tired. Try avocados, hummus, fish, nuts and seeds. They are rich in protein.

One of the great difficulties of WFH and conducting online mediation from home is that although your screen is nearby, so is the fridge.

We all know what calories are. They are those things which if you take in too many you put on weight, and if you don't take in enough you have no energy. In fact, they are units of measure of food energy.

Working online increases that tendency to take in too many. So, think about calorie offset. You will be alarmed when you realise how many calories there are in foods that we have become habituated to eating when mediating.

CHECKLIST

14.08	**Calories**
3 Digestive biscuits – the UK's favourite	213
3 chocolate Hobnobs	279
2 rows of Green and Blacks 70% dark chocolate	208
Two KitKat fingers	106
Bag of Walkers ready salted crisps	171
2 handfuls of cheese Doritos	180
One banana	105
Milky coffee machine coffee	123
Slice of toast with marmite and butter	99
Bowl of chicken soup	168
Four tablespoonfuls of hummus and carrot sticks	108
A handful of almonds	68

Sandwiches

Mediation – in person or online – without sandwiches is practically impossible.

Watch them for calories. White sliced bread, submarine rolls or white baguettes are made from highly processed white flour. This causes blood sugar to shoot up, spike and then crash.

According to researchers at the University of Birmingham.

- A triple pack sandwich has an average of 657 calories
- Filled baguettes have an average of 528 calories
- A cheese and pickle sandwich on artisan bread can provide the equivalent of more than three teaspoons of sugar.

What are good ideas for sandwiches? This is of course a matter of personal taste – some suggestions are:

- Mozzarella cheese, avocado and tomato on rye
- Houmous and salad wrap
- Egg mayo with cress
- Smoked salmon and cream cheese bagel
- Tuna mayonnaise with sweetcorn
- Cheese and tomato toastie
- Coronation chicken.

Salad days

If you can, go for a salad – tuna, egg, cheese or couscous are good bets.

Power naps

14.09 One of the secret benefits of online mediation is the power nap. Especially after lunch. Absolute maximum 20 minutes. Any longer and you end up in a deep sleep and wake feeling worse, with sleep inertia.

Just 5–10 minutes works wonders. Set your alarm during a lunch break.

Zoomed out?

14.10 (See **Chapter 7**.)

Does Zoom make you more tired? Is there such a thing as 'Zoom fatigue'? During lockdown plenty of people posted about feeling tired working on screen.

This was reinforced by being at home – often alone, and with the general worry about catching Covid and not being able to get out. Things have changed. We have grown more used to working online and on Zoom. There are fewer complaints being posted now. So it looks as though the problem has reduced but has it gone away? Not entirely.

Engaging with people in-person at any sort of meeting can be tiring. We know that. So can engaging with people online. The big difference is the 'constant gaze'. An interesting finding from research about people working on screen is that when we are on video, we tend to spend most of the time gazing at our own face. If you are looking at the camera, as I advise, you will not be looking at yourself rather than at the faces of the other participants. You won't be looking at anyone i.e. you won't be seeing their faces but they will be seeing you looking directly at them. You need to practise scanning the screen (see **Chapter 12**).

As explained in **Chapter 12** on Communicating in online mediations, you need to look at the camera. You have to pay more attention. During an in-person meeting you don't keep uninterrupted eye contact. You look away, glance out of the window or at the ceiling. That is not seen as rude. Looking away from the screen can be interpreted as not paying attention. So, there are fewer visual breaks. That can make us tired. Which is why you need to take more frequent breaks on Zoom.

People have different social capacities. There is the classic introvert and extrovert distinction. Some people just find it more tiring interacting with others. Extroverts tend to draw energy from interaction. This is true of both in-person and online encounters and applies to mediations just as much as to business meetings or social gatherings.

Some people object to being on camera. They don't like it. Being camera shy is part of their behavioural make up. They are quite happy to participate in the mediation so long as they are not on screen. They can see and hear you, but you can't see them. Of course, they cannot see or hear you if you have your mic and camera switched off.

Does this place you at a disadvantage as the mediator? Does it give them an edge in negotiation? Theoretically it might. In practice it doesn't. Talking to someone who has their camera off is really no different from talking to them on the phone. Except you know that they can see you. So smile (see **12.04**).

We all live more distracted lives. We multitask. We use split screens. We scroll on our phones while watching TV. We look at one screen while doing something else on another screen and so on. Screen switching happens at mediations, but you can control it. One of the advantages of online mediation is leveraging your time. We discuss this in **Chapter 9**.

But switching back and forth from task to task is mentally draining. To see for yourself try this exercise suggested by Professor Mark Williams and Dr Danny Penman authors of '*Deeper Mindfulness*'.

- Time how long it takes you to count to 11.
- Recite 'Mary had a Little Lamb'.

- Try interweaving both: one – Mary – two – had – 3–A' etc.

Thanks to the switching it takes longer.

> **TOP TIP**
>
> - Zoom now has a Hide Self view option.
> - Click View in top right-hand corner.
> - Click on Hide Self view in drop-down menu.

Ten minutes is the magic number

14.11 Ten minutes of deliberate activity or inactivity can boost your mental and physical well-being.

Here are some examples:

- Ten minutes outside in the fresh air in a natural setting. David Attenborough swears by this. He would – he spends a lot of the time looking at animals in the wild.

  Researchers at Cornell University reported in 2020 that as little as ten minutes in a natural setting left people feeling happier with reduced effects of physical and mental stress. So, at mediations go outside for ten minutes.
- If you are feeling anxious, try meditation:
  - Just ten minutes of daily mindful meditation prevents anxious thoughts for the rest of the day. Who says this? Researchers at the University of Waterloo in Canada in their 2017 study.
- If you really want to get your mood up or boost your serotonin levels, try dancing.
- Best to turn off the video and the mic if you do this during an online mediation. At one mediation a participant returned to screen after the lunch break breathing slightly heavily and explained they had done 15 minutes zumba. This is something that you can't really do at in-person mediation.
- High levels of serotonin improve memory, reduces stress and helps develop neural connections. All very valuable at mediation.

Move

14.12 Sitting down has a bad name. Experts constantly exhort us to stand up and not sit too much.

But according to Harvard Professor Daniel Lieberman author of *Exercised: The Science of Physical Activity, Rest and Health* the idea that sitting is inherently bad for you is not true. And he is all in favour of physical exercise. It's good for us.

Humans are born to be lazy. Exercise is unnatural. We must recognise this. Sitting itself is not harmful. It is how you sit those matters. Long periods of inactivity are not good for you. Recall the horror of stories of passengers on long haul flights developing deep vein thrombosis.

Mediators must not just listen actively. They must sit actively. That means move around, fidget and stand up regularly. Standing desks by themselves are not inherently healthier. Using them means that you change your posture, and it is the physical activity of standing up rather than continued standing which is helpful.

James Davies the osteopath and author of *Body* recommends doing repeated calf raises under the desk

- place your feet on the floor, slightly apart,
- right raise and lower your heels as if standing on tiptoe.
- do this for ten repetitions several times during the day to improve circulation and prevent swelling in the lower leg and calf.

TOP TIP

- Don't sit at the screen for hour after hour.
- Stand up and move away from the screen every 30 minutes minimum.
- Try a full body stretch.

If you have the skill, try yoga or tai chi. This will help your flexibility and your memory as well. Of course, if you are in the middle of a constructive private session or joint meeting you can't do this. But as soon as it is over, give yourself a break.

You can do all these things if you are mediating online. Not so easy to do them at in-person mediations.

60 seconds

14.13 Even if you cannot manage ten minutes, one minute walking up and down the stairs or more importantly one minute of meditation will help.

Posture

14.14 Re-read **Chapter 12** about posture.

Watch your back.

- If you are working on a laptop, use an external keyboard and mouse.
- The top of your laptop screen should be at eyelevel and an arm's length away straight ahead of you.

- Buy a laptop stand. Or improvise with some books.
- Having your screen in the correct position will help your back neck and avoid eyestrain.
- Your back has a natural curve. Don't forget that. So, no slouching. Put a cushion behind your lower back top perching right at the front of your chair will encourage your back into the right shape.
- Your shoulders should be directly above your hips. Your full arms and hands should be in a straight line as you type.
- Feet are the flat on the floor or resting on something if you can't reach them. Don't have them dangling in mid-air.
- Standing desks – some people swear by them, others swear at them.

The NHS website has a great five-minute video of exercises nhs.uk/conditions/back-pain/treatment.

Relieving pain

- Keep active. Use the same exercises.
- Try hot and cold compresses – hot water bottle and frozen peas.

Power poses

14.15 Power poses were very popular. Amy Cuddy, a social psychologist, conducted a study at the Harvard Business School. They suggested that adopting a power pose improves people's confidence by

- altering their body chemistry,
- increasing confidence through boosting testosterone
- reducing the stress hormone cortisol.

That study has been attacked but more recent research has suggested that how you hold yourself can influence how you feel and how others react to you.

Poppy Brown, a doctoral researcher in Psychiatry at the University of Oxford, reported in the September 2020 issue of *Behaviour Research and Therapy* that 'we found statistically significant, if small, increases in feelings of power among people who did the power poses compared with those who didn't. What we think might be important for raising confidence is not holding wide, expansive power poses but rather to avoid contractive postures, such as crossing your hands or rounding your shoulders which seem to reduce self-belief and self- assurance.'

Professor Elizabeth Broadbent from the University of Auckland reported that her research shows that: 'Our posture influences our blood pressure and heart rate and how we feel about stress. Upright participants had a healthier pulse pressure overall during and after a stressor test than those who were slumping.'

So, sit up and stand up.

TOP TIP

- Hold a strap behind your back, hands body width apart, palms downwards.
- Inhale and raise the strap keeping your arms straight and avoiding moving forwards.
- Exhale back to the start position.
- Repeat five times.

In a nutshell

14.16

- Sit up and stand up.
- Drink up – choose water.
- Take breaks – and even power naps.
- Breathe from your stomach.
- Avoid too many carbs.
- Get enough sleep.

Part D

Getting mediations in

Chapter 15

Marketing

In this chapter you will learn:

- Why people will do business with you – The Universal Truth.
- Why online marketing is different.
- How to do a simple business plan.

'How do I get mediations?' The question most mediators ask most of the time. Mediation is a crowded marketplace. The 2023 CEDR audit said that there were 17,000 commercial mediations done in the year to September 2022. They concluded that 'there is considerable surplus capacity within the mediation market place'.

Marketing and mediation is a huge subject. I wrote a book about it – *Setting Up in Business as a Mediator.* In this chapter I am not just repeating what I said in that book. There are some overlaps with what we are now discussing – digital mediation and digital marketing. I have given the cross references. Please refer to the book.

What is marketing for mediators?

15.01 It's two words: name recognition. You remember the Texas paradox. 'There are two reasons why you don't get work. People haven't heard of you, or they have.'

The Universal Truth is that people do business with people that they know, like and trust. People cannot trust you if they don't know who you are. They will find it hard to trust you if they don't like you. So, your marketing must be all about getting people to know, like and trust you. In other words, they want to see the two faithful behavioural markers: warmth and competence.

Can people get to know you online? Learn to like and trust you online? Sure, they can. Think of the huge online dating industry. At the start of 2023 the global market size of the online dating industry was US$ 4475.28 million with more than 8000 online dating sites globally. 323 million people worldwide use dating apps. 54% of American online daters said relationships from dating platforms were just as successful as those with people they met through their social circles. So, if people looking for love go online where do you think they will go when looking for a mediator?

15.02 *Marketing*

Marketing is about getting business. As mediators you are selling a service. A service that people cannot see. In Harry Beckwith's phrase: you are selling the invisible. People cannot test it in advance. They cannot taste it, touch it, feel it, try it on or take it for a test drive. They have to take it on trust from you. Trust is the key word.

The first question is:

Have you got what it takes?

Do you have the resources to do what you want to do? The way to find out is to do a business plan. Don't panic. Don't let your brain switch off as you imagine that business plans are what you have to prepare for venture capitalists, loan applications and MBA studies. They are not.

Regards them as aids to clear thinking. Just think of the benefits that a business plan will bring you and then look at **15.03**. If you want more help in drawing up a business plan, see Chapter 7 in my book on *Setting up in Business as a Mediator.*

Benefits of a business plan

15.02 Not having a written business plan is the biggest single cause of business failure. The benefit to you is not the plan itself but the planning. Just drawing one up:

- Sharpens up your thinking.
- Test drives your ideas.
- Gives you a route map.
- Shows you the costs.
- Shows you the time needed.
- Manages your expectations.

The secret is to keep it short and simple

15.03 What resources do I need? How much money, time and energy do I have to invest in my new business?

Money

15.04 If you are new to mediation and want to know how to set up, see **Chapter 7** of my book *Setting up in Business as a Mediator***.** That will tell you what is involved in setting up and how much money you will need.

It can cost you very little. If you are operating from your home, you will not have much extra expense. If mediation is a secondary activity, you will not need much money at all to start with. But if you want it to be a self-sustaining business you need to be clear what your costs will be.

In any case starting a mediation business, even as a quasi-hobby, still costs money.

It is easy to overlook costs that you will incur.

CHECKLIST FOR IN-PERSON MEDIATION COSTS

15.05

Training	This covers your initial training and advanced training as you progress.
Membership fees	For example, to be registered with the Civil Mediation Council or to be a member of a panel of ADR providers.
Subscriptions	Some of the services that you may want to use are not entirely free, for example the premium service for LinkedIn.
Conference fees	As described in **Chapter 12** attending conferences and workshops is a useful way of learning about the mediation market, what your competitors are doing and simply keeping yourself on people's radar. Not many of them are totally free. Even if they are there will be your fares and drinks to buy for people to build better relationships.
Networking expenses	This is linked with attending conferences but you can network in all sorts of circumstances. One of the keys to networking as we discussed in **Chapter 21** is to follow up. This usually means inviting someone you have met for coffee/lunch/drink on another occasion. This will cost you money.
Stationery:	Business cards are essential. They may not be very expensive but it is still an expense. If you decide to have any sort of image of yourself on the card it is best to have a good quality, professionally-taken photograph. You may decide to print marketing material such as leaflets or booklets for distribution and the photograph could be useful for those.
Travel	You will need to travel to events and with any luck you will also need to travel to mediations. Certainly, your observations while you are still in the apprenticeship stage and before you are fully accredited will be unpaid. You may also undertake pro bono work as a volunteer. Sometimes you will be paid your travel expenses; usually you will have to pay yourself.
Mobile phone and broadband:	Your usage will go up. You may have to buy a more expensive plan.

Insurance	Most reputable panels and, certainly the CMC or IMI require their members to have professional indemnity insurance (see para **3.12**).
Room hire	If you decide to stage events yourself to promote your business you may have to pay for room hire as well as refreshments. You need to budget for this. Quite often the mediator is expected to provide premises for the mediation. They often want a neutral venue. You will have a commercial decision to take: do you include the cost of room hire in your fee or charge separately? Certainly, being able to provide room hire at no or very low cost is a definite commercial advantage in attracting mediation business.

Working out your costs is an essential step to calculating how much you will charge (see **Chapter 16** on Pricing).

Online mediation costs

15.06 There are differences for online mediation:

Savings

15.07

- Travel and accommodation.
- Clothes
- Food and drink

Increases

15.08

- Upgrades for LinkedIn, ChatGPT and Hootsuite.
- Upgrades for your chair, external cameras, mics and lights.
- Outside help. Most mediators are not competent at designing websites or fixing computer problems (see **Chapters 18** and **19**).

You will still spend money buying lunches and coffees. Don't give up on in-person events – meeting and greeting, schmoozing and boozing, shaking and faking all still count.

Time

15.09 Mediating online and setting up an online mediation business takes time.

As a minimum you need two hours a week and ideally not less than 20 minutes a day. How do you find the time? You will have to sacrifice some other activities or get up two hours earlier. Ask yourself: 'What would I be doing if I wasn't mediating?'

How long can you wait? Expecting to be mediating twice a month within six months of your accreditation is unrealistic. Adopt a three-year timescale.

Energy

15.10 If you are working full-time or are engaged in another activity, your time and energy will be limited. Perhaps you will only have weekends and the occasional day's leave. Be realistic. You will have other demands on your time (see **Chapter 14**).

In the end marketing is about making a noise. Establishing Name Recognition. Is it better to make a noise yourself? Or do you want someone else to do it for you? Help is available. Mediation panels are now offering marketing services for mediators. For example, Comsgate, Mediator Network, aka The Dispute Resolution Agency.

TOP TIP

To start with, join a panel that provides online mediation. You will have access to their licensed software and be covered by their insurance.

ALERT

The bad news is: Mediation is a hard sell. Mediators cannot understand this. But it is.

Why? Many mediators find this a really difficult question. They cannot understand why litigation and arbitration are easier sells than mediation. To them the positive benefits of mediation are so obvious. See Chapter 13 in my book *Setting up in Business*.

And there is more bad news. Online mediation is an even harder sell. At least among some parts of your potential market. **See Chapter 7.** If you are mediating digitally, you are selling both mediation and online. Here we are dealing with selling digitally.

Why don't people like online? Read **Chapter 7** of this book. What are the advantages of online? Read **Chapter 8** of this book.

15.11 *Marketing*

To help you overcome objections to online mediation see the suggested scripts in **Chapter 20** on Pitching.

In a nutshell

15.11

- Name recognition is the name of the game.
- Get your name out there.
- Make a noise.
- Get busy on social media.
- Give people the chance to know you, like you and trust you.

Chapter 16

Selling yourself

In this chapter you will learn:

- The seven factors that count.
- How to get the best out of LinkedIn.

You want to appoint a mediator. What do you look for? What is important? Over the years in the UK the biannual CEDR Audit has given us insights into the factors that matter. Some of them you can influence. Some you cannot. Here are the ones that you can influence.

If you are selling yourself, you need a clear idea of how you might appeal. How do you do that? Apply RAPPELL.

There are seven things which you can control.

1 R – Reputation

2 A – Availability

3 P – Presence

4 P – Price

5 E – Experience

6 L – LinkedIn

7 L – Lawyers

Reputation

16.01 You have two reputations: your online one and your real world one.

Your online reputation is the image that you promote through your social media presence – where you talk about yourself. Your real-world reputation is the one that you have because people talk about you having met you either online or in person.

If you are mediating online, you will spend more time online promoting yourself. That is the medium. There will be less buying lunches and coffees. Less shaking and faking. Although if you have the chance to do this, do it (see **Chapter 15** on Marketing and **Chapter 21** on Networking).

Brand/reputation: what is the difference?

What is your brand?

16.02 Marketing consultants urge mediators to build their own individual brand.

Tom Peters, the author of *In Search of Excellence*, has been saying this for over 20 years:

> 'Regardless of age, regardless of position, regardless of the business we happen to be in all of us need to understand the importance of branding. We are CEOs of our own companies: *Me Inc.* To be in business today our most important job is to be head marketer of the brand called You.'

Apart from taking responsibilities for your own career what does it mean? Especially, what does it mean to mediators? With limited exceptions, mediators are not well-known. They are not celebrities – although for some it is not for want of trying. You can see how David Beckham, Gwyneth Paltrow or Harry Styles have a brand. But mediators?

Is brand just another word for reputation?

16.03 In a way yes. Although it is probably more. Reputation connotes people's assessment of your competence, standing and experience and whether you are good value for money and easy to work with. Brand encompasses all of these plus something not expressly mentioned in the CEDR factors – personality.

Having a personal brand means:

- People have heard **of** you.
- People have heard you.
- People have heard others talk **about** you.

Plus they know what to expect from you and how you will make them **feel**. Reputation is how people mark you. Brand is how people feel about you. It is a fine distinction, but it does exist, and it is important.

The good news is that thanks to social media personal branding has never been easier.

> **ALERT**
>
> DIY (do it yourself) in social media has the same charms and dangers as DIY in housebuilding or car maintenance. It can be done. It will cost you less initially but take longer, will not be as good and will be expensive to redo. You need to think D I P (do it professionally).

Where do you start? You start with your profile. 'Profile is everything' is the mantra repeated by business development consultants who advise mediators. Profile has two different meanings:

- Profile as a CV
- Profile as a reputation

Profile as a CV

16.04 Compiling a profile/ CV requires thought and time. You are not formally applying for a job so you are not submitting your CV anywhere. But you still need to make sure that if someone wants to know about you, they can find out what they want to know. Where will they do that? On your website (see **Chapter 17**). Post your profile or CV on your website. Remember there will be two versions: text and image (see **Chapter 18** on video).

You can find consultants who make a living writing profiles and CVs for people. For detailed guidance on doing yourself see Chapter 9 in my book *Setting Up in Business*.

Here is a quick guide.

The key things are:

- Have a structure.
- Keep it simple.
- Keep it short.

CHECKLIST FOR PROFILE/CV

16.05

- Name and contact details
- What you are doing now.
- Mediation experience – including qualifications.
- Testimonials, recommendations, mentions in directories etc.

Publications/Videos/Podcasts.

- Other life experience – focus on those parts relevant to mediation.

Be clear about

- How many words you have.
- Who your audience is.
- Answer these four questions.

HOW LONG SHOULD IT BE?

16.06 Shorter is better than longer.

Visitors don't dwell on your website's landing page. Make sure that your key information is 'above the fold', i.e. that part of the screen that can be read without scrolling down.

Refer to other pages for more details. But try keep it to one page.

Remember what it is for:

- to tell people about you.
- to give them good reasons for not rejecting you.
- to show what you can do for them.
- to persuade them that they can trust you to deliver.

WHAT DO I PUT IN IT?

16.07 Keep your CV/profile up to date. Visitors are interested in what you are doing now and what you have done recently. Awards for excellence as an innovative mediator 25 years ago have limited appeal today. So do citations of articles written ten years ago.

Keep personal information to a minimum. People will see what you are like from your photo and video (see **Chapter 18**).

HOW OFTEN DO I UPDATE IT?

16.08 As a rule of thumb, head-hunters/recruiters advise that your CV should be updated every three months as a minimum.

That is hard work. You need to schedule it (see **Chapter 17**).

DO I NEED A PHOTO?

16.09 Yes. No question. We all judge people by their appearance. Sometimes we make snap judgements, which become indelible. Recall what Steven Pinker said about sounds fading and images remaining. You must have a photograph (see **Chapter 12**).

- Make sure that it is high resolution.
- Make sure that it is recent.
- Use a professional photographer if possible. They just take much better images. They are also more skilled at retouching which for most of us is a vital post-production service (see **Chapter 17**).

Stop Press

- Try using AI-generated images. For great examples see Fotor.com (photo editing), Gencraft.com and capcut.com (portrait generator).

Profile as reputation

Directories

16.10 Directories for lawyers, both solicitors and barristers, have existed for many years. In the UK the two best-known are *Chambers and Partners* and the *Legal 500*. Both now include mediators.

Each year they issue their rankings. The *Legal 500* is published in September and *Chambers* in October. There is a detailed application procedure, which can be found on their websites. If you want to apply, you will have to provide examples of mediations, references, and names of referees.

Chambers is longer established and has more researchers and a wider reach of users beyond the legal market. *Legal 500* tends to be more limited to the legal market.

See

chambers.com>legal-rankings>mediators

legal500.com>london>dispute-resolution

Applying for entry into directories is a painstaking business. If you cannot face it, you can hire someone to do it for you. There are various consultants who do this. They charge for their services. Expect to be quoted a day rate of £250–500 plus VAT and to pay for 5-10 days. It is not cheap, but it is quicker and more efficient than doing it yourself and you can allocate the cost to your marketing spend.

If you are only going to apply to one directory *Chambers* is the better bet in the UK, especially if you are not a lawyer-mediator or want to appeal to the non-lawyer market.

Are they worth it?

16.11 The process of applying is tedious and time-consuming. If you are ranked, you are entitled to use a thumbnail image of the publication in your publicity material and to cite quotations from your entry. For an additional fee you can also have a more detailed profile.

Not everyone thinks that they are worth it. In the words of a well-known property disputes lawyer:

> 'I have to say that since they have started charging silly amounts of money to be listed, I will have no part of it. They still seem to list me, though!'

The directories used to be published in hardcopy volumes each year. Now they are online. People do sometimes consult them when looking for mediators. On balance it is better to be in than out.

Availability

16.12 Availability is key. You could be the best mediator in the world but if the mediation must take place on 4 July and you are not available you do not get the job. In short, the more dates you have available the more mediations you will get.

Mediating online makes you more available (see **Chapter 9**).

1 Fewer geographical limitations.

   Mediating online allows you to mediate anywhere in the world. You are not limited by geography. Even if you don't do big ticket international mediations you are available for mediations anywhere in the country. In other words, your market grows.

2 More mediation days.

   Having to travel to mediations eats into your number of available days in a week. Especially if you travel overnight to and/or from the mediation. This makes it difficult to do another mediation the day before or the day after (see **Chapter 8**).

   Online this is more feasible. Also, because online is less tiring not least because of the lack of travel you have more energy (see **Chapter 14**).

3 Online diaries.

   Mediators are divided about putting their diary online. The convenience for anyone looking to see if a mediator is free on a particular date is obvious. They click on your website and look at your diary.

The downsides are:

- You need to keep the diary updated. Constantly. This can be more difficult than you think if you are moving around.
- Although it encourages people to visit your website it doesn't provide a point of personal interaction. Enquiries about mediations split equally between by phone or email. Either way you have a chance to connect with the person making the enquiry. That is not available is they are just checking your website online.
- You can build some data capture on your website. For example, to access your diary they must first enter their email and contact details. Is this off-putting? It depends on how salesy you want website to be (see **Chapter 17**).

Price

How do you charge?

16.13 There are three factors to consider:

- Your cost structure
- The market rates
- What your competitors charge.

Start with

How much do you want to earn?

16.14 Set yourself realistic targets for your milestones – 6 months, 12 months, 24 months and 36 months. Bear in mind:

- the number of mediations that you think that you can complete at these milestones.
- the comparative figures in the latest 2023 CEDR Audit.

In the Audit

- 76% of respondents described themselves as Advanced.
- 16% as Intermediate.
- 8% as Novices.

No of mediations In-person/online	Average earnings £K	Range of earnings £K
20-30	81	20–145
30-50	175	110–390
50+	312	50–660

Most Novices do fewer than four mediations a year. 49% of Advanced mediators do fewer than ten mediations a year.

This information helps set your base figure.

Online

16.15 Whatever your base rate is, reduce it for online mediations. Why? It is a selling point.

Services are cheaper if you buy them online. Your customers, whether they are lawyers or their clients, will expect online mediation to be cheaper. After all you do not incur the same accommodation and travel expenses as you do when mediating in person. You also save travel time.

You may think that this is a self-evident. But many mediators posted their objections on LinkedIn when the idea was first mooted during Lockdown.' 'Should I charge less because I'm doing online mediation? A client has asked me if I will. I have said no. My time and expertise remain the same.' This was a post by one indignant and highly entrepreneurial mediator.

I took a different view. I charged an average of 10-15% less if mediating online. I enjoyed two of my busiest and most profitable years in 2021 and 2022 and the upward trend has continued.

Also, you save time by not having to travel which will leave you with both more hours and more energy to do mediations. Your turnover should increase simply because you are more available. As a well-known, busy mediator who often does two or three mediations a week said. 'It's a lot easier to fit more mediations per week into the diary if all I have to do in the morning is go downstairs and switch on the computer. I have more time and energy to mediate.'

Your turnover should increase and therefore your profits. Be aware that your profitability will be affected by some of the extra expenses of mediating online. You will not have the travel and accommodation costs. But you will have the cost of upgrading your IT (see **Chapter 11**) and buying extra licenses for example for Zoom and DocuSign. These are of course deductible business expenses (see **Chapter 15**).

Presence

16.16 As I said in **Chapter 15**, focus on three things: becoming known, liked and trusted. So how do you do it? Answer: social media and your website. Your posts, tweets and images help people get to know you and hopefully like you. Your website is where they learn to trust you.

As a mediator the two reasons for having a social media presence:

- to achieve name recognition
- to drive people to your website.

Your website is the magic button. It is your shop window. People can see you there and sample the wares. Drive them to your website (see **Chapter 17**). How? Activity on social media. This is the same driving principle as for all mediation marketing, but it is on steroids in the world of digital mediation (see **Chapter 19**).

Experience

16.17

- Use online. Get trained. Feel comfortable. (See **4.22**.)
- Do as many mediations as you can. Regard the first 10–20 mediations as your paid apprenticeship. Even do pro-bono ones. It is all about getting your hours in.
- Observe as many mediations as you can whether real ones or role-play simulated ones. It is all useful experience. It gives you confidence in your own competence. That is what people want to see in a mediator – confidence and competence.

L = LinkedIn

16.18 Pre-Covid, professionals loved LinkedIn – aka 'Facebook for Suits'. It became the accepted platform for professionals who wanted to connect and generate business. Lawyers and mediators loved it – it was not too salesy.

Lockdown changed this. Everybody was posting on LinkedIn. What else was there to do? Many users start to turn away from it. They felt saturated with pictures of dogs, children, cakes and awards.

There was too much over-sharing of irrelevant information. Well, that is what some people thought. Others disagreed and valued the expansion. Now lockdown is over there has been a return to a more pre-Covid use pattern.

The truth is that if you are mediating online, you cannot avoid LinkedIn. You may not like it much, but it is the only game in town. Start taking your first steps on the LinkedIn ladder of engagement.

The ladder of engagement

1. **Liking** other peoples' content.
2. **Sharing that content** with your connections and followers.
3. **Adding your comments** to others that are produced.
4. **Posting questions** to your followers and connections. Polls are a quick way of generating engagement.
5. **Generating your own content** – posts, blogs, updates, tweets and films. To learn about effective blogging see **Chapter 19.** Use them to

TOP TIP

Posting on LinkedIn helps you:

- Get known – putting your name out there.
- Get liked and become familiar; people like what they know.
- Get trusted – establish your credentials as an expert.

Polls

16.19 These are a quick way to generate content. To create a poll from your homepage:

1. Click **Start a post**.
2. Click **Create a poll**.
3. In the **Create a poll** window, type your questions and fill in the options.
   - There is a minimum of two options and a maximum of four options on a poll.
   - Click **+Add option** to add another option.
4. Select the **Poll duration** from the dropdown.
   - The default duration is one week.
5. Click **Next**.

6. Click the **Edit** icon to edit the post.
    - Select who you want to **share the poll with**.
7. You can add more to the post in the **What do you want to talk about?** field (optional).
8. Click **Post**.

The scheduling platform HootSuite provides useful research findings about LinkedIn.

Is there a best time to post on LinkedIn?

16.20 There is no universal best time or best day to post that guarantees high reach and engagement. Audiences are different in different time zones, active on social media at different times during the day.

Some things seem to work for everyone. Like most social media algorithms, LinkedIn's recommendation system prioritises recency — so post when your audience is online. Check your analytics data to help narrow down your followers' activity patterns.

When looking for the best time to post, keep your goals in mind.

- Are you trying to build brand awareness?
- Drive traffic to your site?
- Establish authority?
- Generate leads?

Overall best time to post

16.21 The best overall time to post on LinkedIn is 9:00 am on Tuesdays and Wednesdays.

Weekends are typically the worst days of the week to post. This may be because people regard LinkedIn as a work-related social media platform and therefore avoid it on their days off. If we have days off anymore.

If you plan to post more than once or twice a week look at this breakdown of the best posting times based on what the Hootsuite social team found:

The best times to post on LinkedIn are:

Monday	**11:00 am** between mid-morning and lunchtime.
Tuesday	Between **6:00-8:00 am**. Tends to generate the highest engagement.
Wednesday	**12:00 pm**. Lunch breaks are a good time.
Thursday	**2:00 pm**. Unlike the other days of the week, Thursday sees the highest engagement in the early afternoon.

Friday	**8:00 am**. Posting before work hours results in the best engagement as people seem to check LinkedIn earlier in the day.
Saturday	**4:00-5:00 am**. Posting early helps.
Sunday	**6:00 am**. Early mornings are your best bet on both Saturday and Sunday.

ALERT

These timings are not specifically concerned with Mediation. They are more generic and brand selling something. But use them as a guideline. Try monitor your results. Work out your own timetable.

Three tips for finding your best time to post

16.22 Have these in mind when monitoring your analytics.

Review your top-performing posts

16.23 Your historical performance data provides insights about your audience. Review your top-performing posts and look for trends. Is there a common denominator? Were most of your top posts published on a specific time or day?

LinkedIn has a native analytics tool you can use for free to pin down your top performers (see **Chapter 17**).

Monitor your results

16.24 To find the best time to post on LinkedIn you must monitor. Adjust your posting schedule to track your evolving audience and strategy.

Regularly reviewing your LinkedIn analytics shows whether your strategy is working or if new trends are emerging. Be prepared to and try a new schedule. Change is part of social media!

Be consistent

16.25 Posting consistently has three benefits:

- it keeps your audience engaged.
- it helps you collect even more analytics data. More data means more opportunities to learn about what your audience likes.
- it helps your business become more recognisable on LinkedIn and helps your audience feel more connected to your brand and values.

> **ALERT**
>
> Consistent posting requires a lot of self-discipline and organisation. Check how much time and energy you have available to devote to it. See your business plan (**Chapter 10**).
>
> If you create a connection with your audience, LinkedIn's algorithm notices it and so should your profitability.

L = lawyers

16.26 They are the main source of mediations for mediators. In the UK they are still the gatekeepers for civil and commercial mediations. They are usually pressed for time. So, make sure that your website is easy to find and navigate. Make sure that it is mobile phone friendly (see **Chapter 17**).

Lawyers want to be reassured about the competence of the mediators that they are suggesting to their clients and they draw comfort if you are in a directory.

Lawyers struggle to keep up to date with the flow of information. If you do posts or even newsletters for lawyers, make them short and specific.

> **ALERT**
>
> - Testimonials are gold dust.
> - Don't sell yourself short (see **Chapter 19**).

In a nutshell

16.27

- Keep your charges competitive.
- Be active on LinkedIn.
- Keep your profile and website up to date.
- Generate content that you give away.

Chapter 17

Website

In this chapter you will learn:

- What makes a good website.
- How to have one.
- Most common mistakes.
- How to brief a website designer.
- How to generate content.

The mantra

17.01 Back to the mantra: people do business with people they know, like and trust.

First, they have to find you. Where will they look for you? On the Internet.

Where will they find you? On your website, social media and YouTube.

If you don't have a website, you don't have a digital presence. You have a digital absence. Which means you don't have a business. You need a website.

Google will produce lots of advice about websites. Most of it is generic and aimed at businesses selling something. This chapter is about mediators' websites. Some of the generic advice applies but there are mediator-specific issues to consider.

Any site – Stonehenge, Machu Picchu, Hadrian's Wall – needs visitors. Websites are no different. How do mediators get visitors? From social media. See **Chapter 19.**

TOP TIP

- Integrate your website and your social media activity.
- They are not stand-alones. They are interdependent.

Are you a digital immigrant or a digital native?

17.02 According to Marc Perensky if you were born before 1980 you are a digital immigrant. This next section is for you.

What is a website?

17.03 Let's clear away some of the confusion.

17.04 A website is a collection of web pages hosted on a server and accessible via the internet. Businesses regard them as indispensable and use them to increase credibility, brand awareness and customers.

How do websites work?

17.05 When you enter a web address, or domain name, into your web browser, your computer sends a request to the server that hosts the website. The server sends back the requested web page, together with associated images and other files, to your computer. The time a website takes to load depends on the speed of the server, the quality of your internet connection and the size and complexity of the website.

What are the differences between a website, a web page and a home page?

17.06 A website is a collection of web pages.

A web page is a single page that is part of the website. If you navigate to the home page, you are on a different web page, but still on the same website. The home page is also a web page.

A home page is usually the first page that you will see when visiting a website. It contains an overview of the website with links to the other pages within the website.

A landing page is a web page designed to capture a visitor's attention and persuade them to take a specific action, eg signing up for a newsletter or making a purchase. Landing pages are typically used in online advertising campaigns and are often the first page that visitors see when they visit a website.

What makes websites work is code

17.07 Source code is what you need to have access to (see para **17.34**).

What is a good website?

17.08 As mediators we are interested in why people disagree. Websites incite disagreements. If you have ever been on a committee or a part of a group trying to design a new website, you will know this.

Your goal for any website is that your users do not have to think. Make the process easy, simple and speedy. Visit a website and ask if it does these three things? If yes, it is a long way there.

How do you build a good website?

17.09 These generic tips apply to all websites but there are some mediation-specific websites tips. Work through this list.

Clear purpose

17.10 Be certain what your site is for. And what it is not for.

Two things to bear in mind:

1 Most mediators are sole practitioners in a cottage industry. They don't need a big flashy website.

2 They are not selling product. They are selling themselves. To do that they need a site that builds name recognition and authority to help users know, like and trust them.

What do you want your website to do?

17.11 Websites have different purposes:

- As a digital business card. At its simplest a website is a business card that potential customers can look at on a computer screen which helps you get known. They are sometimes referred to as 'brochureware'. They give the minimum of information about the business in the same way that a business card or a small leaflet brochure does.
- To build your brand. Just by being there when people search for 'mediator '. They may find you. The main aim is not to generate leads or sales directly but to do it indirectly.
- To build relationships. This is usually achieved by blogposts or podcasts being available to viewers.
- To generate leads. Being more direct – getting them to contact you or you them.
- To give information about your services and how to book them. Sometimes this can be done online. More usually the site invites a visitor to contact the business through email or telephone.

- To generate revenue through sales. Some sites can offer other products and services, which can be purchased online, for example books or courses, podcasts and webinars.
- To generate revenue through advertising: although this is common in non-mediation sectors it is rare in mediation.
- To book appointments. More and more mediators offer an online facility for asking about availability and making a mediation booking. For the novice mediator this is probably an optional extra (see **Chapter 16**).

What am I selling?

17.12 You are not really selling mediation You are selling trust. You want people to get to know you, like you and trust you. If they do, they will buy you and mediation from you.

What are visitors to your website looking for? The first thing is an image of you. They want to see you and hear you. Then they can get to know you and decide whether they like you and could trust you.

Ask yourself what image of yourself are you projecting? What message are you sending?

Try this: what words describe how you want someone who has visited your website to feel about you? This is a simple question but not always an easy one to answer.

Do you want to be thought of as:

- authoritative?
- accessible?
- authentic?
- experienced?
- empathetic?
- friendly?
- good value?
- elite?
- specialist?
- generalist?

Distil your answer into two or three words. You now have what will underpin your website. You want to appear authoritative? Don't have an image of yourself on the beach playing with your dog. If you want to be seen as friendly, you might choose that image.

What resources do you have? – blogs and links

17.13 This comes back to the basic business question: how much money time and effort have you got to invest? Most people are overambitious. They think they have more time and energy to update their website that they in fact have.

If you are successful as a mediator and become busy doing mediations every week you will find you have less time and energy. You may have more content but someone has to turn that into blogs and content for you (see **Chapter 19**).

If you are on a mediation panel or a member of a firm or barristers' chambers, you will have a corporate website. You will appear on it. Although, this will not be your own individual website. But at least you will avoid some of the worries that having your own website brings. Do you want to rely on this or have something in your own name? See **Chapter 16**.

> **ALERT**
>
> Mediators' websites are different from retailers' websites. But clarity of purpose is still paramount. How salesy do you want it to be?

Who is my audience?

17.14 Who are you trying to attract? Who is your target audience? Why would they come to your website? You need to appeal to searches – they are looking for something specific – hopefully you and browsers who are just looking.

Mediators have five main audiences:

17.15

1 Lawyers.

2 Non-lawyer advisors such as accountants.

3 Professional clients such as insurers, insolvency practitioners who are regular mediation users.

4 Non-professional clients who may not know anything about mediation at all.

5 Members of the mediation community. For example, your competitors, mediation providers who are looking to recruit new panel members, publishers who are looking for new authors etc.

You need to have something for each of these five groups. You cannot be all things to all people but try to ensure that there is something on your website that each will find useful.

What is my domain name?

17.16 Choosing a domain name, (which is sometimes called a URL – uniform resource locator) is an important marketing decision. Your first problem is availability. Find out whether your name is available by searching one of the registration sites such as Network Solutions.

A good domain name is easy to:

- Dictate –Try and avoid having to say digit or hyphen.
- Hear – Some words our easily confused. Letters such as D/T, M/N, B/P, V/B. The letter 'S' can be confused with 'ess.'
- Spell – Avoid eccentric spelling such as 'lite' for 'light 'and 'nu' for 'new'.
- Type – The more characters there are in your URL the more typos there will be. Tests have shown that the average unskilled typist makes a typo every seven strokes.
- Read on-screen – Some colour combinations are easier to read than others. Black/ white and red / white are good choices. Blue/grey and green/red are difficult.
- Read in the address toolbar – some combinations of characters are are easy to confuse. For example: m, n, r or l, I, 1 and l.

TOP TIP

If you are using your name, as many mediators do, this is not always easy. Do you have a name that is easily misspelled? If you do, also register common misspellings, e.g. Maciver, McIvor, Macivor.

Visuals

17.17 Websites are essentially a visual medium. Online, people will be dealing with your image on the screen, not with you as a person, in person. So how you appear on the screen is vital.

Will your images be taken professionally? How long will they be there before being updated?

Will you be formal or informal? Would it just be head and shoulders or full length?

Poor quality images mean a poor-quality site. Blurry images and sterile stock images shriek amateur website.

A cartoon sketch, a passport size photo tells them something. A short video – even 15 seconds – tells and shows so much more. Frankly, if you don't have a video, why bother having a website?

Most people don't have the visual skills and experience to design a website. You can see that when you look at the ones that have been put together using a relatively simple web builder. Are there stock photos of London Bridge or skyscrapers at night and blocks of text? They do a job, but not a very good one.

> **TOP TIP**
>
> Integrate your website with your video offering as well as your social media activity. Your website is not a stand alone (see **Chapter 18**).

The right fonts

17.18 Match your font to your general style. Make it easy to read.

Typefaces are not trivial. Users spend most of their time on a website scanning text.

Do you use serif or sans serif? Sans-serif fonts are more attention-grabbing, easier to read. And seem more modern, with cleaner, less cluttered designs.

Try out different styles. Remember to always keep your site's purpose and users in mind. Avoid long paragraphs of text in cursive style fonts.

Is your site well designed and functional? Is it visually appealing and with a professional look? Use white space, quality photographs and graphics. Let your message show through.

Make your site distinctive but still appealing to your users.

The right words

17.19 Great looking sites can be ruined by poor text. You cannot design away bad copy.

Writing copy is a skill. Talk to copywriters (see **17.41**).

Tech

Straightforward navigation

17.20 Is it easy to get around your site? Good websites don't require users to think. Make it as easy as possible for users to move to the parts of the site that you want them to see – whether that is making an appointment or sending you an email.

Visitors are always in a hurry. Don't make them work for information. Create obvious, logical navigation with a clear hierarchy. Remember your site should satisfy both searchers – looking for something specific, and browsers – just looking.

Does the site work quickly, correctly and as visitors expect? Proofread carefully and test regularly for problems with speed or functionality Potential customers form a first impression – only once. Make sure their user experience is a good one. Once visitors become frustrated, they leave the site.

Look at Amazon. It is easy to use to buy something. But try cancelling your Amazon account. Difficult or what? It is deliberately not made easy. So, you give up. Make your website easy to use.

Fast page speeds

17.21 Visitors demand fast speeds to keep them engaged. So does Google.

The data tells us:

- 1 in 4 visitors abandon a website after waiting for 4 seconds.
- 46% of visitors will never revisit a slow web page.

Google takes page speeds into account when it comes to search engine optimisation, which means you need to have a fast website to rank in search results. Search Google for 'Open Internet speed test". You will find several. Try speedtest.net.

Mobile friendly

17.22 We use our smartphones to access websites.

Check that your website is mobile friendly.

Resource: Go to support.google.com and type in mobile-friendly test.

TOP TIP

- DIY or DIP – do it yourself or do it professionally? See para **17.23**.
- Not sure what to do? Look at websites that you like. Ask are they DIY or DIP?

Building your website

17.23 The secret is to be clear about what you want. This applies whether you are doing it yourself or using a website designer.

Here is a list of the key questions to ask yourself. Try to formulate as clear an answer as you can. This takes time and effort but it will save you much more time, effort and stress later. It is worth doing.

Here are the key questions:

What is my website to do?

17.24

- Build brand awareness i.e. name recognition.
- Establish authority.
- Generate business.

What is your budget?

17.25 Websites cost money. Work out how much you have available to spend. This is why having a business plan with a budget is it is so important (re-read **Chapter 15**).

You don't have to spend a fortune on your website. You can if you want to. How much you spend will depend on what you want to achieve. You probably will not be able to avoid spending at least £100 for even the simplest most basic website where you (and ChatGPT) do the work yourself. You can easily spend £5000 or more for a bespoke site that a web designer builds for you. You will see the difference. Just like feeling the difference when you wear a bespoke outfit instead of an off- the- peg one.

The big question is whether you are going to do it yourself or not. Most people unless they have an IT or design background will not have the experience, skills, or aptitude to design a good quality website. What makes a good quality website is a much-debated question (see **17.08**).

DIY

17.26 Even if you are building the website yourself you will need some basic tools.

- Domain name
- Web hosting
- Content
- Website security

Website builders

17.27 If you are going to do it yourself, think about using a website builder. There are lots of them. For example godaddy, Wix, Squarespace. Their prices vary.

17.28 *Website*

They change all the time with deals and packages. Go to their websites. Here are some useful websites.

- Uk.godaddy.com
- Wix.com
- Squarespace.com
- Bluehost.com
- Hostinger-zyro.com
- Weebly.com

Website builders make it easy to create an off-the-shelf website that looks professional enough to give you basic start with templates which you populate with text and images using drag-and-drop editors. Be aware that the basic price is just a basic price. For advanced features and add-ons, you will pay more. You may also have to do more work yourself and even learn some basic coding skills. That may excite you or it may terrify you.

To differentiate your services in the competitive mediation market, you need a bespoke website that is designed for you, not assembled by you (see **17.17**).

What is the timeline?

17.28 As a rule of thumb all tasks, whether building websites or drafting a mediation statement, take at least 40% longer than you think they will. Always leave more time to get your website up and running than you think you will need. If you are in a hurry expect to pay a premium if you are using some outside help. Or spend hours and hours at your computer if you do it yourself.

Who will host it?

17.29 Next, you need to choose a web hosting service, which is where your website's files will be stored. Resist going for the cheapest just because it is the cheapest. The Internet is awash with companies offering hosting services at low prices. Not all of them are well established and resourced. Go for the best that you can afford.

Who will maintain it?

17.30 Who will look after the website? This means who is going to make sure it works? Who is going to update it, i.e. provide new content? Can you do this yourself? Be honest. Or will you need help?

Why will visitors stay on your website?

17.31 What do you give them? Not sell them. Give them.

Make your website a resource centre. Somewhere they can learn information not just about you as a mediator but about things that can help them when they go to mediation.

What's the process?

Look around

17.32 First step have a look at other websites. Work out which ones you like and which ones you don't. Bear in mind you are looking at them as potential competitors. Try some imaginative reconstruction and see websites through the eyes of potential purchasers.

Find a website designer

17.33 There are thousands of them. Search the Internet. There are hordes of freelance website designers all over the world.

You find a good one in the same way that you find a good plumber, doctor or mediator. Ask people that you know for recommendations. Ask friends and contacts.

Ask for references. Contact people they worked with. Was the designer helpful, on time, responsive etc. Make sure you get the pricing right. Is this a fixed price project? Or do they charge by the hour or by the day? Day rates are the most common.

Ask yourself if you want to be able to actually talk to your work website designer in person either on Zoom or on the phone? Would you want to meet them?

Look at mediators' websites. If you like one, take a note of who designed, it. Their name will be at the foot of the pages by the © sign. If there is no email or telephone number contact the mediator and ask. If they will not tell you, make a note that they are not someone to waste time on.

ALERT

Don't just copy the opposition. Recall you are trying to establish your personal brand.

Go bespoke (see **Chapter 15**).

What will they hand over?

17.34 What will the deliverables be? Who keeps the source code? Who has the intellectual property rights in the design? Make sure that you have a written agreement that covers these points (see **Appendix 2**). What after-sale services will the designer provide – advice, troubleshooting, maintenance, updating etc. How will they charge?

What is your brief?

17.35 How big will the website be? How many pages? What will the topics be? Do you have testimonials – will you list them?

What are you willing to spend? Reread your business plan (see **Chapter 15**).

Work out a website brief. Your designer can help with this, but you need to think about what you want in advance. Find examples of other websites that you like and ones that you don't like and show them to your designer.

Here is a checklist of key questions. You need to ask them even if you are building your own website.

Checklist of website design questions

17.36

1 What is my domain name See **17.16**.

2 What is the website for? See **17.23**.

3 Who will host the site?

If you use a web designer, they often arrange hosting and support for your site. This will not usually be expensive. Check around for prices.

A hosting service is the online world's landlord. You rent space for your business in a building that your landlord owns. You rent space for your business online from a hosting service which operates web servers that are constantly connected to the internet.

Some are free. But most experts advise using a paid-for hosting service. These often offer additional facilities such as helplines and backup if the server goes down. You can find a hosting service by going online.

4 Who will maintain the site?

Website maintenance includes the following:

- Updating content

  This is vital. See **17.40**.

  It is not difficult to do yourself, but it does take time and self-discipline.

- Backing up your website

  Your hosting service should do this, but it is as well to have your own backup as well.

- Link Checking

  Links can be broken if you make changes to your site or references.
- Testing website speed

  Good download speed is crucial. You do not want visitors becoming bored waiting for content to download.
- Software updates

  If you use third-party software such as Word Press, you will see that they are constantly updating. You need to install the updates promptly.

5 Search engine results

Use Google Analytics (see para **17.46**)

6 Reputation management

Use Google Alerts to monitor your website name, your name and your content on the Web.

You can do this yourself or have someone do it for you. Your website designer may offer this service. Many of them do for small businesses or individuals. Or go online and see who is offering the service. There is a lot of choice out there.

What to put on your website

17.37 Content is king. Follow the golden rules:

- Four seconds is the average time that someone stays on a Home Page.
- Grab them by the eyeballs and keep them on the page.

The 10 Commandments of website content

17.38

1 Use bullet points. You are not writing feature articles or essays.

2 Keep it short. Use short words, short sentences and short paragraphs. You only need three punctuation marks – the hyphen, the full stop and the question mark.

3 Put key information at the top. Use the inverted pyramid. All the important information goes at the start of each page.

4 Keep key information 'above the fold'. Screen readers spend 80% of their time reading what they can immediately see on the web page without scrolling down. That is 'the fold'. Avoid long scrolling pages. Readers' attention spans are measured in micro-seconds.

5 Grab the readers' eyeballs with a headline. Be specific. 'Three tax tips.' Is better than 'How to minimise your tax bill'.

6 Write strong leads. The first sentence answers the six questions: who, what, why, when, where, and how? As mediators we live on these questions at mediations. We use them to explore issues and generate solutions. Do the same in your blogs.

7 Use the second person, not the first or third. 'You' or 'Your' focuses your writing on the reader. 'I' focuses on yourself or your service. This is not what readers want. They want to know what is in it for them.

8 Use the active not the passive. For example: 'Mediation saves you time and money.' is active. 'Money and time are saved by using mediation.' is passive. Cut down on using 'there is,' 'there are,' or 'it is'.

9 Include text links. Use lots of links to other parts of your site within the text. These help readers find in-depth in information more quickly. Search engines like them.

10 Keep it fresh. See **17.40**.

Good writing tips

17.39 The golden rules of good writing still apply online.

1 Keep it lively – use specific nouns and verbs not general nouns and adjectives and adverbs.

2 Avoid jargon – use plain English.

3 Express your personality – this is difficult but don't try to be someone that you are not. Just write in a style that feels natural and easy. Remember your visitors want to see warmth and competence.

4 Check spelling and grammar – use a spell check on your computer. Grammarly is a good one. See https://app.grammarly.com/

5 Proofread – proofreading your own work is difficult. You see what you wanted to write, not what you wrote. Read it out loud to yourself or have someone else do it.

Images

17.40 See **17.17**.

We live in an image-saturated world. Use them or lose your visitors. The minimum you need is

- A professionally taken image of yourself.
- For other images, you can use stock ones. Some are free. Others you pay for. You can search for them online. It is much better to take your own and use them. Modern cameras, even the one in your phone, take images that are plenty good enough.
- Videos. Put some on your website (see **Chapter 18**).

Refresh your content

17.41 Online content is like fish. Once it's stale it puts people off.

You cannot just put up your website and leave it. Don't think that visitors will be magnetically drawn to it or business will just roll in. Not so. You have to attract them. Keep updating your website. Why?

- Search engines thrive on novelty. The more often you update the higher your website will be ranked.
- Visitors are put off by out-of-date information. Seeing that the site was last updated two years ago will not impress. They will just go to another site.
- Up-to-date content impresses them. They are reassured that there is something substantial behind the website. There is still widespread suspicion about websites. Are they just a front? Anybody can have an impressive website but is there an impressive business or service on offer behind it?
- Refreshing content is good for you as well. You stay engaged in your project as you think of new material and review what you have done and what you are going to do.

How do you refresh content?

17.42 There are several options:

- If you used a developer for your website, they can do it. They will charge but it is not expensive.
- Do it yourself. If you have a template or blog-based site this is straightforward.
- Buy a commercial CMS (Content Management System) or use an open-source CMS. Open source simply means source code that is available to users without charge. There is a bewilderingly wide choice Wordpress, Drupal, Zoom. Take a look

  https://wordpress.com/

  https://www.drupal.org/

  https://zooma.agency/en/learn/what-is-wcms-and-why-should-you-use-one

How often do you update content?

17.43 Work out what needs to be updated. How frequently you do it depends on the nature of the content. Timetable it.

A rule of thumb: update some aspect of your website at least once a month. This is not as difficult as it sounds.

- If you have a blog, writing 750 words on a mediation related topic is not too onerous. It should not take more than three/four hours in total (see **19.14.)**
- If you provide tips and advice to mediation users, refining them or adding new ones should take 30/45 minutes.
- If you provide snippets of information and news, updating takes only 15–20 minutes.

17.44 *Website*

The secret is planning and sticking to your plan. Think about using a scheduling app such as HootSuite (see **Chapter 19**). LinkedIn now has a scheduling function.

Resource: Go to Linkedin.com in help

How often do I update my website?

17.44 From time to time, you will need to revamp your website. Fashion and styles change. As mediators we do not need to be as cutting edge as graphic designers, but we don't want to appear dated, old-fashioned and out of touch.

TOP TIP

- Look at your market's websites. Make sure that you are in tune with their look and overall style.
- Carry out a reconnaissance of your competitors' websites. Knowing what the opposition/competition is doing is always useful. But don't just copy them.

CHECKLIST: WEBSITE UPDATING SCHEDULE

17.45

Every two years	Redesign the site. Add new features and content. Incorporate feedback.
Every year	Review and update all content including photographs – especially photographs. Often the person walking into the mediation room bears scant resemblance to the beaming face on their website.
Each quarter	Review your Profile/CV.
Each month	Update at least one page with a blog or testimonial.
Each week	If you have received a new testimonial add it straightaway. If a significant development happens, eg a new Court of Appeal case about mediation tell visitors about it.
As needed	Big breaking news, eg you have just been awarded the Mediator of the Year prize.
	Changes in your charges, if you show them on your website.
	Changes in your contact details.

UPDATING CHECKLIST

What do I update?

17.46 Do not be overwhelmed. You do not have to do everything at once. Any small change updates your site. If you are stuck, use this checklist:

Profile

Review this every three months. If your profile stays the same year after year visitors will think that you are not active.

Testimonials

Seek them out and use them.

Blog

This is the obvious one to update regularly.

Terms and conditions

Keep an eye on what the competition is doing and make sure that you are not out of step with market trends. If you are not following a trend formulate a good reason in case a potential customer asks.

Rates

Stay competitive. In the end you can only charge what the market will bear. The market is dynamic.

Tips

Make a list of tips, say 20, and work through them by posting one on your website each week/month.

Publications/videos/podcasts

Tell visitors about publications that you have written or are working on.

How do I know if my website is working?

17.47 If the number of people offering you mediations shoots through the roof, you might reasonably infer that your website is working. But even that is not a safe assumption. Your increasing work may simply be result of two or three influential satisfied customers mentioning your name.

17.48 *Website*

A quick, cheap, and fairly reliable way of finding out if your website is effective is to use Google Analytics. The world refers to statistics but on the Web, they are called analytics. They are the same thing: figures and numbers.

Google Analytics

- It is free;
- It gives you more in-depth analysis on competing services; and
- You do not need their paid Ad Words campaign to use it.

Go to marketing platform.google.com>Analytics.

> **ALERT**
>
> From 1 July 2023 Google Analytics 4 replaced Universal Analytics. Go to support.google.com for the latest information.
>
> Try some qualitative analysis by:
>
> - Going on to your own website and navigating around it.
> - Asking friends to do the same.
>
> Then do the same thing with other mediators' websites and systematically compare the experience.

The silver bullet: Search Engine Optimisation

17.48 For digital immigrants certainly, and possibly also for digital natives, Search Engine Optimisation ('SEO') is a mysterious and arcane practice. Consultancies specialising in SEO will tell you that they can increase your page rankings. In other words when someone goes online and looks for mediators, your name and website will come up higher in the list.

They say that you will not achieve top ranking without paying for it. But you can achieve a higher ranking by using SEO.

If you ask SEO consultants what they do, they are vague. They assure you they can achieve great outcomes but are not specific about the methods that they use. This is not to suggest that they use underhand methods. Understandably they are reluctant to reveal their trade secrets. Other Internet gurus are sceptical about the services offered by SEO consultants and have described them as 'snake oil salesmen'.

A good place to start is by downloading Google's SEO starter guide. It comes in Adobe PDF format. Google have done their best for digital exiles to make it reasonably reader friendly, but it is likely that you will have to work through it more than once. There are useful and easy-to-follow diagrams to help you. At the time of going to press you can download it from www.google.com/webmasters/docs/search-engine-optimisation-starter-guide.pdf.

Google dominates the market. In practice you do not need to bother with any other search engines.

But Google do not tell you everything. They want to minimise others manipulating the rankings. If you want to try and gain an insight into the Google approach, try going online and searching for blogs. Tom Demers writes a useful one. Go to tom demers@tomdemers. And you can follow him on Twitter. I do.

If all else fails, you will have to find yourself an SEO consultant. You find one in the same. way that people find mediators. Ask colleagues for references, research the Internet and look in directories.

Readily accessible contact and location

17.49 Your audience will not chase you down. Make it easy to engage, of a multiple point of contact: phone, email, social media and maybe an easy-to-use contact form.

In a nutshell

17.50

- Get your website up. Do it now. Do it quickly. A half-built website is not a website.
- Websites are never finished. They are always works in progress.
- Update, maintain and review.
- Buy in as much professional help as you can afford.
- Look after your website and your website will look after you.

Appendix 3

This is drafted from the point of view of the designer. It is based on a template that is made available by:

Tiago Lavis-Fernandes. Freelance Web Designer 83 Ducie Street Manchester, M1 2JQ United Kingdom

tiago@diviwebdesigner.co.uk

Insert template for web design contract

Between {company name} and {client company}.

Agreement

You {contact_first name} {contact_last name}, representing {client_company}

("You") are hiring me {company name} ("I or me") to design and develop a website for the estimated total price of {contract_contract_value} as outlined in our previous correspondence.

What do both parties agree?

You:

You have the authority to enter into this contract on behalf of yourself, your company or your organisation.

You'll give me the assets and information I tell you I need to complete the project.

You'll do this when I ask and provide it in the formats I ask for. You'll review my work, provide feedback and approval in a timely manner too. Deadlines work two ways, so you'll also be bound by dates we set together.

You also agree to stick to the payment schedule set out at the end of this contract.

Me:

I have the experience and ability to do everything I've agreed with you, and I'll do it all in a professional and timely manner.

I'll endeavour to meet every deadline that is set, and on top of that,

I'll maintain the confidentiality of everything you give me.

Design

I create look-and-feel designs and flexible layouts that adapt to the capabilities of many devices and screen sizes.

I create designs interactively and use predominantly HTML and CSS so I won't waste time mocking up every template as a static visual. I may use visuals to indicate a creative direction (colour, texture and typography.) I call that 'atmosphere.'

You'll have plenty of opportunities to review my work and provide feedback. I'll either share a Google Drive folder or development site with you, and we'll have regular, possibly daily contact.

If, at any stage, you change your mind about what you want to be delivered and are not happy with the direction my work is taking you'll pay me in full for the time I've spent working with you until that point and terminate this contract.

Text content

Unless agreed separately, I'm not responsible for inputting text or images into your content management system or creating every page on your website.

I provide professional copywriting and editing services, so if you'd like me to create new content or input content for you, I can provide a separate estimate for that.

Graphics and photographs

You should supply graphic files in an editable, vector digital format. You should provide photographs in a high-resolution digital format.

If you choose to buy stock images, I can suggest stock libraries.

If you'd like me to search images for you, I can provide a separate estimate for that.

Browser testing

Browser testing no longer means attempting to make a website look the same in browsers of different capabilities or on devices with different size screens. It does mean ensuring that a person's experience of a design should be appropriate to the capabilities of a browser or device.

I test my work in current versions of major desktop browsers, including those made by Google (Chrome).

I wouldn't test in other older browsers unless we agreed separately. If you need an enhanced design for an older browser, I can provide a separate estimate for that.

Mobile browser testing

Mobile browser testing using popular smaller screen devices is essential in ensuring that a person's experience of a design is appropriate to the capabilities of the device they're using. I test my designs in iOS (Safari) and Android (Google Chrome.)

I wouldn't test in Blackberry, Opera Mini/Mobile, specific Android devices, Windows or other mobile browsers unless we agreed separately. If you need me to test using these, I can provide a separate estimate for that.

Technical support

Unless you subscribed to my hosting package, I don't offer support for website hosting, email or other services related to hosting.

You may already have professional hosting, and you might even manage that hosting in-house; if you do, great.

If you don't, I can set up an account for you at one of my preferred hosting providers. I can set up your website on a server, plus any statistics software such as Google Analytics and I can provide a separate estimate for that.

The updates to, and management of that server will be up to you unless you subscribe to my hosting package and pay a yearly fee of £150 or a monthly fee of £15. If so, all the above hosting support is included. If you decide to use my server to host your website, the first year of hosting for your first website designed by me is free of charge.

Search engine optimisation (SEO)

I don't guarantee improvements to your website's search engine ranking, but the web pages that I develop are accessible to search engines.

I also provide SEO services, so if you'd like me to help you reach higher positions on search engines such as Google or Bing, I can provide a separate estimate for that.

Changes and revisions

I don't want to limit your ability to change your mind.

The price at the beginning of this contract is based on the number of weeks that I estimate I will need to accomplish everything you've told me you want to achieve, but I'm happy to be flexible.

I offer 3 free revisions of your project which means that after delivering the first draft, you can send me one e-mail with all the changes you would like to make and that counts as your first free revision.

Once the final version of your website is delivered, I will send it for your approval and you can send me another e-mail with all the changes you would like to make – that counts as your second revision. You will still have an extra free revision just in case you need to send me another e-mail with the final set of changes.

Any additional revisions will be charged at a rate of £50/hour. If you wish to change your mind or add anything new, that won't be a problem as I'll provide a separate estimate for those additional weeks.

Legality

I'll carry out my work in accordance with good industry practice and at the standard expected from a suitably qualified person with relevant experience. With that said, I can't guarantee that my work will be error-free. So I can't be liable to you or any third-party for damages, including lost profits, lost savings or other incidental, consequential or special damages, even if you've advised me of them.

Your liability to me will also be limited to the number of fees payable under this contract, and you won't be liable to me or any third-party for damages, including lost profits, lost savings or other incidental, consequential or special damages, even if I've advised you of them.

Finally, if any provision of this contract shall be unlawful, void, or for any reason is unenforceable, then that provision shall be deemed severable from this contract and shall not affect the validity and enforceability of any remaining provisions.

Intellectual property rights

Just to be clear, "Intellectual property rights" means all patents, rights to inventions, copyright (including rights in software) and related rights, trademarks, service marks, get up and trade names, internet domain names, rights to goodwill or to sue for passing off, rights in designs, database rights, rights in confidential information (including know-how) and any other intellectual property rights, in each case whether registered or unregistered and including all applications (or rights to apply) for, and renewals or extensions of such rights and all similar or equivalent rights or forms of protection which subsist or shall subsist now or in the future in any part of the world.

First, you guarantee that all elements of text, images or other artwork you provide are either owned by your good selves or that you have permission to use them.

When you provide text, images or other artwork to me, you agree to protect me from any claim by a third party that I'm using their intellectual property.

I guarantee that all elements of the work I deliver to you are either owned by me or I've obtained permission to provide them to you. When I provide text, images or other artwork to you, I agree to protect you from any claim by a third party that you're using their intellectual property.

Provided you've paid for the work, and that this contract hasn't been terminated, I'll assign all intellectual property rights to you as follows:

You'll own the website I design for you plus the visual elements that I create for it. I'll give you source files and finished files, and you should keep them somewhere safe as I'm not required to keep a copy.

You own all intellectual property rights of text, images, site specification and data you provided unless someone else owns them.

I'll own any intellectual property rights I've developed prior to, or developed separately from this project and not paid for by you. I'll own the unique combination of these elements that constitutes a complete design, and I'll license its use to you, exclusively and in perpetuity for this project only, unless we agree otherwise.

Displaying my work

I love to show off my work, so I reserve the right to display all aspects of my creative work, including sketches, work-in-progress designs and the completed project on my portfolio and in articles on websites, in magazine articles and books. I also reserve the right to include a discreet copyright mark on your footer (e.g. Designed by FWD).

Payment schedule

I'm sure you understand how important it is as a small business that you pay the invoices that I send you promptly. As I am also sure you'll want to stay friends, you agree to stick tight to the following payment schedule.

To start this project, I require the first payment of £ xx as a deposit. Once I have sent you the first draft of your website, you will be able to request your first set of changes or approve the first draft. I will then send you the second invoice of £xx, do the changes you asked for and continue with the construction of your website.

When I complete the project, you will receive the final version for approval, request the second and third sets of changes, and receive the final invoice of £xx to put your website live.

I issue invoices electronically. All proposals are quoted in British Pounds and payments will be made at the equivalent conversion rate at the date the transfer is made. Any payments made in accordance with this agreement shall, once they are paid, not be refundable nor creditable for any reason whatsoever.

You agree to pay all charges associated with international transfers of funds. The appropriate payment details will be printed on my electronic invoice. I reserve the right to charge interest on all overdue debts at the rate of 25% per week.

Payment details

You can pay using the following options:

- Via bank transfer using the Account Number 00000000 and the Sort Code 00-00-00
- By card using my website's payment page https://shop.freelance-webdesign.co.uk/make-a-payment
- Via PayPal using the link https://www.paypal.me/freelancewebdesignUK/300

General

Neither of us can transfer this contract to anyone else without the other's permission.

We both agree that we will adhere to all relevant laws and regulations in relation to our activities under this contract and not cause the other to breach any relevant laws or regulations.

This contract stays in place and doesn't need to be renewed. If for some reason one part of this contract becomes invalid or unenforceable, the remaining parts of it remain in place.

Although the language is simple, the intentions are serious, and this contract is a legal document under exclusive jurisdiction of the English and Welsh courts.

If you agree with the terms of this contract, please press the green "SIGN" button at the top, fill in your details and use the digital signature field for handwriting your name with your mouse (or finger if you have a touch screen), so I can jump on your project straight away.

Chapter 18

Videos/podcasts

In this chapter you will learn:

- How to go about making videos
- How to go about making podcasts

Videos

18.01 Recall what Steven Pinker said about sound speeding and images remaining. A widely cited statistic is the viewers retain 95% of what they watch on video but only 10% of what they read in text.[1] And we watch a staggering number of videos every day. Around 3.7 million new videos are uploaded to YouTube every day. That is 720,000 hours of fresh video content per day. YouTube has 2 billion active monthly users who watch over 5 billion videos a day.

Mind-blowing figures. Not all of them are music and cat videos. Admittedly not many are mediation videos. The point is that videos are a much used, and much-liked medium of communication.

If you want to have a dynamic website, not a static one, put a video on it. How do you start? Revisit the questions you asked yourself about your website in **Chapter 17.** Ask the same ones about videos.

1 How much money, time and effort do you have to invest?

2 Are you going to DIY or DIP?

Then, think in terms of these three categories:

- Production values
- Performance
- Content

1 https://www.popvideo.com/blog/looking-at-the-facts-why-video-content-has-the-highest-retention-rate#:~:text=Studies%20have%20shown%20that%20adding,it%20in%20text%20(insivia).

In other words, how do you want the video to look and sound? How do you want you to look and sound? What do you want to say? What's your message?

Making a video is not just a question of switching on your camera, pressing record and talking. You can do that. But, as with writing, editing is all important. Post-production is as important as pre-production and production.

Can you edit? Can you insert music or title cards? Be honest about your technical capability. If you can fine; if you cannot, find help.

Production values

18.02 During lockdown there was a craze for people posting short videos on LinkedIn using their iPhones. They were really just extended selfies. Their selling point was that they had an immediacy and honest authenticity. Some are very appealing. Most were dire.

Some people are naturally more photogenic and better in front of a camera than others. Others think that they are naturals but ....! The hard lesson is that not many of us are naturally photogenic or confident in front of a camera. Most of us cannot get it right first time. We need to learn how to do it and rehearse.

Posting selfies on LinkedIn is one thing. Putting up a video on your website is another. One is ephemeral. The other is there to stay, at least for a time (see **Chapter 17**).

If you want to do better than DIY, you will need help and advice. In all filming, lighting and sound are key. You can see immediately the difference that professional standard lighting and sound makes. That is quite apart from the skill in placing the lights and the mics.

ALERT

You will be astonished if you go to a studio to see how sensitive mics are and how important soundproofing is. It is known as solid sound.

Professional standards are difficult to achieve outside a purpose-built studio.

So, what do you need?

People

Cameraman

18.03 You will need someone to shoot the video and edit it for you. Often they are the same person. Sometimes the cameraman and the editor are different.

Director

18.04 Do you also need a director? That is someone who helps you prepare for the shoot, supervises it, and signs off on it. Directors charge. Is it worth it? It depends on:

- how confident you are about being in front of camera.
- the three questions – how much money, time and energy do you have to invest in the project.

A director will also help with your script. Making a video is not the same as turning up to the workshop and ad-libbing your way through a presentation. You need to get it right. There are tips and tricks involved in producing an appealing script (see **Chapter 12** on speaking).

They will also recommend studios and cameramen and editors.

Time

18.05 Rehearse. Rehearse. Rehearse. You cannot read out your script in a monotone. It is a performance. From the start to finish of your project allow plenty of time for rehearsal and editing. Both take longer than you expect.

Clarity

18.06 Be clear who your audience is and what message you are sending to them. You are appearing on video so that people can see what you are like as a mediator. We see with our ears as well as our eyes. It is not enough to look good: you must sound good.

Recall the mantra: people do business with people that they know, like and trust.

Are you the sort of person they can come to like and trust? Do you display warmth, confidence, and competence? High production values suggest competence. You need to be able to perform your script in a way that radiates confidence and competence. How you speak and what do you say will show viewers whether you have confidence, competence and warmth.

What do you wear? When do you smile? When do you pause? These are all a part of presenting a character, persona or personality that someone wants to hire as their mediator.

Money

18.07 What does it cost to make a video? As of 2023 you can expect in London studio rates to be:

- a cameraman. £375–£475 a day depending on the equipment and the same for an additional sound recordist with audio mixer kit.

- film editors £300 a day
- directors £150–£500 a day
- make up £80–£250 a day

Outside London the rates are cheaper.

You can, as with your website, use freelancers in other parts the world and do the whole thing on Zoom. It can work. I have done it. Is it as good as turning up in the studio in London with your own cameraman and director? No. It is harder as an experience and the outcome is not as good.

2 Performance

How do you say it?

18.08 Go back to **Chapter 12 and** re-read the section on voice. The advice there about presenting on Zoom applies when making a video.

You don't have to memorise your script or even look at your notes online. You can use a teleprompt such as DVD prompt. The basic version is free and enables you to use your iPad as a teleprompter. It works very well. Go to the App Store and download DVD prompt.

There is a knack to being able to look at the camera and read the text at the same time but with practice it comes. You still need to maintain eye contact and pause for breath and speak to the end of the line just as you do in person.

You must articulate your words more clearly and speak a little more slowly than you might do in person. This is because the sound quality online is sometimes not as good as it is in person. You also need to rely upon your voice more because your use of hand gestures, which can be very useful when in person, is restricted when you are being filmed (see **Chapter 12**).

Content

18.09 You can post two types of videos on your website. Those which are about you. Those which are about something else.

Introducing yourself is relatively easy. You know who you are. You don't have to research yourself. But you may not realise how you come across to others. That is where a director helps.

You don't just have to identify who your audience is. You also have to identify what they are looking for. What do they want?

Videos on other topics are more difficult. You must do research. Find out what is already available. What does it do well and what doesn't it do? Are there gaps that you can fill? Once you have an idea, turn into a script.

> **ALERT**
>
> What do you say?
>
> The content of your video is your choice. The key questions are:
>
> - who is your audience?
> - what do you want them to take away having watched your video?
> - what would you like them to do?

Are you making just one video introducing yourself and your services or are you going to make a series about different topics?

Whatever you choose, provide viewers with something that is useful to them. As one client emailed me after a shareholder dispute mediation:

> 'I found your website videos very useful in preparation; the trouble when you Google mediation is you just get top level articles about why you should mediate a legal issue, but you are helping people who are about to mediate.'

Making your own video

18.10 You can find lots of help online. To start with go to:

- wikihow.com How to make a video
- Vimeo go to vimeo.com>blog>post>how-to-make- a video

Distribute your videos

18.11 Don't just post them on your website. Consider the two main channels YouTube and Vimeo.

YouTube

18.12 Setting up a channel is easy.

- Sign in to YouTube on a computer or the mobile site.
- Click on your profile picture. Click create a channel.
- You'll be asked to create a channel.
- Check the details (with your Google account name and photo) and confirm to create your channel.

There are lots of helpful videos. Go to:

- youtube.com>creators> getting started, and
- youtube.com>watch

18.13 *Videos/podcasts*

Definitely worth considering. Reread **Chapter 12**. Again you can find lots of help on the internet – eg https://m.wikihow.com/Make-a-YouTube-Video.

Just as there are website builders there are video builders.

See for example:

- Vimeo.com>create
- Adobe.com >express>createvideo.
- Invideo.io

Vimeo

18.13 Setting up in Vimeo is easy as well.

Go to www.vimeo.com.

- Click 'Join'.
- Create a username and password and into your email.
- Confirm your email by following the instructions sent to your inbox.
- Upload a profile photo or your logo – recommended size is 600×600 PX.

There are lots of helpful videos. Go to vimeo.com>join.

Look at the Vimeo website and as mentioned above you will find lots of products available to help you produce your own videos. Much like the web builder sites such as Wix (see **Chapter 17**). For both Vimeo and YouTube there are free basic options and more advanced ones that you pay for. What are the main differences between YouTube and Vimeo?

- The big difference is the size. YouTube is enormous with over 1 billion users who watch hundreds of hours of content every day. Vimeo is much smaller: 200 million of which about 25% are in the US.
- YouTube has a much bigger and more diverse user base. The risk is that you receive negative comments and feedback. Vimeo is a more mature audience that often offers constructive feedback.
- Both of them offer free versions with upgrades. With YouTube you cannot replace a video with a new version and retain your analytics about who has viewed it. On Vimeo you can.
- YouTube makes its money through ads which you find everywhere. You can upgrade to an ad-free version. Vimeo doesn't have ads.

Podcasts – audio

18.14 More and more people are using podcasts to keep up to date or to learn about new subjects. They are another distribution channel for your brand. Why make a sound podcast when you can make a video?

Three reasons

1 It is easier. You only need a microphone. You don't have to worry about lighting and cameras.

2 It is cheaper.

3 People like them. They are less distracting than videos. You can be doing something else while listening to a podcast – driving, sitting on the train, or activities around the house.

Making your own podcasts

18.15 If you want to make your own podcasts you will need to spend time learning how to do it. There are very useful websites that will help you, eg wikihow.com/start-your-own-podcast.

An alternative is to approach a company that makes them. They will either make them for you to upload onto your website or onto YouTube or they will ask you to record a podcast for them which they will distribute. Either way you are generating name recognition.

CHECKLIST TO START A PODCAST

Pick a theme

18.16 Stress test it. How many podcasts can you make about this theme before you run out of steam? Then ask yourself the sub-questions.

- What is your goal? Is it to generate leads, build authority or earn a passive income through subscription?
- What is the message you want to share with the world.
- Who is the show for? What is your audience? Imagine an avatar of your ideal listener. See that person when you talk about them.
- What will make your podcast stand out?

Format

18.17 Which format are you going to use?

- Scripted?
- News?
- Educational?
- Will you be doing the interviews, or will you be the interviewee?
- Will you have a co-host?
- How long should the episode be? How often should you broadcast the? As with blogs consistency not quantity is important. Choose a schedule you

can keep to (see **Chapter 17**).You can always scale up. Predictability not unpredictability is what you need.

Create your podcast brand

18.18 Just pick a name. Here are some hints.

- Choose four words or less.
- Keep it short and intriguing.
- Make it easy to spell and pronounce.
- Decide on a name you like saying out loud.
- Make sure someone else is not already using it.

Create an episode description. Different podcast apps have different character limits. Apple Podcasts give you 4000 characters. Between 400 and 600 is ideal.

Include:

- Tell your listeners what to expect.
- When a new episode will come out
- Answers to their questions
- Insights from mediation practice and theory.
- Make it engaging.
- Ask a question.
- Tell them what it's about. Include your podcast value proposition.

Remember podcast platforms or search engines as well. Include relevant keywords.

Choose your equipment

18.19 Use external USB mics that plug into your computer. The Blue Yeti is a popular choice.

If you are interviewing people use headphones. Try the Sony MDR 7506.

Recording software

18.20 You can use Adobe audition for $30 a month or you can use Audacity which is free.

If you are on a Mac, Garage Band is fine.

Outline your first episode

18.21 You don't need to script the whole thing. You can if you want to. It depends what type of podcast you are making but you must have a structure.

- This list also applies to video podcasts.

CHECKLIST FOR PODCAST STRUCTURE*

18.22

- Hook
- Intro
- Welcome/episode overview
- Interview – talk
- Outro

*This can also be used for video podcasts.

> **TOP TIP**
>
> You need good quality content and a confident performance. Without those two things you'll be wasting your time and money. It is the same as making a video (see **Chapters 12** and **17**).

Record your podcast

18.23 This is the question of taking steps. It is not as complicated as it seems, but you need to take care.

1. Choose a room with minimal noise. Sometimes referred to as a room with solid sound.
2. Cover hard surfaces with soft materials blankets cushions and so on.
3. Adjust your sound system. Set a conservative recording level. Don't record too loud. You can always make things louder.
4. Use a high-quality audio file. Try WAV or AIFF file. Resolutions of 24 bit, 408KHZ are good.
5. Keep your mouth placement and tone consistent and constant.
6. Make a test recording.
7. Always record 30 seconds of silence.

> **TOP TIP**
>
> Don't be self-conscious. Nobody likes listening to themselves or hearing the sound of their own voice.

Record bumpers

18.24 These are an Intro and an Outro.

Intro

18.25 A good intro will say in one sentence

- who you are.
- what is your experience.
- why your point of view matters.

In two sentences say

- What your podcast is about.
- How they'll benefit from listening.
- Tell them how it's going to make their life better.

Outro

18.26 Always thank people for listening. Include a tagline and give them something to do next. In other words leave them with a CTA – Call To Action.

It could be to

- Leave a review on Apple podcasts.
- Follow you on social media.

> **TOP TIP**
>
> - Only give them one Call To Action. One thing at a time.
> - Give them too many choices and they will not do any.

Edit your podcast

18.27 This is the boring fiddly bit. But you need to do it. Why? Conversations can result in tangents. Less is more. Cut out the waffle.

Poor quality audio can cause listener fatigue. When you spend too much energy listening you get tired and leave.

The most common editing mistakes

- Intro is too long.
- The music is too loud.
- Forgetting not to use copyrighted music.

Listen to some other podcasts. Take notes, learn, steal but don't copy.

In a nutshell

18.28

- Put videos on your website.
- Use podcasts video and audio on social media.
- Audio podcasts are easier and cheaper to make than video. They are still effective marketing tools.

Useful resources

18.29 lmimediation.org>resources.

Podcasts.apple.com>applepodcasts.

Chapter 19

Social media

In this chapter you will lean

- Which platform is best for you
- Six tips for successful blogging
- Six blogging pitfalls.
- How to give talks online

Putting the media into mediation

19.01 Don't think about being able to engage in digital mediation without engaging in social media; in fact, don't think about engaging in mediation at all without it. It is impossible. Just look at the size of the social media usage.

According to DataSage:

1 There are **4.9 billion** social media users in the world as of March 2023. It is forecasted that there will be **5.85 billion** social media users worldwide by the year 2027.

2 The global social network penetration rate is **59.4%** as of January 2023.

3 **Facebook** is the biggest social media platform in terms of user base. It has **2.958 billion** users as of March 2023.

4 On average, the typical social media user interacts with **6.6 social media platforms**.

5 Social media is used by **85%** of the world's 5.27 billion mobile phone users.

6 An average person uses social media for **two hours and thirty-five minutes** every day around the globe.

7 **Millennials** and **Gen Z** are the most frequent users of social media platforms (see **Chapter 1**).

How many social media users are there globally in 2023?

19.02 Over 4.9 billion people are accessing social media worldwide as of 2023. An average social media user hops between six and seven social media every month.

Let us see the number of social media users in the world over the years:

Year	Number of Social Media Users
2017	2.73 billion
2018	3.1 billion
2019	3.51 billion
2020	3.9 billion
2021	4.26 billion
2022	4.59 billion
2023	4.90 billion
2024*	5.17 billion
2025*	5.42 billion
2026*	5.64 billion
2027*	5.85 billion

Which is the biggest social media platform in 2023?

19.03 The top three, as of 2023, are:

1 Facebook (91 billion Monthly Active Users (MAUs)).

2 Youtube (2.56 billion MAUs)

3 Whatsapp (2 billion MAUs)

The fastest-growing social network is TikTok But how much use are TikTok and Instagram to mediators? Some mediators post on them. There are very few. Probably not worth bothering with for most mediators.

Online tools

19.04 (See **Chapter 16**.)

The platforms compared:

	Global users	Features	Best time to post
LinkedIn	850m	B2B and professional networking	Tuesday, 10.00–11.00

	Global users	Features	Best time to post
X (formerly Twitter)	450m	Microblogs Sharing updates and comments	12.00–18.00
YouTube	2.96bn	Second most used site	14.00–16.00 weekdays
Facebook	2.95bn	Most used site	13.00 for most shares 15.00 for most clicks

That's the global picture but what is relevant to mediators? The standard advice used to be:

LinkedIn: use this to:

- build professional networks
- devise lead generation programmes
- create groups to generate debate and conversation
- connect with sector influencers (see **Chapter 16**).

X (formerly Twitter): use this to:

- break news
- spot and follow trends
- broadcast special events or time-limited deals
- reach sector influencers

Be realistic – most people, unless they are celebrities, don't generate high levels of engagement.

YouTube: use this to:

- promote yourself through video
- create a resource for potential customers looking for advice and information about mediation

Things have changed (see **Chapter 1**).

- LinkedIn has become much more personal, subjective and social and less about work. There are more posts about emotional upheavals, personal vulnerabilities and disadvantages overcome. Tom Skinner of London marketing agency Go Up defined this trend as a symptom of 'a society that celebrates people who can self-publicise above all else' (see **Chapter 16**).
- **X (formerly Twitter)**was founded in 2006. It has never been the most popular of social networks. But as the Economist says 'it has been an efficient means for discovering links to important news and big ideas.' Elon Musk bought it for US$44 billion. He thinks that he overpaid for it and he's changing it. Now it is called X. Most people still refer to it as Twitter.
- **Facebook** launched a rival via Instagram called Threads. It was billed as a kinder alternative to Twitter/X. After an explosive start it seems to have plateaued or even begun to peter out.

Content

19.05 What do you use social media for? Two things:

- to drive users to your website.
- to build name recognition.

You need something for people to look at, hear and read. In other words, **Content is king** (see **Chapter 17**). Mediators now have a new best friend. Who is that? ChatGPT. Content generation is a big business. The same question arises: DIY or DIP? Why struggle coming up with great content, when you can ask ChatGPT to do a blog for you?

As we saw in **Chapters 5** and **6** the work product from ChatGPT tends to be generic and bland. If the name of the game is a presence on social media and getting your name out there to gain name recognition, it could be a useful tool. You may be getting the name out there, but are you building a brand? You might need more bespoke and distinctive content (see **Chapter 16**).

ChatGPT

19.06 (See **Chapters 5** and **6**.)

Already, experienced and well regarded keynote speakers are using ChatGPT to produce an outline or first draft of their talks. This could be very useful. Regular mediation bloggers on LinkedIn are already using it.

Mediators who blog a lot will no doubt use ChatGPT to compile their blogs for them. This might be an improvement. The quality of blogs varies enormously. Some already read as though a machine has produced them. This may be unfair and what has happened is that the mediator has used a blog writing agency. You can tell agency blogs because they tend to lack individuality or quirkiness. Many are regurgitations of articles in *The Economist* or *The Harvard Business Review*. Useful without doubt, but often lacking individual insight or originality. Will ChatGPT do the same? And also save you money, time, energy and stress?

One thing is becoming clearer. The quality of ChatGPT's output depends on the quality of the input. In other words, the better your prompts the better the response. So, we are all going to have to learn prompt engineering (see **Chapter 5**).

So, will ChatGPT help you? Let's try it for an answer.

Question

19.07 Please draft a blog of 400–450 words on whether mandatory mediation is good for mediation.

Response

19.08

'Mediation is a form of alternative dispute resolution that involves a neutral third party, known as a mediator, who helps parties to reach a mutually satisfactory agreement. Mediation is often used in civil disputes, such as divorce and custody cases, but it can also be used in other areas such as business, employment, and healthcare. In recent years, there has been a push towards mandatory mediation in certain situations, but is mandatory mediation a good thing?

On the one hand, mandatory mediation can be seen as a positive development. For one, it can help to reduce the burden on the courts. With court dockets already crowded, mandatory mediation can help to free up court resources by allowing disputes to be resolved outside of the courtroom. This can also help to reduce the cost of litigation for all parties involved. Additionally, mandatory mediation can help to promote communication and cooperation between parties. By requiring parties to engage in mediation, they may be more willing to come to the table and work towards a solution, rather than resorting to adversarial tactics.

However, there are also potential downsides to mandatory mediation. For one, it can be seen as a violation of individual rights. Parties may feel that they are being forced to participate in a process that they do not want to be a part of. Additionally, mandatory mediation may not always be effective. In some cases, parties may simply be unwilling to come to an agreement, regardless of the efforts of the mediator. In these situations, mandatory mediation may simply delay the resolution of the dispute and may not ultimately result in a satisfactory outcome.

Another potential issue with mandatory mediation is that it may not be suitable for all types of disputes. For example, in cases involving domestic violence, mandatory mediation may not be appropriate. The power imbalance between the parties may make it difficult for mediation to be effective, and there may be safety concerns that need to be taken into account. Additionally, in cases involving complex legal issues, such as patent disputes or securities litigation, mediation may not be the best option. These types of cases may require more specialized knowledge and expertise than a mediator can provide.

In conclusion, while mandatory mediation may have some benefits, it is not always the best option. It is important to consider the specific circumstances of each case and determine whether mediation is likely to be effective. Additionally, it is important to ensure that parties are not being forced to participate in a process that they do not want to be a part of. Ultimately, the goal should be to find the most effective and efficient way to resolve disputes, whether that is through mediation, arbitration, or litigation.'

Comment

19.09 How do you rate it?

Will it make people want to follow you? I suspect not. But could you use it as a draft or an outline. Let's try again.

19.10 *Social media*

Question

19.10 Please draft an outline of a blog of 400 words on whether mandatory mediation is good for mediation.

Response

19.11

'Certainly! Here's an outline for a blog post on the topic of mandatory mediation:

I. Introduction

- Explanation of mandatory mediation
- Statement of purpose for the blog post

II. Arguments in Favor of Mandatory Mediation

- Provides an opportunity for parties to resolve disputes before resorting to costly and time-consuming litigation
- Encourages parties to communicate and negotiate in good faith
- Can lead to more creative and mutually beneficial solutions than those imposed by a court

III. Arguments Against Mandatory Mediation

- May not be effective in cases where parties are unwilling or unable to negotiate
- Can be coercive, particularly if parties are required to participate against their will
- May be an added expense for parties who are already facing financial strain

IV. Potential Impact of Mandatory Mediation on Mediators

- Could lead to an influx of cases and an increase in demand for mediators
- May require mediators to be more directive and assertive in order to facilitate negotiations
- Could result in more standardized mediation practices, which could be beneficial or detrimental depending on the circumstances

V. Conclusion

- Summary of arguments for and against mandatory mediation
- Discussion of the need for more research and data on the effectiveness of mandatory mediation
- Final thoughts on the role of mandatory mediation in the larger landscape of alternative dispute resolution

VI. Additional Resources

- Links to relevant studies and articles on mandatory mediation
- Contact information for local mediation organizations and resources for finding a mediator.'

Comment

19.12 Now we are getting somewhere. This shows how AI can support mediators and bloggers: it cannot replace them. Not yet anyway.

With this in mind read on.

LinkedIn and website-blogging

19.13 Bear these maxims in mind:

- Don't blog a dead horse.
- Make sure that your blogs contain something that is either new, useful or relevant -preferably all three.

(See **Chapters 16** and **17**.)

Six steps for successful blogging

Set up a blogging calendar

19.14

- Put in your diary the date your blog will be published.
- Seven days before that date – write the blog.
- Seven days before *that* date – start thinking about what to write.
- Compile a running list of topics you can cover over the next three or four months.
- Some of these will suggest themselves. For example, if you are going to the CMC conference, blog about the programme and what you expect to learn. Then your next blog can be about what happened. What was the news? Who did you meet? Two blogs out of one event. Perhaps even more.
- If you have recently attended a talk or mediation support group, blog about the key topics.

Hootsuite

19.15

- You can find scheduling help with an app such as Hootsuite. You can start with the free version. Experiment with it. You'll find it easy to set up. You will need to have already set up your social media accounts. If you like it, you can upgrade.
- Visit hootsuite: https://hootsuite.com/en-gb/plans/free-offerings.

Choose your point

19.16

- Every blog must have a point.
- Make sure that you can summarise in one sentence of not more than 10 words, what the blog is about.
- The point is really the takeaway that you want your readers to have when they have finished reading your blog.

Pick your keywords

19.17 Work out what specific keywords you want to include in your online material before you start to blog.

But make sure that you include some of them:

- in the title.
- early on in the blog.
- right at the end in the takeaway.

Choose your structure

19.18 This is a blog, not a discursive essay or a stream of consciousness. Use headings and bullet points.

Here is a suggested template:

CHECKLIST FOR A BLOG

Introduction

19.19

- Say what you're going to discuss. Remember the six key questions the first paragraph sentence should answer: Why, When, Who, Where, What and How.
- Make your point. Explain it.
- Move onto your next point. Make it. Explain it.
- Keep doing this until you have finished.

Conclusion

19.20

- Remind the reader of the key points.
- Repeat the takeaway.

Call to action (CTA)

19.21

- A blog without a CTA is a waste of time. You want to promote connections. You do this provoking reaction.
- Ask for a comment. End with a question. It can be a simple as: 'Do you agree?'

Chose your length

19.22 Opinions among expert bloggers vary. The length will depend on:

- how complicated the topic is.
- how often you blog.

When	Words	Where
Daily	200-300	LinkedIn
Weekly	300-600	LinkedIn
Monthly/Bi-monthly	1000-1500	Website

In practice, given our shrinking attention spans, 600–800 words is about right.

Include links and mentions

19.23 Readers want unique and relevant content.

- The uniqueness comes from you as the blogger.
- Relevant content can be from other sources, either from pages on your website or from links to external sources.
- Be generous with your links and acknowledgements.
- Give names of individuals and organisations.
- Don't forget that some people set up Google or social media alert tracking systems and will be able see that you mentioned them. They will have a look at what you said about them. They may even cross-refer to you.

Respond to comments

19.24 Remember you are writing a blog to promote your mediation business to potential customers.

It is about your customers.

- Answer the questions that they are asking. By doing that you establish connections with your readers.
- Acknowledge their comments.

Six blogging pitfalls

19.25

1 **Bad writing.**

Poor grammar, punctuation and spelling put readers off.

2 **Laying down the law.**

Instead of laying down the law invite comments and conversation. Ask questions.

3 **Over-promoting.**

- You are selling your services as a mediator. So are all the other mediators in the world.
- Attract customers by getting them to see you, your website and blogs as resources that they can use and not just as PR outlets.

4 **Writing as an expert.**

When you write as an expert you are writing for yourself, not for your clients. Your self-esteem might increase but will your mediation enquiries?

5 **Lack of focus**

This means

- badly organised individual blogs.
- not having an overall strategy of what your blogs are trying to achieve.
- not having a recognisable voice or style.

This doesn't mean having the same approach to every issue or using the same language every time. It means showing what makes you different from all the other mediators. Not an easy thing to do. It takes time and practice (see **Chapters 15** and **16**).

6 **Binge blogging**

- You start to blog. You do a few. You become better at it. You find it easier. You come to like it. You have spare time, so you do three or four blogs in a week.
- Then some mediations come in. You overlook your blog calendar because you now have your mediation diary to worry about. You don't blog for 3 months. You have lost your audience.
- Readers like consistency. They will come to expect a blog from you on the first Friday every month or every other day.

This is why you should consider using a scheduler app such as Hootsuite (see para **19.15**).

LinkedIn how has a scheduling function. The instructions for how to use it are on their website. Hootsuite allows you to schedule over different platforms.

How to write a book

19.26 Blogging is one thing. Writing a book is an entirely different matter. Why even think of writing one? Ask yourself.

- Will writing a book give you credibility? The answer is yes.
- Do books help build your brand. Again, the answer is yes.
- Do people still read books? Talk to a publisher.
- Will you make money? Some but not much from royalties. Much more from mediations that have come to you because of your name, reputation and brand (see **Chapter 15**).

If you are keen, then go to **Chapter 14** in my book *Setting Up in Business as a Mediator.*

Talks, workshops, webinars and conferences

19.27 Giving talks, seminars and lectures is a standard way of making a noise. But what about glossophobia, the fear of public speaking?

Most of us don't like talking in public. As has been said many times most people at a funeral would prefer to be in the coffin than give the eulogy. A slight exaggeration perhaps but we have a natural reticence and reluctance. Usually this is based upon fear.

Read Chapter 14 in my book *Setting up In Business as a Mediator* about how to give a talk in person. This chapter concentrates on the differences between doing it in person and online. First a few basics which are set out in more detail in my book. Philip Collins, a well-known journalist and speech writer, uses the mnemonic DETAIL. What does the mnemonic mean? (Delivery, Expectations, Topic, Audience, Individual, Language and length.) Doing it online means you need to adapt.

Delivery

In person

19.28 Your speech is written to be spoken. It is not an essay or an article. It is a performance.

- Stick to the script. Speaking without notes appears impressive. But it is difficult to do.
- Don't read out the text. Use cards to prompt you. Always have a full text of the speech but don't use it unless catastrophe strikes.
- Don't speak and read at the same time. Read: pause: look up: engage the audience in eye contact. Only then, speak.
- Always write out your opening and closing paragraphs. Learn them off by heart and stick to them to the letter.

19.29 *Social media*

Online

19.29 You don't have to memorise your script or even look at your notes online (see **Chapter 16**).

You can use a teleprompter such as DVD prompt. This is free and enables you to use your iPad as a teleprompter. It works very well. Go to the App Store and download DVD prompt (see **Chapter 12**).There is a knack to being able to look at the camera and read the text at the same time but with practice it comes (see **Chapter 18**).

Three tips

19.30 Maintain eye contact and pause for breath and speak to the end of the line just as you do in person.

Articulate your words more clearly and speak more slowly than you do in person. This is because the sound quality online is sometimes not as good as it is in person.

You will rely upon your voice more because your use of hand gestures (which can be very useful in person) is restricted online (see **Chapter 12**).

Expectations

In person

19.31 Work out:

- What your audience expects of you and what you expect of them.
- What you expect people to do once they have listened to your speech.
- Is your speech meant to be informative, inspirational or persuasive?

Online

19.32 This advice still applies online. However, online audiences tend to be bigger and more diverse. People can join from all over the world. Working out what their expectations are can be much harder. You will have to take your cue from the person who asked you to give the talk. Be prepared to be rather more generic.

Topic

In person

19.33 What is your speech about? If you cannot say what it is about in one 15-word sentence you have not got a speech. Chris Anderson TED talks calls it the 'throughline' – what you are going to say about the subject, ie the key message that you want the audience to take away.

Online

19.34 This applies even more online. Online talks need to be tighter and more structured than in-person ones. Why?

- You are using your DVD prompt.
- A more diverse audience may not be able to follow an ad hoc, impromptu speech in quite the same way
- Any conversation online tends to be slower with longer gaps (see **Chapter 12**).
- You don't pick up the energy from the audience in the same way.

> **TOP TIP**
>
> - Be ultra-clear what it is you are talking about.
> - Re-cap more often.

Audience

In person

19.35 Whom are you trying to address? Who will be there? What is on their mind? What questions do they want answered? What do they already know?

Online

19.36 As we have seen your audience will be much more of an unknown quantity. Learn about them. Following posts on LinkedIn and Twitter. You can see trends and pick up market intelligence. This helps you frame your talks in a way that is new, relevant and useful.

You will not be able to draw energy from the audience as you can in person. You cannot pick up cues from the audience's response in the same way. Because you are looking at the camera you will not be looking at the audience's faces.

You cannot scan the screen in the same way you can scan the room. You can do it but it is not easy if you are concentrating on the camera or your teleprompter.

Being interactive is harder online. You rely upon hands up emojis and questions in the chat function. You don't get the free-flowing interplay that you can get in person. Remember everything is a little more stilted. Don't try and force the tempo.

Leave time during your presentation for questions. Pause before answering them, so you don't cut off the questioners. Repeat or summarise the question to make sure that everyone has heard it.

Polls are a useful energiser and attention generator. Make sure that you have someone to help you handle the tech.

19.37 *Social media*

Individual

In person

19.37 This is hard to define. It means coming across to your audience as someone they like and might, in time, trust.

Online

19.38 Making a personal impression is different online. Many think it is more difficult. It might be. How comfortable are you in front of camera talking to people that you cannot always see? Even if you find this difficult you can still make an impression. Just think of all the online dating referred to in **Chapter 1**.

Language and length

In person

19.39 Keep it simple and clear. Avoid jargon and in-jokes. Choosing the right words and tone is much easier once you have worked out the structure of your speech.

Short speeches are better than long ones. Be very clear how long your speech will last. Between five and ten minutes is plenty if you want to stimulate lots of discussion

Never talk for more than 20 minutes. Aim for 18 minutes. After that people's attention wanders. According to Chris Anderson of TED Talks, 18 minutes is 'short enough to hold people's attention, including on the Internet, and precise enough to be taken seriously. But it's also long enough to say something that matters'.

> **TOP TIP**
>
> Stand/sit up. Speak up. Shut up.
>
> Reread **Chapter 12** on presenting yourself and practise the exercises in the Endnote.

Online

19.40 This advice applies even more online. Attention spans are shorter. Your audience will find it easier to become distracted and unfocused online. Time seems to pass more slowly online. Don't let it drag.

Keep everything shorter. Remember the three S's; speak slowly, shortly and sweetly.

Keep PowerPoint to an absolute minimum. Try and avoid it even in person. Many speakers abuse it. Reading wodges of text displayed on the screen is mind-numbing and loses your audience for you.

You want the audience to concentrate on you. You are selling yourself as an online mediator. You don't want them reading some text off the screen. You need them to be looking at you.

Action plan

- Open a LinkedIn Account. Post regularly at least once a week.
- Join LinkedIn Groups and post comments. Be careful. It can be addictive.
- Open an X (Twitter) account. Post regularly, at least once a week.
- Do the same with a Threads account.
- Create a YouTube channel.
- Stick to your social media content schedule.

In a nutshell

19.41

- Online talks are different. Less interactive. Less energy.
- Keep the talk shorter. Recap more.
- Use chat functions and polls – much easier if you have someone to do the tech for you.
- Give a link to your website for any follow-up or handouts.

Chapter 20

Pitching

In this chapter you will learn

- What a pitch is.
- How to pitch.
- How to overcome objections to online mediation.

'Life's a pitch' is the great title of a great book by Roger Mavity and Stephen Bayley.[1]

For admen life is truly a pitch. What about mediators? Mediation doesn't sell itself. You have to sell it. You also need to sell yourself. Who are you selling to? Selling for mediators is pitching. You will not be pitching a start-up to venture capitalists or seeking investment from Dragons' Den. But you will be pitching yourself to potential clients and their lawyers

How to pitch

20.01 Be clear about your goals. If you are not clear, you cannot pitch successfully.

Try this exercise:

- Write a 50 word description of your online offering.
- Edit it down to 20 words.
- Now try it in 10 words.

Work on your pitches. How you pitch will depend on your audience. Your pitch to someone who has never been to mediation will be different from a pitch to the claims director of an insurance company. Calibrate your pitches. Have a portfolio of them ready.

1 Bayley and Mavity *Life's a Pitch: How to Sell Yourself and Your Brilliant Ideas* (Corgi, 2017).

Five Pitches

The elevator pitch

20.02 We are all told to develop this one.

The idea is to explain your proposal/business/project/yourself to anybody within two minutes. This being what two New York journalists worked out was the average time you travel in a lift between floors.

Work on it. Crafting one is not as easy as it sounds.

The high concept pitch

20.03 This comes from Hollywood where people don't have time to listen to you in the lift. They have five seconds in between phone calls.

You need an easy-to-grasp idea. So, when the studio boss asks you what your film is about you can say 'Snakes on a Plane' (concept *and* title) or 'A bus with a bomb' (*Speed*).

Can you write your concept on the back of your business card? That does not mean you use the whole of the card.

So, for example the high concept for LinkedIn is 'Facebook for business'. For X (formerly Twitter) it is 'Blogs for ADD sufferers'.

A good high concept pitch is:

- Brief: one short sentence is the ideal.
- Uses building blocks that people already know, eg Jaws, space, blog.

As a mediator you are not pitching studio bosses. But you are pitching decision makers. Bring them solutions to their problems. Work out what is bugging them and how they can debug their lives.

The one-word pitch.

20.04 In the online world of ever-shrinking attention spans the need for speed increases. Only brutally simple ideas get through to people. They travel further and faster. You need one word.

For example, Barack Obama's presidential campaign strategy was one word: 'Forward'.

What is your one-word pitch for mediation? Think about it. Benett G Pitcher, a renowned and highly experienced commercial mediator, in a keynote address to the Florence International Mediation Chamber and IMI said his one word was 'Opportunity'.

Work out yours.

The question pitch

20.05 We are often persuaded more by questions than by statements. Aren't we? Questions make us think more. Don't they?

The headline pitch

20.06 You need this for emails. Does the headline grab your attention or not? People read emails either because they look useful or because they are intrigued.

Research shows that people who receive lots of emails go for utility. People with fewer emails read them out of curiosity.

Give yourself a chance by being specific. Instead of: 'Improve your chances of successful outcome at mediation', say '3 tips for good mediation outcomes.'

Meeting objections

20.07 When you pitch about mediation you will meet objections.

The F Triangle is a helpful device in overcoming them. Fundraisers use it all the time – Feel, Felt, Found.

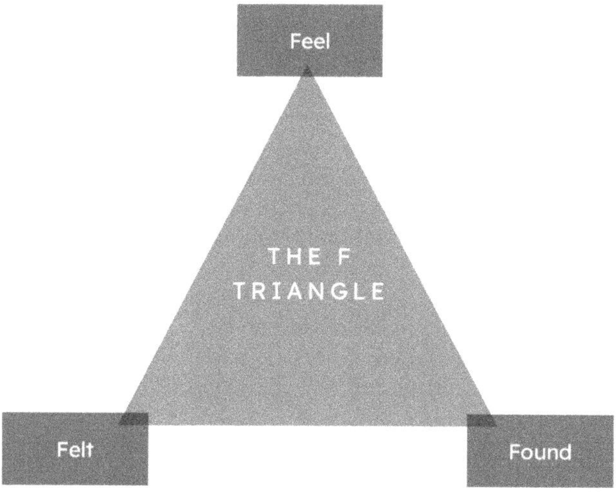

Use the three elements to frame a response along these lines:

> 'I know how you *feel*. Others have told us that they *felt* like that. What we have *found* is that…'

20.08 *Pitching*

Have your pitch ready. Don't try and meet objections off the cuff. Remember what it is like facing difficult interview questions. You don't want to hear them, but you know that they will be coming. So, prepare.

Pitching and promoting for mediators

20.08 Promoting and pitching go hand in hand. But they have the same goal: mediations for you. For more information and advice see Chapter 3 of my book *Setting Up in Business as a Mediator.*

Let's look at what's different about pitching online.

Where do I do my pitching?

On the phone and when you network

20.09 Pitching online is different from pitching in person. Building relationships online is harder and slower. But it can be done. I know from my own experience. I was contacted on LinkedIn by a newly trained mediator, Jon Whitworth, who wanted to undertake some observations. He was not a lawyer but had an interesting background in negotiation.

Jon attended three online mediations with me. We got on well. We talked about the differences between mediation of the sort that I was doing, civil and commercial, and negotiation of the sort that he used to do – hostage release. He explained the difference to me between a hostage negotiator and a hostage consultant. A hostage negotiator keeps the hostage-taker talking and hopefully the hostages alive until Special Forces arrive and storm the building and release the hostages. A hostage consultant negotiates a commercial deal. Money is paid to the hostage-takers, and they release the prisoners. It is a completely different mindset and outcome.

Our discussions led us to think about offering co-mediation. There is a market for it in the Kidnap and Ransom world (K&R). Disputes arise between the employers of the hostages, their insurers and the consultants who negotiate the outcome. Could we offer a service there? Jon knew about K&R's problems. I knew about mediation.

To promote this offering, we decided to make a series of videos. All this took place during Covid. We never met. Not even when we made the videos. They were shot on Zoom. You can see the results on my website: swalkermediation.com. Click the Resources tab.

When lockdown finished and the videos had been shot and posted on our website, we eventually had lunch at Wilton's. I am pleased to say that when we met, I felt as though I had known him for years. He said the same thing. We still have lunch regularly. And Jon's mediation practice is developing really well. Have a look at his website::jonwhitworthmediation.com

Think about how the context affects the output.

Online it takes more effort to convey the same energy and feeling you naturally give out during a face-to-face pitch. You need to work harder to keep attention. If something is not engaging, people switch off both mentally and physically. One click and they are gone.

Turbo charge your output.

CHECKLIST FOR TURBO CHARGING

20.10

- Focus on your key points. Streamline. Nail the important stuff.
- Use your facial expression, tone of voice, eye contact (look at the camera), and words to inject energy and emotion. Reread **Chapter 12**.
- Review Your Pitch:
  - Do you need to make changes? Fewer words, More recaps. Memorable stories.
- If you have to use slides – and in most cases, you don't – use them sparingly.
  - Use fewer words on each slide.
  - Use more slides with less on them.
  - Simple words. Single words. Not blocks of text.
- Stand Up:
  - When you are pitching in person, you stand up. Do the same online.
  - Standing up will allow you to breathe better as you speak and engage your body, add energy to your delivery (see **Chapter 12**).
- Angle your computer so that the camera is slightly higher than eye level. It is a more attractive angle for your face on camera.
- Check your lighting – you don't want to be in the shadows. Nor do you want to be squinting at a bright light.
- Check Your Tech:
  - Always do this whether this is your first time or you 101st time. Make sure that you are familiar with the technology.
  - Practise with friends to make sure you can seamlessly move around on it.
- Log on early. Test your mic and video camera.

As recommended **in Chapter 11**, buy an external camera and a better mic. Upgrading them is not expensive and makes a world of difference.

This checklist can be used when giving any sort of presentation.

Online Q&A

20.11 Q&As are more complicated than in-person. You might have to unmute people, respond to a message in the chat function, share their screen with you. Get comfortable with these functions so it feels seamless to the audience.

Use active listening to demonstrate that you are hearing them – nodding, taking notes, summarising what you heard before answering. This shows, both physically and mentally, that you are listening to their questions, and being thoughtful about your answers.

There will be more pauses in an online conversation. Don't panic. It's normal.

Overcoming objections to online mediation

20.12

1 Objection

'I'm a technophobe. I'm hopeless at computers.'

Response

'You don't have to do anything. I am the mediator and act as host. I have the professional version of Zoom. I will send you an email with a link on it. All you have to do is click on the link. That's it. I will let you into the session and put you in your private breakout room.'

2 Objection

'I like to see the white of their eyes. You can't do that on screen.'

Response

'A lot of people say they feel that. What I have found is that once they have been on Zoom they have felt that they can engage with everybody else.

If you're not sure let us have a dummy run. I will show you how it works.

You will be able to see everybody on the screen. Sometimes you can see people better on screen than if they are speaking to you across a crowded table.'

3 Objection

'You can't express emotions on screen.'

Response

'A lot of people feel that. I have found that in fact people can express their emotions even more openly on screen. They feel less intimidated because they are in their own environment and safe. People have told me they have said things on the screen that they would not have felt able to say if we had been in person.'

4 Objection

'You can't establish rapport online.'

Response

'You're right, it's different. We can't shake hands or share a plate of biscuits. I know that a lot of people feel that this means you can't establish rapport.

I have found that once you start looking at each other and talking, you can. After all, rapport just means getting along with someone.

5 Objection

'What happens if my broadband goes down?'

Response

'Don't panic. We just use our mobile phones instead. We always use them as back up. Either you can plug your mobile phone into your computer and use the mobile mobiles network or we just talk on the phone. You can log into Zoom from your phone.'

6 Objection

'I can't sit at a computer all day. I hate them.'

Response

'A lot of people feel that way about their computers. I feel that way about my computer. The great thing about online mediation is that you don't have to sit at your computer all day long.

You can just click Stop Video and Mute icons and have a break. We have lots of breaks at online mediation. Taking breaks online is much easier than when you are in a windowless room on the 19th floor of a lawyer's office.

There's a lot less downtime at online mediations. When I'm with the other room you can take a break or get on with something else.'

7 Wrap up

Let me send you a Zoom invite for a quick demo. Won't take more than 5 to 10 minutes. No obligation. No hard feelings if you hate it. How about X pm on XX?

In a nutshell

20.13

- Write your pitches.
- Practise them on camera. Record and time yourself.
- Learn the responses to the objections.
- The more you pitch the easier it becomes.

Chapter 21

Networking

In this chapter you will learn:

- Why we network
- Secrets of successful networkers
- What to avoid

Networking: a good thing or a bad one?

21.01 Most of us hate it. Researchers in 2014 found that people felt physically dirtier when they networked. They saw networking as morally impure. This is known the Macbeth effect after the scene in the Shakespeare play where Lady Macbeth describes wiping imaginary blood stains off her hands.

George Soros, the legendary international financier, finds it a waste of time and energy. He said: 'Networking is not working'.

Julia Hobsbawm the world's first Professor of Networking disagreed. She says: 'You can't work without networking'.

Who is right? Let's see. If you want to network can you do it online? Yes, you can. The question is: how do you do it? That is what this chapter is about.

What is networking?

21.02 Julia Hobsbawm advises that Networking 'is not about running around throwing your business cards like confetti but learning interesting things and having the courage and curiosity to connect with people because you think you might learn from them.'

Networking is especially important for mediators. What do mediators do? They attend mediations. They meet groups of strangers who are not getting on very well and build relationships with them. They call this creating rapport. Out of rapport comes trust. And out of trust come deals.

In essence that is what networking is. The big difference at mediation is that you as mediator have been invited and people want to interact with you. They want you to like them and even be on their side. So, you are not risking humiliation, rejection and boredom. Which are the things that put most people off networking.

Nor are you having to sell yourself. At least not from cold. As a mediator you still have to sell yourself at the mediation, i.e. win over people's trust. But you are not cold calling. In sales speak you are attending on a 'qualified lead'.

Do you have the right mindset?

21.03 Any mediator should have this. Your mediation training equips you to be comfortable networking. Look at Julia Hobsbawm's definition again about exhibiting curiosity and connecting with people because you might learn from them. That is exactly what mediators do. Doing that will help you avoid the biggest mistake that people make with networking.

They approach the whole thing with the wrong attitude. They go with a 'What can you do for me?' approach.

Admittedly networking at a mediation when you **have been appointed** as a mediator is different from networking **in order to be appointed** as a mediator. You don't have the same guaranteed receptive welcome. The risk of rejection is higher. But don't panic.

You can find lots of advice on how to network or work a room. There are specialist coaches. I included a section of it in my book on *Setting Up in Business as a Mediator.* Read **Chapter 13** for lots of useful tips and advice. I am not just repeating them here. Instead let us look at the differences between networking in person and networking online.' Can you network online? Yes, you can. Here is how.

Ten tips for better networking

21.04 Here are tips for networking face-to-face and online networking.

Turn up

In person

21.05 If you are invited to an event, say yes. Put it in the diary. And go. Resist finding reasons not to go.

Find out in advance who else is going. Ask around the people that you know whether any of them are also going.

Online

21.06 The same rule applies. Register for the event. Click on the link at the appointed time. You may not be able to find out who is attending in advance, but you will see who is attending when you are logged on. A list of participants is usually displayed often with titles, showing their faces and names in Gallery View. Or scroll down the participants' panel, which is usually on the right of the screen.

It is easier **not** to attend an online event. You don't have to make the same physical and mental commitment to physically go to the venue. You can either log on or not as your mood takes you. It is also a lot easier to attend an online event. One click, and you are there. No travel or getting ready. So why not log on? You don't have to stay right to the end if you don't want to.

Join in

In person

21.07 Remember Woody Allen's advice: 'Half of life is turning up'. That's true. The other half is: 'When you turn up join in'.

Online

21.08 It is a lot less effort to turn up online but it is more effort to join in. You don't have to face a roomful of strangers or stand on your own, not talking to anybody. But you cannot just turn to someone and say hello and ask them why they are at the event or use whatever chat up line you favour.

But you can join in. Harvard Business Review suggests five ways to successfully engage during a virtual event:

1. **Engage in the first 60 seconds** to hook people into the conversation.
2. **Introduce yourself early.** Introductions are important. Even if you have been connecting through email prior to the meeting, introduce yourself formally on your first face-to-face call.
3. **Don't hide** in a large group. If the meeting has a lot of attendees, resist the urge to dissolve to the 'back of the class'. Get involved, ask questions and make relevant comments.
4. **Keep it high-level** unless you are asked to explain something in greater detail. Avoid long monologues. Summarise your experiences don't describe them at length. This makes the conversation more of a discussion and less of a lecture.
5. **Question in five-minute intervals.** Don't wait to rattle off all your questions at the end. Instead ask a question every five minutes to keep engagement up.

How do you do this?

Use the Chat function:

- Submit questions in advance if asked. This helps get your name in front of the presenters and organisers. Participate during the session. Ask questions.
- Send messages either to the meeting in general or to individual participants who you might have heard of, recognise or already know.
- When in breakout rooms talk to people.

Your 10-second intro

In person

21.09 Practise this before you go to your first networking event.

'My name is XX. ...

Wait for them to say who they are.

I'm YYY ...

Then you say

So, Alex what brings you here?

Try and find out who they are and what they do before you go into your pitch. By doing this you will be able to calibrate your pitch (see **Chapter 20**).

Online

21.10 You may be invited to introduce yourself. This depends on the type of event. If you ask a question, expect to be asked to say who you are and what your background is. In breakout sessions people usually introduce themselves.

Have your intro ready and keep it short.

Forgetting names

In person

21.11 We all do it. It is embarrassing.

You forget names as soon as soon as you have been told them because:

- You didn't hear the name. There was too much noise. They mumbled or spoke into your bad ear.
- You are distracted at the time. Someone else caught your attention or you are thinking about something else. So, focus on the person who is talking to you.
- You were not paying enough attention or showing enough interest. This is the biggest problem.
- Use business cards and check them. If they hand you their business cards, take them and as you are reading, ask them something about themselves while saying their name.

Online

21.12 This doesn't happen. People's names appear by their image on screen. The participants list will show names as well.

If people are doing introductions, listen, take a note. If you cannot hear or missed what they said, ask them to repeat. The sound quality often fluctuates online. That gives you an excuse for asking. It is less embarrassing for you to do this online than in person.

Remember your mediation training: ask about them.

In person

21.13

> 'But enough about me. What about you? What do you think of me?'

Bette Midler raised a laugh with this line in 'Beaches'. Funny but it touches a nerve.

So, restrain your inner extrovert. Listen more than you talk.

Online

21.14 The same thing applies online. And if you find it difficult to get a word in edgeways you can always text on the Chat function.

Give, don't take

In person

21.15 The core value of networking is to establish and activate relationships. You want to establish rapport (or trust). You do this by:

- being open and sharing.
- giving to the other person not by demanding or taking.
- listening and questioning and in this you find out what you could do for them. You are not trying to find out what they could do for you.
- acknowledging with thanks if they offer something to you, whether it is an introduction or a meeting for lunch.

Online

21.16 The same thing applies online but you do it by Zoom meetings, direct messages, texts, WhatsApps, emails and phone calls.

Ask for a card

In person

21.17 Asking 'Do you have a card?' is politer than saying 'Can I give you my card.'

21.18 *Networking*

Enter them in your Contacts immediately. Make a note in the Notes section of where you met them and any other key points.

Online

21.18 You will have their name. Look them up. Are they on LinkedIn or Facebook? If they are, send them a message. Ask them to connect.

Check their website and email. Contact them through that.

Smile

In person

21.19 Nothing works better than a smile.

Smiling energises and emboldens you. So, smile, step forward, give your name and shake their hand.

Online

21.20 Even more true on screen (see **Chapter 12**). Just smile, wave and say 'Hi'

Shoulder surfing

In person

21.21 What you must never do is look over people's shoulders while they are talking to you. This is the number one turn-off.

Maintaining eye contact with your companion while scanning the room with your peripheral vision is an art and skill that you will develop over many hours of networking events.

Online

21.22 There is no shoulder surfing. That is a big plus.

Follow up

21.23 This applies to both in person and online. Remember the two rules.

The 11am rule

21.24 If you meet someone at a networking event and you want to follow up, send them an email before 11am the next day. Tell them that you enjoyed meeting them and that you are interested in what they said. Say that you would like the opportunity of talking further. Ask them if they will have time for a cup of coffee/ lunch within the next two weeks.

Similarly do your thank-you emails or telephone calls before 11am the next day. Otherwise, their impact is lost in the crush of the next day's activities.

The 36-hour rule

21.25 If you receive an email, respond on the same day. Remember the 36-hour rule. Emails that are not answered within 36 hours get lost. Rarely do they resurface.

Where to network?

21.26 Everywhere and anywhere that mediators, lawyers, accountants, surveyors, insurers, architects, medics, company directors, journalists meet.

So, in the UK look out for in particular:

- Conferences such as the Chartered Institute of Arbitrators Mediation Symposium or the CMC Conference which are held each year.
- The annual conferences held by the big trainers such as ADR group and CEDR.
- Workshops, seminars, and role-plays that are put on by various organisations for their members such ads those organised by the RICS.
- Support groups.
- Mediation competitions:
- Use online networks to make connections. Join groups on LinkedIn.

Many universities now run annual competitions for mediators in the same way that they run moots for would-be barristers. The organisers often are desperate both for judges and people prepared to act as mediators.

More and more mediation competitions are being organised. Some are very well-established such as the annual one held in Paris by the International Chamber of Commerce, or the ones organised by the International Academy of Dispute Resolution in the USA and other countries. Others are newer and working hard to establish themselves.

Attend virtual networking events.

Virtual events including video and Web conferencing are now established parts of business life. More people are returning to in-person events, according to the Benchmark Report 2023 from the Influencer Marketing Hub. Pre-Covid 18.9% of all events were virtual. Hybrid events are now the most popular. 57% of people say that they would attend a hybrid event. These look like being the norm is for the foreseeable future.

Last resort

21.27 If all else fails and you still feel that you can't face networking, try this advice from the greatbusinessschools.org website.

Drop the word 'networking' from your vocabulary.

Self-talk matters in stressful situations. A 1995 study reported in the *Journal of Support Behavior* found that people who were self-assured and boosted themselves with useful self-talk performed better during a round of darts. You might not be throwing darts when networking, but you ought to be focused on hitting the target. Reinforcing positivity is vital. So, if the word 'networking' sounds negative, drop it.

Replace 'networking' with 'opportunity'.

The two tips about following up and keeping in touch apply Online as much as in the physical world.

So,

- follow up;
- keep in touch; and
- always check if they are on X (formerly Twitter), LinkedIn or Facebook and connect with them.

In a nutshell

21.28

- George Soros is right: networking is not working. It is preparation for working.
- Julia Hobsbawm is right: you cannot work without networking. If you don't network, you won't get work.
- Woody Allen is right: Half of life is logging on. The other half is joining in.

Useful resources

21.28

Van Raalte, Judy L; Brewer, Britton W; Lewis, Brian P; Linder, Darwyn E; et al. *Journal of Sport Behavior*; Mobile Vol. 18, Iss. 1, (Mar 1995):

Index

[All references are to paragraph numbers]